Transportation
and Behavior

Human Behavior and Environment

ADVANCES IN THEORY AND RESEARCH

Transportation and Behavior

EDITED BY

IRWIN ALTMAN

University of Utah
Salt Lake City, Utah

JOACHIM F. WOHLWILL
AND
PETER B. EVERETT

Pennsylvania State University
University Park, Pennsylvania

PLENUM PRESS · NEW YORK AND LONDON

Library of Congress Cataloging in Publication Data

Main entry under title:

Human behavior and environment.

    Vol. 5 edited by I. Altman, J.F. Wohlwill, and P. Everett.
    Includes bibliographies and indexes.
    PARTIAL CONTENTS: v. 3. Children and the environment.—v. 4. Environ-
ment and culture.—v. 5. Transportation and behavior.
    1. Environmental psychology—Collected works. I. Altman, Irwin. II. Wohlwill,
Joachim F. III. Everett, Peter B. (Peter Ben), 1943-
BF353.H85   304.2   76-382942
ISBN 0-306-40773-6   AACR1

© 1981 Plenum Press, New York
A Division of Plenum Publishing Corporation
233 Spring Street, New York, N.Y. 10013

Printed in the United States of America

Articles Planned for Volume 6
BEHAVIOR AND THE
NATURAL ENVIRONMENT
Editors: Irwin Altman and Joachim F. Wohlwill

Contributors

MARK BALDASSARE • Sociology Department and Center for the Social Sciences, Columbia University, New York, New York

PETER B. EVERETT • Program in Man-Environment Relations, The Pennsylvania Transportation Institute, The Pennsylvania State University, University Park, Pennsylvania

DAVID T. HARTGEN • Transportation Data and Analysis, New York State Department of Transportation, Albany, New York

IRWIN P. LEVIN • Department of Psychology, University of Iowa, Iowa City, Iowa

LYNN G. LLEWELLYN • Division of Program Plans, U.S. Fish and Wildlife Service, Department of the Interior, Washington, D.C.

JORDAN J. LOUVIERE • Department of Marketing, University of Iowa, Iowa City, Iowa

RICHARD M. MICHAELS • Urban Transportation Center, University of Illinois at Chicago Circle, Chicago, Illinois

RAYMOND W. NOVACO • Program in Social Ecology, University of California, Irvine, California

RICHARD A. OLSEN • Lockheed Missiles and Space Company, Sunnyvale, California

DANIEL STOKOLS • Program in Social Ecology, University of California, Irvine, California

Preface

The present volume in our series, *Human Behavior and Environment,* is devoted to a specific topic, continuing the pattern established in the last two volumes. The current theme is behavioral science aspects of transportation. This topic was chosen to exemplify a problem area of practical import to which psychologists, sociologists, and other behavioral and social scientists can make and have been making notable contributions. Our volume includes papers from a variety of psychological perspectives, including human factors, environmental psychology, and behavior modification, along with other contributions from a sociologist and a transportation engineer interested in behavioral science contributions to transportation. Joining us as guest editor for this volume is Peter Everett, an environmental psychologist whose area of specialty is the study of behavioral components of transportation systems.

Volume 6 of our series, currently in preparation, will be devoted to behavior and the natural environment. A provisional table of contents for that volume appears on page v.

Irwin Altman
Joachim F. Wohlwill
Peter B. Everett

Contents

CHAPTER 1

TRANSPORTATION AND THE BEHAVIORAL SCIENCES

DAVID T. HARTGEN

CHAPTER 2

PSYCHOLOGICAL CONTRIBUTIONS TO TRAVEL DEMAND MODELING

IRWIN P. LEVIN
JORDAN J. LOUVIERE

CHAPTER 3

REINFORCEMENT THEORY STRATEGIES FOR MODIFYING TRANSIT RIDERSHIP

PETER B. EVERETT

CHAPTER 4

TRANSPORTATION AND WELL-BEING: AN ECOLOGICAL PERSPECTIVE

DANIEL STOKOLS
RAYMOND W. NOVACO

Chapter 5

Human Factors Engineering and Psychology in Highway Safety

RICHARD A. OLSEN

CHAPTER 6

THE SOCIAL COST OF URBAN TRANSPORTATION

LYNN G. LLEWELLYN

CHAPTER 7

THE EFFECTS OF A MODERN RAPID-TRANSIT SYSTEM ON NEARBY RESIDENTS: A CASE STUDY OF BART IN THE SAN FRANCISCO AREA

MARK BALDASSARE

CHAPTER 8

FUTURE TRANSPORTATION:
ORGANIZATION OF THE DESIGN PROCESS

RICHARD M. MICHAELS

Introduction

The cost of transportation in the United States approximates one-fifth of our gross national product. Furthermore, one of every six individuals is employed directly by transportation industries such as automobile production, traffic control, and highway construction. In a larger sense, virtually all jobs in modern society are dependent on some aspect of transportation; for example, regardless of occupation, almost all of us must travel to and from work. There are also many enterprises that are specifically dependent on transportation systems, such as drive-in banks, large suburban shopping malls, and motels along interstate highways. Thus, the figure of one in six people who are directly employed by the transportation industry underestimates the degree to which we depend on transportation in almost every facet of our lives.

Energy consumption figures offer a corresponding picture of the impact of transportation on our economy and society. Currently, in these energy-constrained times, 52% of the daily petroleum consumption in the United States occurs in various transportation systems. Of that amount, 43% is accounted for by passenger cars. Therefore, it is of little wonder that so much of the impact of our current energy problem is borne by the transportation system.

Quite apart from the dominant place of transportation in our day-to-day lives, it is a topic that brims with behavioral science issues and concerns. Although interest in this area on the part of social and behavioral scientists is comparatively recent, many problems are being studied in a systematic fashion. These include travel mode choices, individual decisions to purchase a vehicle, reaction time to a traffic emergency, and many other topics.

Historically, the study of transportation has been the domain of engineers, who were primarily concerned with the physical design and construction of transportation systems. They have been joined by the

1

legal and economic professions, which address such issues as the pricing and regulation of transportation services. It is only in the last decade that sociologists, geographers, psychologists, marketing specialists, and other professionals have examined transportation topics. As a result, the study of transportation is now highly diversified and eclectic and bridges a number of aspects of contemporary life, including land use, employment, residential location, energy supplies, pollution, recreation, economic vitality, friendship patterns, and overall quality of life.

The present volume illustrates a range of behavioral science perspectives on various transportation topics. The first chapter, by Hartgen, a transportation planner, presents an overview of the diversity of potential behavioral science contributions to transportation, including examples of only partially researched areas. The chapter also reflects the perspectives of those in transportation planning and policy roles. The Levin and Louviere chapter demonstrates the usefulness of social-psychological research and theory (particularly studies of attitudes) in predicting travel demand. The chapter by Everett outlines ways in which behavior-change strategies may be applied to the task of altering individual travel practices, especially of increasing the use of energy-efficient modes of travel such as public transit. In their chapter, Stokols and Novaco present a model for understanding the relationship between transportation and stress. Their approach is buttressed by data that relate various levels of traffic congestion to stress. In the next chapter, Olsen provides an overview of the considerable amount of work in the human factors area that bears on transportation safety.

Two chapters deal with a topic of very recent origin: social impact assessment. Llewellyn illustrates some general approaches to social impact assessment and describes the need for more research and attention to the impact of transportation systems on the quality of life of nearby residents. The next chapter in the volume, written by Baldassare, is a social impact assessment of the Bay Area Rapid Transit (BART) system, which was built in the late 1960s and early 1970s in the San Francisco Bay area.

In the final chapter, Michaels reviews the potential future role of behavioral science in relation to transportation issues, and he offers a general approach to incorporating human characteristics into the transportation design process.

Many of the contributions of behavioral scientists to transportation issues were stimulated by the fast pace of technological and social change occurring in our society during recent decades. These changes have included shifts in modes of transportation such as the widespread use of the private automobile as a preferred means of travel, the worsening shortage and high cost of energy, urban sprawl and decay, and growing concerns about quality of life. The variety of issues associated with various facets of transportation will very likely broaden and intensify during the coming decades; certainly, many of the issues are ripe for analysis and research by social and behavioral scientists. The chapters in the present volume offer a glimpse into this new and exciting field.

1

Transportation and the Behavioral Sciences

DAVID T. HARTGEN

INTRODUCTION

The policy-oriented disciplines that serve the functions of government and society (e.g., transportation, housing, health, education, energy, environment) are rapidly changing. Each has evolved at an accelerating pace over the last 20 years, after a period of relative lull in the early 1960s. Until recently, these subjects have been treated as distinct and separate entities, but recent trends indicate a growing tendency by analysts to regard them as interrelated and overlapping.

The methods developed by transportation analysts in the early 1960s were intended to deal with the problem of urban access, that is, major highway construction actions in cities. They were based on highly aggregate theories that viewed travel as a four-step process involving trip generation from small geographic areas analogous to census tracts, trip distribution between origins and destinations, assignment to modes (transit and auto), and finally, route assignment. This process, sub-

A revision of papers presented at the Conference on Applications of Behavioral Science to Transportation, Charleston, South Carolina, October 30–November 2, 1978, and at the Annual Meeting of PTRC, Warwick, England, July 9–13, 1979.

DAVID T. HARTGEN • Transportation Data and Analysis, New York State Department of Transportation, Albany, New York, 12232.

sequently known as UTPS (urban transportation planning system) was widely promulgated by the federal government and was adopted and used in virtually every large city in the United States to forecast long-range travel for proposed transportation systems. The reader is referred to numerous texts (e.g., Stopher & Meyburg, 1975b) for detailed discussion of this system.

The 1970s, however, have focused on the impact of transportation actions on nonusers and, more recently, on the problems that arise from constraints on travel. Many analysts view the procedures developed earlier as inadequate for dealing with current issues (for example, Neels, Cheslow, & Beesley, 1978; Stopher & Meyburg, 1975a), even though they are still in common use. While these methods fall short in a number of ways, criticism is directed primarily at their lack of behavioral content and their artificial complexity and data-intensiveness. In the first instance, a review of methods shows almost no casual structures relating travel to activity, demographic, societal, personality, cognitive, or government policy antecedents. In the second, the methods in their present computerized forms require massive data sets (20,000–30,000 households in a city of 1 million persons) containing highly detailed travel reports by family members. These data sets are aging rapidly, most were collected in the early 1960s, and time and money are not available to repeat them even if that were advisable. Clearly, some better approaches must be found.

Recent improvements in methods have flowed from two major streams of thought, both of which can be regarded as more "behavioral" in content than previous approaches. The first encompasses mathematical modeling using data at the level of the individual trip-maker, that is, disaggregated data (e.g., Atherton & Ben-Akiva, 1976; Charles River Associates, 1976; McFadden, 1978). These methods borrow liberally from economics, psychology, mathematics, and statistics, and as a group, they are highly advanced and perhaps 10 years ahead of transportation planning practice. The second approach takes the view that disaggregation of observations does not in itself constitute behavioral understanding, since one still treats individuals and contexts alike when predicting the behavior of market segments. This approach, rather, emphasizes the social and psychological aspects of travel behavior (e.g., Brog & Erl, 1980; Dobson, 1978; Fried & Havens, 1977; Golob, Horowitz, & Wachs, 1977; Hartgen & Wachs, 1974; Hartgen, 1977; Jones, 1977; Louviere, 1977; Margolin & Misch, 1978). Research is extensive on these topics, particularly in the study of attitudes and behavior. The purpose of this chapter is to review and assess this second stream.

BRIEF OVERVIEW OF THE BEHAVIORAL SCIENCES

Even social and behavioral scientists themselves do not agree on the meaning of the term *behavioral science* (e.g., Britt, 1966). Some are inclined to take a broad, sweeping view and include not only psychology and sociology but also anthropology, economics, education, history and political science, marketing and business, and parts of certain other fields (e.g., geography). Others are inclined to take a narrow view and include only certain elements of the first three fields. Because it is easier to deal with a relatively narrow set, we take the view here that the "behavioral sciences" are those subjects that deal primarily with the individual as an overtly behaving (i.e., observable) entity, viewed both separately and as a member of groups and society, and with the ways in which individuals operate, perceive, synthesize, evaluate, and respond to changing environmental conditions. We would include most of social psychology, a large part of sociology and psychology, and only some of anthropology, economics and geography, and business and marketing.

There are, of course, numerous ways to classify the content of these disciplines. Since I am a transportation analyst and not a behavioral scientist, the classification shown in Table 1 is intended to facilitate an easy map-over between the disciplines. Not much attention has been paid to philosophical questions concerning whether, for example, behavioral intent is really more akin to attitude than to behavior. But perhaps a few points of clarification are in order. Generally, the subjects in cognitive and psychological structure are intended to include all processes that are internal to the individual, that are not directly observable, and that serve to color, warp, or influence one's view of the external world. The implication of separating these processes from those involving learning is that they are assumed to be static over the short run. Any changes that occur in a level of these traits, as in response to an improved transit system, are assumed to be instantaneous. Further, no inherent reference is made to the sources of such traits or to how they evolved in each person. Similarly, *behavior* is taken to mean overt actions, observable by the analyst in an unobtrusive fashion. Actions to modify behavior, such as improvements of transit systems or specific incentives for use, are included, again in static fashion: the *process* of how such actions might result in change is dealt with in learning theory. Social structures include the classical concepts treated in sociology and anthropology. Design of physical systems includes human factors analysis, which concentrates on man–machine interaction, and personal space concepts focusing on vehicle layout and accessibility. Finally, or-

TABLE 1
BEHAVIORAL SCIENCES:
A CLASSIFICATION FOR TRANSPORTATION ANALYSIS

General area	Subjects
Cognitive and psychological structures	Attitude theory and measurement Attitude change Perception Beliefs Emotions Motivation Personality Behavioral intent
Behavior	Attitude–behavior linkages Modification of behavior Behavior (revealed preference)
Learning	Learning theory Decision theory Diffusion theory and innovations Adaptation
Social structures	Roles and norms Status and class Lifestyle Life cycle (family) Culture Society Socialization
Design of physical systems	Human factors Personal space
Groups and organizations	Group dynamics and leadership Organization development

ganization theory and group dynamics contain those subjects relating to the structure and behavior of nonfamily organizations and groups. Undoubtedly, other elements have been overlooked, but these appear to be the major ones.

CURRENT TRANSPORTATION ISSUES: EVOLUTION AND BEHAVIORAL APPLICATIONS

To bring meaning to the discussion, five broad themes in transportation are reviewed below:

1. Urban transit.
2. Rural transit systems.
3. Transportation for the mobility-limited.
4. Environmental and social impact analysis.
5. Energy and transportation.

Numerous other issues for transportation could have been proposed (e.g., Transportation Research Board, 1978b; Wachs, 1977). The selection of these themes is based on their breadth of subject matter and their current relevance.

URBAN TRANSIT

While it would seem that urban transit analysis has always been a central element of transportation planning, this is not the case. In fact, such activities have been a recent arrival in most transportation planning agencies, even transit operators. During the 1960s, spurred by the Federal Aid Highway Act of 1962, virtually every area in the United States with over 50,000 population developed multimodal long-range transportation plans incorporating both transit and highway elements. These plans often described in great detail the intended operation of transportation systems at some distant point in time (usually 20–25 years); they contained much less information concerning the actions needed immediately to get to that future, nor did they address the critical, real, day-to-day problems in either the highway or the transit world.

During the late 1960s, transit costs began to escalate rapidly and ridership continued to decline. As a result, most transit operations, already squeezed by increasing deficits, went from shaky ground to quicksand. Many operations simply went out of business or were taken over by public entities. Federal funds for capital assistance were of little use in stemming the tide of transit company failures, since the issue was not capital fund availability but operating assistance. In the early 1970s, therefore, several states and local governments, and eventually the federal government, began to assist transit operations. In the meantime, transit planning activities at all levels of state and local government expanded rapidly, in response to the availability of federal planning funds and other resources. It is now common to find many large transit operations with at least one resident transit planner, and most urban-area transportation planning staffs and state transportation agencies also employ transit planners.

Since the present deficit situation acts to constrain the services provided, improvements in service and fares must be traded off against the availability of public financing. As transit becomes more dependent on the taxpayer than on the farebox, its role as a public versus a private service must continually be evaluated against increasingly scarce public dollars. The issue of local financial support for transit service (its extent and nature, and the degree to which it can be expected to provide an increasing proportion of subsidies for an ever-decreasing market) is likely to remain the central question that transit planners and analysts will have to deal with over the next 10 years. Closely related is the issue of consolidation and efficiency of transit service, as well as the allocation of the transit services and costs to various geographic and demographic groups. The ability of transit operators to make accurate estimates of demand and cost in response to alternative service arrangements is central to the effective analysis of such questions and is likely to be an issue of considerable concern to transit operators, as well as to transit planners and governments. Table 2 shows how concepts and techniques in the

TABLE 2

MAJOR PRESENT AND POTENTIAL APPLICATIONS OF BEHAVIORAL SCIENCES
TO URBAN TRANSIT OPERATIONS

Subject	Typical applications
Present:	
Attitude theory and measurement	Attitude toward transit service
Behavior and revealed preferences	Mode choice of consumers
	Community views and support
Modification of behavior	Ways to encourage people to use transit services
Decision theory	Change in behavior if service is improved
Potential:	
Organization development	Structure and behavior of transit companies
	Transit management and labor relations
Motivation	Factors influencing transit choice
	Reasons for support of transit services
Learning theory	Experience with transit service may increase its acceptance
Diffusion	Various groups more inclined to try out new services
Status and class	Different user groups tend to use such services at different rates
	Development of specialized marketing campaigns
Life cycle and family	The allocation of roles within households
Human factors	Transit systems design
Personal space	Internal vehicle layout

behavioral sciences relate to the above questions. Without any doubt, the most extensive present applications have been in consumer choice behavior, attitudes, and opinions. For instance, numerous studies exist concerning the structure of mode choice (e.g., Charles River Associates, 1976; Golob, Horowitz, & Wachs, 1977; Golob & Recker, 1977; Gilbert & Foerster, 1976; Hartgen, 1974; Tischer & Phillips, 1979). In each of these studies, the overt behavior of urban commuters in choosing auto or transit modes was correlated with demographic variables and a variety of measures of attitudes toward transportation alternatives. Various scaling procedures—including Thurstone, Likert, Osgood, and occasionally Guttman and certain multidimensional scales—have all been employed in these and other studies (Dobson, 1978; Donnelly, 1975; Golob & Dobson, 1974; Hartgen, 1977; Margolin & Misch, 1978).

These ideas have been extended in mathematical form through the use of individual decision theory from the literature of mathematical psychology (Stopher & Meyburg, 1975a). Extensions of the models of Luce and Raiffa (Restle & Greeno, 1970) have been applied extensively to mode choice. For Instance, McFadden (1978) has demonstrated the flexibility of Luce's share model, in multinomial logit formulations, in predicting commuter mode-choice preferences. Typical variables include travel times and costs, frequency of service, and certain attitudinal measures such as perceptions of comfort, convenience, or reliability. While most of this activity has been oriented to long-range transit planning, it is equally applicable to short-range transit planning and operations.

The viability of transit service will ultimately stand or fall on its utilization by the public. Such utilization is a behavioral phenomenon, subject to the usual rules of perception and evaluation and impinged on by a variety of personal and situational constraints. Thus, it should be apparent that many other concepts and techniques from the behavioral sciences could be useful in transit operations and analysis. These are also shown in Table 2.

Worthy of particular mention is the whole area of labor and management, a field that is well evolved in the behavioral sciences but until recently has not seen significant application in transit operations. Two examples may serve to illustrate the point. Many individuals in transit management came up from the ranks of employees and often do not possess extensive management-oriented skills or education (Smerk, 1976). Therefore, they are often ill-equipped to deal with the intricacies of a basically shrinking industry, beset by financial problems and dependent on public funding. If one adds the need for political astuteness, sensitivity to public concerns, and sound technical knowledge, the requisite training for transit managers would seem to be immense. Such skills, however, can be taught, and the knowledge to teach them generally resides in the behavioral sciences, particularly in marketing and business.

Another obvious application of behavioral sciences is in encouraging transit use. Experience has shown that it is very difficult to improve transit in such a way that the general public is induced to use it. The primary problem is that in most cities and contexts, the burdens associated with automobile use are not so onerous as to outweight its great advantages: individual freedom and independence, personalized expression of self, and flexibility of travel choice. The problem of how to induce change—in attitude, in behavior, or both—is conceptually akin to similar problems in the behavioral sciences, yet until recently (e.g., Everett, 1978), very little of the vast body of literature has been applied to transit services planning. The potential for relevant and practical research in this area would appear to be considerable.

RURAL TRANSIT SYSTEMS

Very few issues have been given greater recent attention in transportation than rural transit systems. The heavy urban–suburban emphasis of metropolitan planning and investments in the 1960s and early 1970s meant, among other things, little attention to rural transportation problems in general and rural transit in particular. Awareness of the mobility needs of rural America slowly increased during this period (e.g., Burkhardt, 1972), culminating in modest federal support for transit demonstration projects in the early 1970s (Federal Aid Highway Act, 1973). Later legislation (Surface Transportation Assistance Act, 1978) has formalized the program and provided both capital and operating-assistance funds.

The premise of such programs, put simply, is that the economic, locational, and demographic characteristics of rural America mean reduced mobility levels for large population groups. Particularly, those without access to autos, because of age, income, physical handicap, or preemption of auto use by other family members, are major population segments of interest (Pennsylvania Transportation Institute, 1977; U.S. Department of Transportation, 1976a). Transportation access problems are a central concern in rural environments (Burkhardt & Lago, 1977), but particularly for such groups.

The issue, essentially, is the extent to which government can and should alleviate such deprivation. Since population density is low, the clients are dispersed, and trip lengths are often long, bus-based systems serving these groups may be expected to operate at low occupancy levels, high costs, and significant deficits (U.S. Department of Transportation, 1976a). Thus, taxpayer support at the local, state, and federal levels is essential. As with transit generally, the appropriate roles at each level are a subject of continuing controversy and change, with a general relative increase of public sector involvement.

Certain technical subissues also warrant attention. The demand potential for rural transit service is generally very low and costs are high (Kidder, 1977; U.S. Department of Transportation, 1976a). But the excess capacity of most systems—at least on paper—suggests that capital investment in additional vehicles may not always make good sense. Private nonprofit and public client-agency transportation systems often provide duplicating but uncoordinated services, all of which are underutilized and are high in taxpayer costs. The services, which may be known locally by many different names (e.g., Meals on Wheels, FISH), do not generally provide transportation as their primary service; nevertheless, their combined transportation budgets are often many times greater than the budget of the regular transit system. The degree to which such services can be consolidated to provide effective services at fair and adequate levels is an evolving technical and administrative question.

Surprisingly little direct use of the behavioral sciences has been made in rural transit services. While the literature on the sociology of rural environments is vast, most of it deals only indirectly with transportation, insofar as isolation generates a number of economic, psychological, and social problems (Kay, 1975). Surveys of rural populations often contain transportation-related questions, but until recently, few such studies have been oriented primarily toward transportation services. Some application of marketing and business principles in setting up rural transit systems has also begun (Gerstenberger, 1977; McKelvey, 1975; Transportation Research Board, 1978a), but these operations have not emphasized—or generally even incorporated—behavioral science principles. The potential for applications of the behavioral sciences here is extensive and generally untapped.

Table 3 shows certain possible applications. Perhaps the largest potential area is the direct use, by transit service planners and operators, of the literature on the structure of rural society. It may be quite rightly pointed out, for instance, that the second- and third-order impacts on the individual of rural transit service provision extend far beyond the quantifiable increase in mobility that is provided. These positive impacts—particularly changes in economic status, reduction of isolation and its associated social problems, and changes in attitudes—are, of

TABLE 3
MAJOR PRESENT AND POTENTIAL APPLICATIONS OF BEHAVIORAL SCIENCES
TO RURAL TRANSIT SERVICES

Subject	Typical applications
Present:	
Opinion measurement	Community views of transit service needs
Social structure	Effect of transportation and isolation on rural society
Consumer choice theory	Marketing transit services
Potential:	
Attitude measurement and change	Probable relationship between isolation and transportation services
Perception	Views of needed services
Motivation	Factors underlying behavior
Behavior and behavior modification	Understanding of and change in travel patterns and use of new services
Learning and diffusion of innovations	Marketing new services; increasing usage
Roles–norms–status–class	Factors affecting service use and perceptions
Lifestyles and cycles	Factors affecting service use and perceptions
Culture and society	Impact of social structure on transportation and vice versa
Group dynamics and leadership	Use of in-place group structures to develop and support services

course, major reasons to provide such service, but in measuring service effectiveness, transportation analysts rarely include them. While transportation service is not the only necessary ingredient in improving the quality of rural life, it is clearly an essential one. Conversely, such service may subsequently change the rural society itself, modernizing it and integrating it into a larger social order. Whether this result is bad or good is a value judgment, but the point is that transportation analysts cannot now even make such judgments since they lack the requisite knowledge on impacts.

Consider, as examples, the subjects of attitude measurement and change and of perceptions. In a careful study of attitudes toward transportation service improvements throughout New York, Donnelly (1975) and others used conjoint measurement and multidimensional scaling procedures to determine what kinds of transit service rural residents needed and were willing to pay for. As transportation analysts, not behavioral scientists, these researchers found themselves required to learn and assimilate a large body of literature on attitude scaling to conduct the study. While the results were satisfactory and useful, it is clear that much effort could have been saved if more material on applications of attitude measurement and change to transportation had been available. In addition, it would have been of particular use to have available extensive studies of rural lifestyle and isolation in relation to transportation service, since the study showed that of all problems confronting rural New York residents, transportation was perceived to be the greatest in importance.

TRANSPORTATION FOR THE MOBILITY-LIMITED

Urban area transportation plans in the 1960s were surprisingly devoid of detailed information concerning the travel characteristics or requirements of any special groups, including the mobility-limited. Concern about these groups began to evolve in the late 1960s, as the geographic and temporal scale of transportation planning decreased and more emphasis was placed on the special requirements of various subgroups within the population. Greater interest in transit systems and their accessibility and mobility for special groups also accelerated this trend.

Initial analyses of transportation systems for the mobility-limited were oriented primarily to modifications of existing transit systems. However, it became apparent that in many ways, existing transit systems were inadequate for the special requirements of these groups, because mobility-limited persons were not often capable of taking full advantage of these systems for a variety of physical and psychological reasons. The result was the promulgation of federal laws and regulations describing special requirements for "elderly and handicapped" planning, for the provision of transportation services for the elderly and the handicapped, and for revising existing systems to provide access. Parallel with this activity, the development of fully accessible transit vehicles has also proceeded.

A separate and almost unrelated evolution has also taken place in other (nontransportation) areas. The late 1960s witnessed a significant increase in the vocalization of demands, particularly by the physically handicapped, that a variety of services provided by society be made accessible to them in a fully integrated way. These demands have culminated in recently promulgated guidelines requiring full accessibility to all public buildings and related facilities. It is perhaps unfortunate that the issue of transportation accessibility has not been at the forefront in the evolution of these accessibility issues. Rather, transportation appears to have taken a back seat, and transportation planners and providers have therefore found themselves generally reacting to rather than influencing the direction of policy on this subject.

The key issues in transportation services for the mobility-limited are likely to continue to revolve around broader national questions. It is central to understand and agree on the degree to which access is either a right or a privilege, and what amount of it constitutes fair and equal treatment for specialized user groups. The position of the handicapped-person lobbies has been that separate service, while it may be superior in quality, does not constitute equal service because it is not integrated. In this view, one of the primary objectives of transportation actions should be to encourage and enable the physical and psychological integration of the handicapped person into society, and this simply cannot be done by the provision of separate systems.

But recent studies show that specialized facilities such as subway station elevators or bus wheelchair lifts do not, in fact, lead to significant additional use for a variety of social and psychological reasons. And such actions require large expenditures, particularly for fitting existing vehicles (estimates at $4–$10 billion nationwide). It can be demonstrated that the dollars thus spent could provide a far higher level of service to these groups in other ways, either through chauffeured systems or specialized services, rather than through the removal of physical barriers in existing systems. A central issue, therefore, is cost versus effectiveness.

To deal with such questions, the analyst must understand the nature of demand for transportation systems, the implied particular physical and service requirements for serving different groups, future travel behavior, future lifestyles, and better utilization of existing client-agency transportation services through coordination and cooperation in the use of vehicle fleets. All these questions have behavioral content. Table 4 shows how such issues can be studied with behavioral science methodology. The most extensive use of these principles has been in the human factors area, to assist in the appropriate design of fully accessible transportation systems (e.g., National Cooperative Highway Research Program, 1976). Considerable use has been made of attitude and opinion measurement and theory. For instance, Hartgen, Pasko, and Howe (1977), Miller (1976), and Paaswell and Recker (1976) all used simple attitude-scaling procedures to evaluate the perceived public transit needs of handicapped or carless people. Studies have also focused on travel behavior (Falcocchio, 1977; Hartgen, Pasko, & Howe, 1977), and more recently on lifestyle (Wachs & Blanchard, 1976). Numerous other topical areas would appear to be of potential usefulness to planners, particularly roles and norms, and socialization.

As an example, consider the problem of future lifestyles. As Wachs

TABLE 4
MAJOR PRESENT AND POTENTIAL APPLICATIONS OF BEHAVIORAL SCIENCES
TO TRANSPORTATION FOR THE MOBILITY-LIMITED

Subject	Typical applications
Present:	
Human factors	Design of vehicles and transportation system access
Attitudes	Perception of handicapped and/or elderly toward transit systems
Behavior	Mode choice and trip generation of the elderly
Lifestyle	Evolution of travel patterns as people age
Potential:	
Perception and beliefs	Views of transportation accessibility and mobility
Attitude–behavior link	Perceptions of mobility limitation and their effect on travel choices by handicapped persons
Decision theory	Methods by which the elderly and the handicapped make travel choices
Roles and norms	Behavior in a variety of social and structural contexts
Status and class	Social background for describing travel patterns of the elderly and the handicapped
Socialization	The process by which the elderly and/or the handicapped adopt specific roles and behaviors
Personal space	Interior vehicle design
Group dynamics and organization development	Structure of lobby groups and their activities

noted (Wachs & Blanchard, 1976), transportation planners often make the assumption that the travel needs of today's elderly and/or handicapped are a good indication of tomorrow's requirements. But the lifestyles, attitudes, and travel behavior of tomorrow's elderly are more likely to be those of the people who are working today, with higher average travel rates than today's elderly and hence they are likely to be more mobile in their later years than today's elderly. To the extent that such patterns are constant, we must look to today's middle-aged people, not to today's elderly, to understand tomorrow's elderly. The sociology of aging and its changes would be of obvious and great relevance in understanding these trends, yet except for a few isolated cases, transportation analysts have not incorporated such studies in their work.

ENVIRONMENTAL AND SOCIAL IMPACT ANALYSIS

While it is true that the transportation plans developed in the 1960s included a large number of proposed major facilities for metropolitan areas, these plans generally did not serve as the key impetus for the facilities then in the planning or development stage. Nor did they appear to have a major impact on the decline of highway construction in the 1960s. Highway construction was already being slowed significantly by a variety of broad social and national concerns, caused in part by issues outside highway construction itself. Preeminent among these issues were:

1. Increasing concern on the part of the public about environmental conservation and improvement of air quality.
2. Increasing (in the 1970s) realization of the scarcity of energy resources.
3. Concern about the significant detrimental impact on neighborhoods within urban areas (often accuring to precisely those individuals and communities that did not benefit significantly from the highway project itself).
4. Significant increases in the involvement of citizens in the general activities of government.
5. Realization that escalating construction costs, combined with scarcer public dollars, mean increasing inability of local governments to meet the local share of federal construction projects.
6. Generally tighter federal budgets and greater emphasis on transit systems.

The sum total of all of these trends was to effectively slow urban highway construction and investment to a crawl in the late 1960s and early 1970s. Partially in response, a variety of federal programs were developed to emphasize transit construction and investment and to maximize the use of existing transportation systems. The 1977 Clean Air Act Amendments further accelerated this trend, by requiring the detailed evaluation of a variety of low-capital actions in the transportation sector, particularly van pooling, car pooling, and public transit actions, as well as moderately effective actions. In summary, the heyday of major highway construction is over, at least in urban areas, and with it probably has also died the necessity of evaluating and analyzing on a large scale the impact of major transportation actions on the urban environment and on urban society and communities.

The central issues of transportation investment are demand shifts versus transportation system expansions, and improved maintenance and utilization of existing facilities versus the creation of new facilities. The question of transportation access versus its relative social and environmental costs will continue to be important, but it is likely to decline in relative importance. We should also expect to see increased concern about the relative distribution of costs and benefits of transportation actions among the various demographic and geographic groups in society; these trends will come about primarily in response to increasing concerns about the equity of such distributions, and the degree to which such distributions and services are appropriate for different societal segments.

Clearly, analysis of transportation impacts will continue, although, the scale and complexity of such impacts is likely to shift toward the low-cost noncapital action. This means that new work will be required in the identification and measurement of impact values, their associated weights as viewed by the public and its various lobby groups, and the design of transportation investments in such a way as to make them compatible with both the environment and society. Good examples would be present concerns about changes in the air-pollution potential and the energy efficiency of automobiles, the noise around airports and along major highways, and the maximum use and operating efficiency of existing transportation facilities. As the scale and time frame of transportation investment decreases, current and proposed actions are likely to find an increase in the magnitude of public involvement in transportation. Transportation analysts ought to be readying themselves now for dealing with a variety of new actions that are concerned primarily with the short-term impacts of transportation investments.

The behavioral sciences have much to offer the transportation planner in this area. As Table 5 shows, environmental and social impact

TABLE 5

MAJOR PRESENT AND POTENTIAL APPLICATIONS OF BEHAVIORAL SCIENCES
TO ENVIRONMENTAL AND SOCIAL IMPACTS

Subject	Typical applications
Present:	
Attitudes and opinions	Community views of transportation actions
Community cohesion	Studies of community impact of major facilities
Groups	Citizen involvement in transportation planning
Human factors	Design of transportation facilities to reduce air pollution
Potential:	
Perception and beliefs	Community view of transportation projects
Roles and norms	Positions of actors in citizen groups
Status and class	Differences in communities and neighborhoods
Society and socialization	Highway project impacts on communities
Group structures	Understanding lobbies and pressure groups

analysis to date has utilized only a few central ideas from the behavioral sciences. These applications have concerned attitudes, opinions, and community cohesion related to transportation projects and their impact (e.g., Institute on Man and Science, 1976; U.S. Department of Transportation, 1975). Much work has also been done on the nature of citizen participation and the way in which groups and organizations operate in both the public and the private sector (e.g., Manheim, 1971; Jordan, 1976; Smith, 1975; Yukubousky, 1973). The work is of particular interest since it provides another example of transportation analysts' learning a set of skills already possessed by others rather than having them provide the service. For instance, Yukubousky (1973) reviewed over 50 different methods of citizen participation, including such well-known procedures as focus groups and participant observation. Each method was evaluated for application to transportation planning, development, programming, design, and construction, based on experiences with the method in the social sciences. This major work is still a central reference today. Studies have also been made of transportation impacts on demographic and social groups (e.g., Crane & Partners, 1976), although the procedures used have not been the same as those used by social scientists.

Other applications are also apparent, for instance, the concept of neighborhood. When transportation facilities are constructed in urban areas, a significant amount of disruption generally takes place long before as well as during and after development. In fact, "highway plans" have been cited as a major factor in accelerating the decline of some neighborhoods, as residents hesitate to invest in the face of possible relocation. But parallel examples also exist in which highway construction has served as an impetus for revitalization. Such matters have been of great concern to transportation analysts but have not received much attention in the behavioral sciences.

ENERGY AND TRANSPORTATION

A central shortcoming of most metropolitan-area transportation plans developed in the 1960s is that they failed to consider the possibility of price or supply constraints on transportation fuels. Of the 230+ long-range urban transportation plans prepared in this period, no more than a handful even mention the possibility of energy constraints, and of those that do, none, to the author's knowledge, deal with those constraints in a way that suggests that the concern should be deep. Further, the transportation investment proposals that were developed from these plans generally make no mention of such constraints, nor are the investments themselves based on a realistic estimate of the probability of such constraints. Even today, it is a rare agency that comprehensively studies the nature of the transportation energy supply and its future. Perhaps, then, it is not surprising that the transportation planning profession was caught largely off-guard by the 1973–1974 and the 1979 energy crises. Those crises, while short in duration and small in magnitude, were severe enough to demonstrate the critical dependence of the United States on foreign energy supplies, and particularly the importance of such supplies to the continued growth and viability of the domestic economy. Further, available evidence suggests that it was the availability of energy, rather than gasoline prices, that primarily influenced demand in the 1973–1974 crisis (Hartgen, 1979a; Neveu, 1977; Peskin, 1975). Where possible, individuals reduced discretionary travel and took minor actions to cope with the crisis: there was very little shift to alternative transportation modes, nor did the 1973–74 crisis show evidence of changes in car purchasing or residential moving behavior (Keck, 1974; Stearns, 1975). This evidence was partially reconfirmed by the "crisis" of 1979, which saw a 30% rise in price and an 11% shortfall of supply (Hartgen, 1979a), but a surge in small-car purchasing. Some research has been published on energy constraints and the effectiveness of various energy conservation options in the transportation sector (Rubin, 1975; National Cooperative Highway Research Program, 1977; Gross, 1979).

Recent history (through 1980) suggests that we are entering a period of increasingly stringent requirements with respect to energy conservation for transportation. Recent price rises and shortfalls are likely to be repeated. Eventually, the price of petroleum will very likely be driven up so much that alternative fuels will be viable as substitutes, or that significant shifts in travel behavior and perhaps lifestyles will result. The key issues in the next several years revolve around transportation energy conversion and contingency-based actions, while continuing present or reasonable levels of personal mobility. The actions that should be taken to address these issues in an effective, fair manner will be of great interest to local transportation analysts and operators. Such actions will very likely fall with differential impact on different demographic and geographic groups of society, as occurred during the 1979 energy crisis (Hartgen, 1979a). Allocation of scarce energy resources is likely to produce concern about relative shortfalls and priorities for transportation uses by individuals and families, as well as within and perhaps among rural and urban areas. Over the longer run (15–30 years), we must deal with a conversion from the use of petroleum-based products to other products and with the impact that this conversion is likely to have on travel, the economy, and the society.

Considerable research is needed (e.g., National Cooperative Highway Research Program, 1977) if we are to understand how travel will change in response to energy conservation incentives and disincentives. Critical to this understanding is a knowledge of how individuals and decision-making units place priorities on travel and allocate scarce resources for its completion. Transportation experts will also have to develop approaches to identify and evaluate alternative sources of action to conserve energy at the state and local level.

Energy contingency planning, as opposed to conservation planning, focuses on short-term actions intended to meet a specified shortfall for example, a 10% cut in gasoline supplies. For example, in the spring and summer of 1979, supplies were 11% below the previous year's levels, and prices rose 30% in 12 months. Government response was generally predictable: odd–even, half-tank rules to prevent panic; exhortations to reduce travel; and 55-mph speed-limit enforcement. The public's behavior was also predictable: reductions in discretionary travel; canceled or shortened vacations; and some transit use. Small car purchases surged as people tried to maintain mobility at a constant out-of-pocket gasoline cost. Modifications of behavior were made only to the extent that disruption of lifestyle were prevented.

There are a number of obvious applications of behavioral science principles to the energy issue, which are summarized in Table 6. Consider, for example, behavior modification. Energy conservation in transportation is ultimately a question of whether behavior can be modified so that energy is conserved. The principles of behavior modification and the relationship between attitudes and behavior are critical and obvious links between the energy issue and the behaviorial sciences. For exam-

TABLE 6
MAJOR PRESENT AND POTENTIAL APPLICATIONS OF BEHAVIORAL SCIENCES
TO ENERGY AND TRANSPORTATION

Subject	Typical applications
Present:	
Attitude theory and measurement	Attitudes and opinions about energy use
Behavior	Present energy use patterns
Potential:	
Attitude change	Views toward energy consumption
Lifestyle	Changes in U.S. lifestyle that reduce energy use
Behavior modification	Rapid change in behavior, as in emergencies
Decision theory	Choice under supply constraints
Group structure	Influence of pressure groups and lobbies in energy allocations

ple, during 1979, the public focused on vacation-related actions to conserve gasoline, modifying their choices of destination and mode, while the government generally focused on transit. The public have remained skeptical of the reasons given for the crisis and are inclined to continue to take actions that are consistent with the necessity to conserve (e.g., the purchase of fuel-efficient cars). Critical to this process is an understanding of the ways that individuals perceive the energy crisis and the opportunities for energy use in the transportation sector. Attitude theory and measurement, as well as perception and beliefs, are likely to play important roles in this process. Some headway has already been made in understanding attitudes toward energy conservation (e.g., Meyers, 1979), but the effort has only scratched the surface. Further, since energy usage is in many ways a product of lifestyle and culture, a considerable portion of the behavioral science concepts in these areas are also applicable to the problem. It is fair to say at this point that while very little of such material has been studied and brought into the transportation energy area so far, the potential for payoff in doing so would appear to be very great.

SUMMARY AND CONCLUSIONS

This chapter has described the evolution of central issues in five problem areas relating to transportation, and it has considered how the projected direction of work on these issues is likely to benefit from the input of the behavioral sciences.

These results are summarized in Figure 1, which serves as an overview of the paper. Clearly, in transportation, the most obvious present applications are those concerning attitude theory and structure, with lesser but also important applications in behavior and attitude–behavior links, lifestyle, community, and culture. Personal-space and human factors are also areas that have received considereable attention, and certain management principles are being applied to transit operations.

It should also be apparent that there are a large number of subjects within the behavioral sciences that are, at least on the surface, directly applicable to the kinds of problems and issues that transportation analysts are likely to encounter. Particularly, further work on the attitude–behavioral link, on perception, and especially in the area of social structure—particularly life cycle, family, culture, and society—would all seem fruitful. An overlooked area of application that may have considerable potential for some studies in group structure and organizations, particularly group dynamics, pressure and lobby groups, and principles of management.

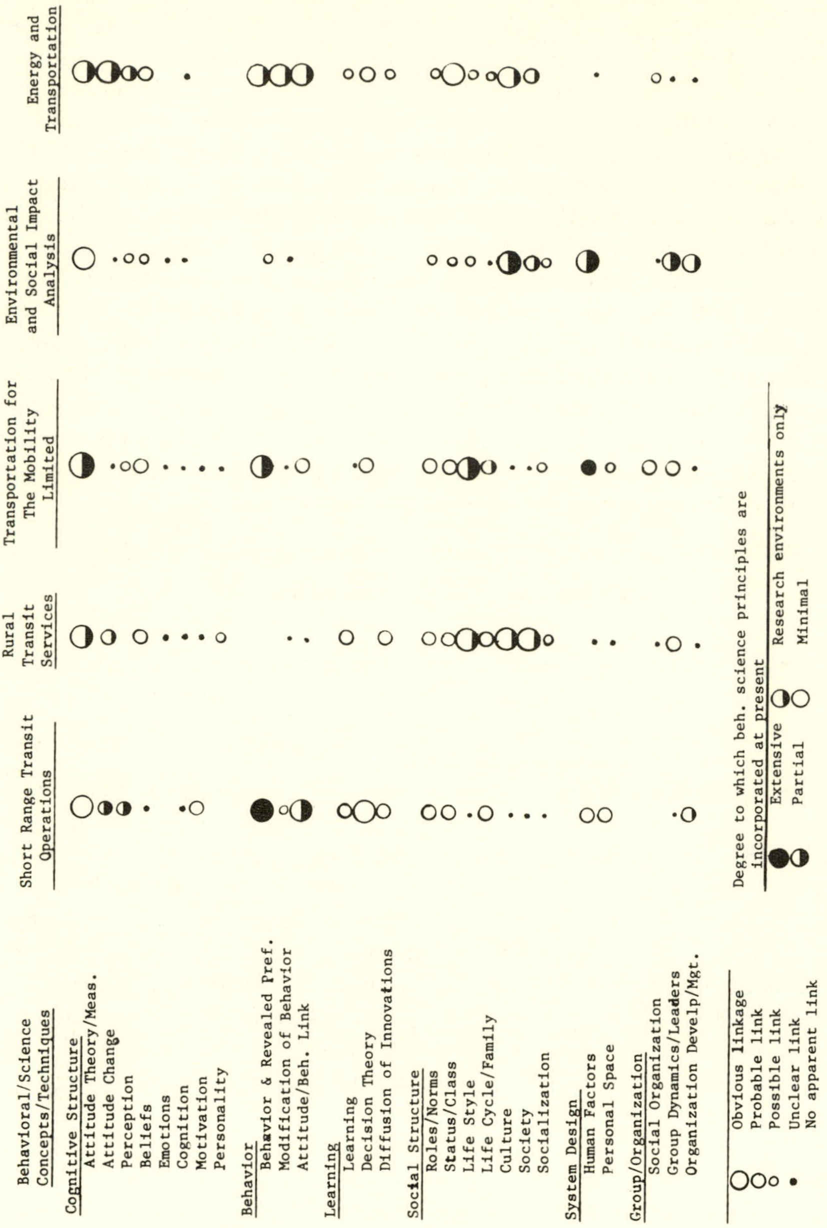

Behavioral/Science
Concepts/Techniques

Cognitive Structure
Attitude Theory/Meas.
Attitude Change
Perception
Beliefs
Emotions
Cognition
Motivation
Personality

Behavior
Behavior & Revealed Pref.
Modification of Behavior
Attitude/Beh. Link

Learning
Learning
Decision Theory
Diffusion of Innovations

Social Structure
Roles/Norms
Status/Class
Life Style
Life Cycle/Family
Culture
Society
Socialization

System Design
Human Factors
Personal Space

Group/Organization
Social Organization
Group Dynamics/Leaders
Organization Develp/Mgt.

Column headers:
Short Range Transit Operations
Rural Transit Services
Transportation for The Mobility Limited
Environmental and Social Impact Analysis
Energy and Transportation

Legend:
◐ Obvious linkage / Probable link
○ Possible link
o Unclear link
• No apparent link

Degree to which beh. science principles are incorporated at present
Extensive | Partial
Research environments only | Minimal

Figure 1. Present and potential links between behavioral science concepts.

We have purposely not dealt in detail with the methodology of the behavioral sciences, since in many ways it is not significantly different than that used in transportation. However, certain approaches might be highlighted for exploration as potentially useful:

- Experimental designs in laboratory settings, such as Louviere's studies of factors affecting mode choice. (e.g., Louviere 1977; Levin & Louviere, 1978).
- Quasi-experimental designs for before–after studies such as for transportation improvements (e.g., Tischer & Phillips, 1979) or for car-pool programs (Brunso & Hartgen, 1979).
- Content analysis of recorded focus group interviews (e.g., Krishman & Golob, 1977).
- Structural equations and path analysis (e.g., Dobson, 1978) to extract causal relationships between attitudes, demographics, and travel behavior.
- Participant–observer methods.
- Social indicators and "unobtrusive measures."

Perhaps one of the richest areas is quasi-experiments. Many "demonstrations" in transportation have been undertaken with only the loosest of experimental controls, the end result being that background effects could not be isolated. The conclusions drawn, of course, were thus misleading. Only recently has specific attention been given to more careful designs to evaluate transportation actions.

Finally, the diffusion of innovation (in this case, the diffusion of behavioral science ideas into transportation) is itself a behavioral process that generally requires positive action on the part of both giver and recipient. This chapter has been prepared in the belief that even the author's superficial knowledge of the behavioral sciences suggests a possible lasting and significant interaction of mutual benefit. It is fair to say that the behavioral sciences have not been overly concerned with such issues as transportation theory and policy making. While it is not suggested that it ought to be otherwise, the applications of behavioral science principles to governmental disciplines, including transportation, should be given more attention. For a variety of reasons, many of which are subsumed in the issues described above, transportation would be an obvious point of contact.

REFERENCES

Atherton, T. J., & Ben-Akiva, M. E. Transferability and updating of disaggregate travel demand models. Transportation Research Board *Record No. 610,* 1976, 12–18.

Britt, S. H. *Consumer behavior and the behavioral sciences*. New York: Wiley, 1966.

Brog, W., & Erl, E. An overview of interactive travel data collection techniques. Paper presented at the Annual Meeting of the Transportation Research Board, Washington, D.C., 1980.

Brunso, J. M., & Hartgen, D. T. Carpool coordinator demonstration study: Final report. New York State Department of Transportation, *Preliminary Research Report No. 171*, Albany, N.Y., 1979.

Burkhardt, J., & Lago, A. *Predicting the demand for rural public transportation systems*. Washington, D.C.: Transportation Research Board, 1977.

Burkhardt, J., *A study of the transportation problems of the rural poor*. Washington, D.C.: U.S. Office of Economic Opportunity, 1972.

Charles River Associates, *Disaggregate travel demand models*, Washington, D.C.: National Cooperative Highway Research Program, 1976.

Crane, D. A., & Partners. *Impact assessment guidelines*. Washington, D.C.. National Cooperative Highway Research Program, 1976.

Dobson, R. D. Structural models for the analysis of traveler attitude–behavior relationships. *Transportation*, 1978, *7*, 351–364.

Donnelly, E. P. Statewide public opinion survey on public transportation. New York State Department of Transportation, *Preliminary Research Report No. 80*, Albany, N.Y., 1975.

Everett, P. B. *A behavioral science approach to transportation systems management*. University Park, Pa. Pennsylvania Transportation Institute, 1978.

Falcocchio, J. Travel patterns and mobility needs of the physically handicapped. Transportation Research Board *Record No. 618*, 1977.

Fried, M., & Havens, J. *Travel behavior: A synthesized theory*. Washington, D.C.: National Highway Cooperative Research Program, 1977.

Gerstenberger, A. *Marketing rural transportation services*. University Park, Pa.: Pennsylvania Transportation Institute, 1977.

Gilbert, G., & Foerster, J. F. The importance of attitudes in the decision to use mass transit. *Transportation*, 1976, *5*, 45–62.

Gillian, J. & Wachs, M. Lifestyles and transportation needs of the elderly in Los Angeles. *Transportation*, 1977, *6*, 321–322.

Golob, T. F., & Dobson, R. Assessment of preferences and perceptions toward attributes of transportation alternatives. Transportation Research Board *Special Report No. 149*, 1974.

Golob, T. F., & Recker, W. W. Mode choice prediction using attitudinal data: A procedure and some results. *Transportation*, 1977, *6*, 265–286.

Golob, T. F., Horowitz, A., & Wachs, M. Attitude–behavior relationships in travel demand models. Paper presented at the 3rd International Conference on Travel Behavior, Tanunda, Austrailia, 1977.

Gross, J. M. Energy impacts of transportation systems management 1978–80. New York State Department of Transportation, *Preliminary Research Report No. 150*, Albany, N.Y., 1979.

Hartgen, D. T. Attitudinal and situational variables influencing urban mode choice: Some empirical findings. *Transportation*, 1974, *3*, 377–392.

Hartgen, D. T. Ridesharing behavior: A review of recent findings. New York State Department of Transportation, *Preliminary Research Report No. 130*, Albany, N.Y., 1977.

Hartgen, D. T. Changes in travel during the 1979 energy crisis. New York State Department of Transportation, *Preliminary Research Report No. 170*, Albany, N.Y., 1979. (a)

Hartgen, D. T. Guidelines for transportation energy contingency planning. New York State Department of transportation, *Preliminary Research Report No. 157*, 1979. (b)

Hartgen, D. T., & Wachs, M. Disaggregate travel demand modes for special context planning: A dissenting view. Transportation Research Board, *Special Report No. 149*, 1974.

Hartgen, D. T., Pasko, M., & Howe, S. M. Forecasting non-work public transit demand by the elderly and handicapped. Transportation Research Board, *Record No. 673*, 1977.

Institute on Man and Science. *Social and economic impacts of highway projects.* Rensselaerville, N.Y., 1976.

Jones, P. M. New approaches to understanding travel behavior: The human activity approach. Paper presented at the 3rd International Conference on Travel Behavior 1977, Tanunda, Australia, 1977.

Jordan, D. *Effective citizen participation in transportation planning.* Washington, D.C.: U.S. Department of Transportation, 1976.

Kaye, I. *Mobility in rural America.* Washington, D.C.: Rural Housing Alliance, 1975.

Keck, C. A., Changes in individual travel during the energy crisis, 1973–74. New York State Department of Transportation, *Preliminary Research Report No. 67*, Albany, N.Y., 1974.

Kidder, A. E. Costs of alternative transportation systems for the elderly and the handicapped in small urban areas. Transportation Research Board, *Record No. 660*, 1977.

Krishman, K. S., & Golob, T. F. Using focus group interviews and workshops to develop transportation concepts. General Motors Research Laboratory, *Paper 2428*, Warren, Mich., 1977.

Levin, I., & Louviere, J. Functional analysis of mode choice. Paper presented at the Annual Meeting of Transportation Research Board, Washington, D.C., 1978.

Louviere, J. *Applications of psychological measurement and modeling to behavioral travel demand analysis.* Center for Behavioral Studies, University of Wyoming, Laramie, 1977.

Manheim, M. *Community values in highway location and design.* Center For Transportation Studies, Massachusetts Institute of Technology, Cambridge, 1971.

Margolin, J. B., & Misch, M. R. *Handbook of behavioral strategies in transportation.* Washington, D.C.: Behavioral Studies Laboratory, George Washington University, 1978.

McFadden, D. Quantitative methods for analyzing travel behavior: Some recent developments. Paper presented at the Annual Meeting of Transportation Research Board, Washington, D.C., 1978.

McKelvey, D. *Transportation systems for older Americans and public systems in rural areas.* Iowa City: Center for Urban and Regional Research, University of Iowa, 1975.

Meyers, C. E. Factors affecting willingness to conserve gasoline. New York State Department of Transportation, *Preliminary Research Report No. 167*, Albany, N.Y., 1979.

Miller, J. Latent travel demand of the handicapped and elderly. Transportation Research Board, *Record No. 618*, 1976.

National Cooperative Highway Research Program. Transportation requirements for the handicapped, elderly and economically disadvantaged. *Synthesis No. 39*, Washington, D.C., 1976.

National Cooperative Highway Research Program. Transportation energy. *Synthesis No. 48*, Washington, D.C., 1977.

Neels, K., Cheslow, M. D., & Beesley, M. *Improving demand forecasts for urban area travel.* Washington, D.C.: Urban Institute, 1978.

Neveu, A. J. The 1973–74 energy crisis: Impact on travel. New York State Department of Transportation, *Preliminary Research Report No. 131*, 1977.

Paaswell, R. E., & Recker, W. W. *Problems of the carless.* Washington, D.C.: Office of University Research, U.S. Department of Transportation, 1976.

Pennsylvania Transportation Institute. *Proceedings of the 2nd National Conference on Rural Public Transportation.* Washington, D.C.: U.S. Department of Transportation, 1977.

Peskin, R. L. *The immediate impact of gasoline shortages on urban travel behavior.* Evanston, Ill.: Department of Civil Engineering, Northwestern University, 1975.

Restle, F., & Greeno, J. G. *Introduction to mathematical psychology.* Evanston, Ill.: Addison-Wesley, 1970.

Rubin, D. *A summary of opportunities to conserve transportation energy.* Cambridge, Mass.: Transportation Systems Center, 1975.

Smerk, G. M. The transit industry: What's right and wrong. *Transit Journal,* 1976, *2,* 31–44.

Smith, D. C. *Manual for community involvement in highway planning and design.* Washington, D.C.: Federal Highway Administration, 1975.

Stearns, M. D. *The behavioral impacts of the energy shortages: Shifts in trip-making characteristics.* Washington, D.C.: U.S. Department of Transportation, 1975.

Stopher, P. R., & Meyburg, A. M. *Behavioral travel demand models.* Concord, Mass.: Lexington Books, 1975. (a)

Stopher, P. R., & Meyburg, A. M. *Urban transportation modeling and planning.* Concord, Mass.: Lexington Books, 1975. (b)

Tischer, M. L., & Phillips, R. V. The relationships between transportation perceptions and behaviors over time. *Transportation,* 1979, *8,* 21–33.

Transportation Research Board. Public transportation in rural and suburban areas. Transportation Research Board, *Record No. 661,* Washington, D.C., 1978. (a)

Transportation Research Board. The ten most critical issues in transportation. *Transportation Research News,* Nov.–Dec. 1978b, 3–6.

Transportation Research Board. Urban travel demand forecasting. *Special Report No. 143,* Washington, D.C., 1978. (c)

Transportation Systems Center. *Transportation energy conservation.* Cambridge, Mass.: Office of Technology Sharing, Transportation Systems Center, 1979.

Ugolik, W. R., & Knighton, R. G. Estimating the effects of alternative service levels on rural transit ridership. New York State Department of transportation, *Preliminary Research Report No. 144,* Albany, N.Y., 1978.

U.S. Department of Transportation. *Environmental assessment notebook.* Washington, D.C., 1975.

U.S. Department of Transportation. *Rural passenger transportation.* Washington, D.C., 1976. (a)

U.S. Department of Transportation, *Social and economic effects of highways.* Washington, D.C., 1976. (b)

U.S. Federal Aid Highway Act, Section 147: Rural Highway Public Transportation Demonstration Program, 1973.

U.S. Surface Transportation Assistance Act, Section 18: Rural Public Transportation Program, 1978.

Wachs, M. Transportation policy in the 1980's. *Transportation,* 1977, *6,* 105–119.

Wachs, M., & Blanchard, R. D. Lifestyles and transportation needs of the elderly in the future. Transportation Research Board, *Record No. 618,* 1976.

Yukubousky, R. Community interaction techniques in transportation systems and projects development. New York State Department of Transportation, *Preliminary Research Report No. 50,* Albany, N.Y., 1973.

2

Psychological Contributions to Travel Demand Modeling

IRWIN P. LEVIN and JORDAN J. LOUVIERE

INTRODUCTION

Travel Demand Modeling: A Historical Overview

The area of travel demand modeling has traditionally been concerned with assessing the determinants of current travel patterns, predicting changes in these patterns as a function of projected changes in transportation systems, and developing more efficient transportation systems based on users' needs and preferences. The concept of a demand for travel is essentially an economic one: Travel is rarely valued for its own sake; rather, it is valued as a means of attaining some other end. Theoretically, it should be possible to map out the quantities of travel that are purchased at each of a range of prices. Normative planning goals could then be achieved by setting supply of transportation and demand for transportation in equilibrium. Although this is an attractive concept, firmly grounded in the well-developed area of consumer theory in economics, a range of problems plagues most attempts to put it into operation in transportation planning. Indeed, research in the general area of travel demand modeling has been moving rapidly toward theory and methods that may be broadly viewed as attempts to develop

IRWIN P. LEVIN • Department of Psychology, University of Iowa, Iowa City, Iowa 52242.
JORDAN J. LOUVIERE • Department of Marketing, University of Iowa, Iowa City, Iowa 52242.

explanations of human travel behavior, in general, and human travel choices, in particular. As will be described in this chapter, such research relies heavily on the contributions of psychological measurement and modeling.

The early history of travel demand modeling was characterized by a focus on highly aggregate measures of transportation system behavior and traveler behavior: Areal units termed *traffic zones* served as the basic unit of observation and analysis (Hill & von Cube, 1963). Statistical explanations, usually in the form of multiple linear regression equations, were sought for four broad areas of traffic-zonal travel behavior:

1. *Trip generation:* the process whereby travel is generated in traffic zones. Typical assumptions were that the number of trips originating in a particular traffic zone was associated with household activity- and need-related factors such as average family size, the number of automobiles owned by inhabitants of the zone, and the income levels of the zonal inhabitants (Wooton & Pick, 1967).

2. *Trip distribution:* the process whereby trips generated in a traffic zone are distributed or allocated to other zones as destinations. The most theoretical of the four areas of aggregate travel behavior analysis, the movement of trips between origin and destination zones is usually conceived of in terms of what is called a *gravity function* (Carrothers, 1956). Such a function receives its name from the analogy that was once drawn with Newton's notion of gravitational attraction: The force of attraction between any two masses or bodies is directly proportional to the product of their masses and inversely proportional to the square of the intervening distance between them. Despite rather sophisticated attempts to rationalize so-called gravity regularities in trip distributions by recourse to the theory of utility maximization or the theory of entropy maximization (Wilson, 1967), the derived functions basically postulate that the number of trips moving from one traffic zone to another is some positive function of the generation of trips in each zone (the "masses") and some negative function of distance or travel effort between the zones (measured in time, distance, or money).

3. *Mode split:* a concern with explaining how aggregate trip flows "split" themselves between available transportation modes (private auto, bus, train, etc.) (Quandt, 1968). In traditional aggregate transportation-planning analyses, mode split is sometimes forecast after trip generation and other times after trip distribution, with little available theory to suggest which phase would be most appropriate. Typical explanatory variables include zonal aggregate measures, for each travel mode of interest, of the zone-center-to-zone-center travel times and costs, the average access (on and off) distance to various mass transit modes, and the like.

4. *Traffic assignment:* the development of sophisticated computer algorithms to trace the shortest time paths through the main links in the transportation network; to calculate volume-to-capacity ratios on the links; and to divert trips to second, third, etc., best least-time routes as travel times on the shortest route change with increasing volume–capacity ratios (Dial, 1971). This phase of travel analysis invariably involves assumptions that travelers always select least-time and cost paths and instantly adjust to congestion by diverting their trips to the next least-time path.

Much of the transportation analysis and forecasting effort of the United States and a number of other major Western nations still relies heavily on this type of approach to understanding and forecasting travel patterns. However, the aggregate modeling approach has generally fallen short of its goals of forecasting accuracy and policy sensitivity. Since 1970, some major new developments in the scientific understanding of travel behavior have come gradually to have an impact, and the contributions of psychological theory and methods have been largely within these new approaches. These new approaches have been termed *behavioral,* apparently for two reasons: (1) they focus on individual travelers and their trip-making behavior as the unit of observation and analysis; and (2) they seek to develop "behavioral" theory to explain the travel behavior of individuals.

BEHAVIORAL TRAVEL MODELING

The leading source of theory in the area of *behavioral travel modeling,* as we will now term it, is a blend of consumer theory from economics and choice theory from psychology. Much of the work has been accomplished by Daniel McFadden, Moshe Ben-Akiva, Richard Westin, Joel Horowitz, Will Recker, and others (e.g., Ben-Akiva, 1974; Horowitz, 1979; McFadden, 1974; Recker & Golob, 1976; Watson & Westin, 1975). The general choice theoretical notions of Luce (1959) and Restle (1961) have been shown to be consistent with consumer theory in economics, and by making appropriate assumptions about the composition of a utility or value function and the distribution of errors associated with its observations, tractable statistical model forms have been derived to test hypotheses about variables that are associated with choices. Because so much of our own research and thinking has been conceptually similar and also has been influenced by this work, we shall briefly outline its conceptual basis.

We begin by assuming that each individual uses some utility or value function to evaluate alternatives among which a choice must be made. Consistent with much work in both psychology and economics,

we assume the existence of a so-called multiattribute value function.
That is, we assume that the individual has a number of criteria against
which alternatives are compared and evaluated. If there are i total individuals sampled, and we assume that they share a common form of the
value function with common parameters, or at least that k homogeneous
subgroups of individuals can be identified that share a common
functional form and common parameters, then we can write:

$$V_{ij} = f(v_{ijl} + \epsilon_{ij})$$

where V_{ij} represents the overall evaluation given by individual i to
alternative j; v_{ijl} represents the systematic part of the value function of
individual i for the j alternatives based on l observable attributes that are
possessed by the alternatives, and ϵ_{ij} represents the unobserved or non-
systematic component of the value function.

By making appropriate assumptions about the ϵ_{ij}, different statistical choice models may be derived. For example, assuming that the ϵ's
are doubly exponentially distributed (so-called Gumbel distributions)
results in various forms of multiple Logit (or logistics curve) models,
while assuming jointly normal distributions results in Probit models.
The function, f, in Equation 1 is usually assumed to be additive in the
coefficients and errors; hence, it is similar in form to multiple regression
equations.

Statistically estimable choice models have been developed that relate choice probabilities to subjective evaluation of alternatives through
an equation such as the following (Richards & Ben-Akiva, 1975):

$$P_i(j|m) = e^{V_{ij}} / \sum_{j \in m} e^{V_{im}}$$

where $p_i(j|m)$ is the probability of individual i selecting alternative j,
given m available alternatives; e is the base of the natural logarithms;
and the right-hand side is simply a transform of Luce's choice axiom.

To illustrate how such choice models may be derived, consider the
current interest in modeling individuals' choices among alternative
modes of transportation for various trip purposes. Such a situation may
be conceptualized as a discrete choice where each alternative can be
defined by a set of attributes. The problem then becomes one of developing models that relate attribute levels to choice probabilities. In order to
do this, we must postulate that $V_{ij} = g(A)$, where V_{ij} is as defined
previously, A is a multidimensional vector of attribute measures, and g
is a mapping from A to V_{ij}. The measures in A are either obtained from
direct observation and measurement of attributes associated with a particular choice j from a choice set m, or they are fixed values manipulated

in a controlled, simulated choice task. In either case, the resulting value of V_{ij} can be entered into the choice model to predict choice probability. Each of these research strategies for modeling mode choice has unique strengths for contributing to the application of basic behavioral theory to travel demand modeling. The contrasting strengths and weaknesses of these two research strategies, as well as their possible complementary use, will be discussed in a later section.

The last decade has witnessed considerable development and refinement of basic behavioral theory applied to transportation problems, as well as an ever-increasing number of applications. Despite all the progress that has been made, however, almost all research and application have been strongly influenced and guided by the economic roots of the theory—most of the factors hypothesized to influence choice have roots in economic theory, and there has been little evidence of serious attempts to incorporate other explanatory variables of more direct interest and relevance to psychology. Rather, the influence of psychology is largely represented by the choice theory contributions mentioned earlier, and in the development of different approaches to the solution of problems in understanding and predicting travel behavior that currently stand largely outside the mainstream of travel behavior research.

Psychologists can make further contributions to this important social research area by demonstrating and capitalizing on complementarity, rather than emphasizing competition and differences between approaches. Psychology has much to offer the field of travel behavior research, and such research has much to offer psychology, in turn: The chance to test theory and method in real field settings in which behavior can be observed and, more importantly in our view, the chance to revise theory and approach in light of field observations and tests—a reward all too often traded off for the comfort and security of laboratory controls.

The goals of travel behavior modeling are commensurate with those of both scientific and practitioner psychologists:

1. To understand the bases of human travel behavior.
2. To use this understanding to forecast future patterns of behavior to provide information for informed decision making and planning.
3. To blend Goals 1 and 2 in order to develop approaches that are sensitive to the needs of policy makers at all levels: local, state, and national.

There are two major areas of contributions to which we will devote our attention: (1) contributions related to the application of behavioral research approaches and psychological measurement techniques; and

(2) contributions related to the application of behavioral models for understanding decision and choice processes. For organizational purposes, the chapter has separate sections on behavioral research approaches, psychological measurement methods, and psychological process theories, although it is recognized that theory development goes hand in hand with the refinement of research methods and measurement techniques. An additional section is included on attitudinal models to reflect the growing interest in this area of application.

The U.S. Department of Transportation recently recognized the role of psychology and the behavioral sciences in transportation by sponsoring a conference entitled, "Applying Behavioral Science to Transportation Planning, Policy and Management." However, the history of psychological contributions to travel–demand modeling has been a short one, and future contributions should outweigh past accomplishments. Thus, the chapter concludes with a discussion of recent developments and suggestions for potential further contributions.

OUR CONCEPTUALIZATION OF BEHAVIORAL TRAVEL MODELING

In order to organize the discussion in this chapter, we present a formal conceptual view of the concerns of travel behavior research. It represents our preferred paradigm for research in this area, but we provide it here only to focus discussion on the component processes underlying travel decisions. We assume that there are the following four relationships of interest at any particular point in time:

1. A set of perceptual relationships that map objective, observable attributes into individual subjective beliefs and perceptions. For example, if travel times and costs of alternative modes or to alternative destinations are major determinants of choice, then how are objective values of time and cost transformed into "believed" or "perceived" times and costs? Solutions to this problem involve both measurement and analytical capability. As we shall note, it is one of the underresearched areas of travel behavior analysis.

2. A set of "marginal value" relationships that map the "believed" or "perceived" values of Number 1 above into scale values that have meaning on a common psychological dimension, such as "goodness" or "desirability." For example, an individual can evaluate how desirable a bus system is that takes 20 minutes to get to work at a cost of 50¢, and with proper analytic and design tools, the researcher can determine the relationship between travel time and desirability and the relationship between bus fare and desirability. Solutions to this problem involve both measurement and modeling capability, and it is a research area of grow-

ing interest and importance. It is the area covered by the general "value assignment" problem.

3. A set of "overall value" relationships that map the "marginal" scale values of several attributes into a single, common, overall dimension. For example, what is the relative importance or weight of cost and time factors in evaluating alternative transportation systems, and how are subjective cost values and subjective time values *combined* to affect the perceived desirability of the alternative systems? These questions require both measurement and process modeling capability and are currently areas of high interest and importance in transportation research.

4. A set of choice relationships that map "overall values" into choices or choice probabilities. For example, once we have asked an individual to assign "overall values" to a set of alternatives among which the individual regularly chooses, we want to know how these overall values relate to the individual's choices over time or to the choices and values of a number of individuals at one point in time. Personal and situational constraints enter here, where preferences and choices may not coincide. This is a high-priority research area, only now beginning to receive considerable attention.

These relationships may be formalized as follows:

(1) $\quad x = f_1(X)$
(2) $\quad v = f_2(x)$
(3) $\quad V = f_3(v_1, v_2, \ldots, v_k)$
(4) $\quad C = f_4(V)$

where x represents the "believed" or "perceived" value of an attribute, and X represents its observable, measurable counterpart; v represents a "marginal value" or "scale value" of an attribute on some evaluative dimension, and V represents an "overall value" of an alternative on that dimension; and C represents choice, either discrete or continuous (e.g., number of trips per month by a particular mode). A graphic schematization of the relationships expressed in Equations 1–4 is presented in Figure 1, where the function f_1 represents the perceptual transformation, f_2

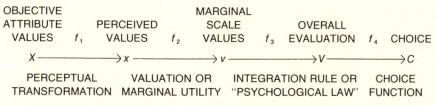

Figure 1. Component processes in individual mode choice behavior.

represents the valuation process, f_3 represents the rule by which scale values are integrated into an overall evaluation of a transportation alternative (Anderson, 1979, refers to this as the "psychological law."), and f_4 represents the transformation of evaluations into choices.

We may substitute within the system of equations as logic permits. For example, we may substitute backwards from Equation 4 to derive:

$$(5) \quad C = f_4(f_3\{f_2[f_1(X)]\})$$

Equation 5 suggests that we can directly model choices as a composite function of observable reality. Indeed, much current econometric modeling practice is predicated on the existence of Equation 5, thereby assuming knowledge of or ability to ignore Equations 1–4. Because of the functional forms used in the statistical modeling, it is easy to demonstrate that very unrealistic assumptions are currently being made about Equations 1–3 in particular. We will address this problem later in the chapter.

RESEARCH APPROACHES

The research approaches or strategies by which behavioral constructs are introduced into transportation research are often tied to the discipline or background of the researcher. When geographers, planners, and engineers incorporate behavioral constructs such as attitudes and perceptions into their research, it is usually accomplished by statistically relating such measures to observations of individuals' travel behavior. This has led to a stream of research emphasizing measurement over experimental design. The prevailing research paradigm within this strategy is characterized by a belief that one measures all of the psychological variables of interest first and then one tries to find statistical relationships between these measures and some measures of travel behavior. We shall call this research strategy the *observational approach*, although it is sometimes labeled *revealed preference* because observed behavior is used to infer travelers' preferences.

Psychologists or persons trained in psychological theory and transportation research use psychological theory to model and explain traveler behavior. This has led to a stream of research emphasizing experimental methods to develop and test theories of traveler choice and decision making. By contrast to the first research strategy, this approach begins by postulating models that describe the processes underlying travel decisions, and then it uses these models to derive the psychological measures of interest in understanding a particular form of behavior.

We shall call this strategy the *controlled experimental approach* because the emphasis here is on tightly controlled experimental designs that allow the isolation of factors and factor combinations that influence travel decisions.

It is useful to note that the first approach attempts to measure the psychological variables involved in Equations 1–3 and to relate them statistically to the behavior in Equation 4 of our schematic conceptualization of behavioral travel modeling. The second approach, on the other hand, seeks to define independently each of the functions involved in Equations 2–4 and then uses these functions to derive the necessary measurements. (Direct evaluation of Equation 1, as we shall see, requires a unique research methodology.)

OBSERVATIONAL APPROACH

The observational approach is by far the most common research strategy in studying travel behavior. This strategy has a number of desirable features. Reliable objective measures can be obtained, such as how often the respondent used a particular mode for the work trip during the past week. Attitudinal measures such as the perceived comfort of the respondent's most frequently used mode can be obtained under conditions where respondents can relate their attitude measures to their own personal experiences (Hartgen & Tanner, 1971). Respondents can report their experiences with and preferences for different transportation systems so that researchers can readily obtain, for example, empirical relationships between preferences and current behavior (Hauser & Koppelman, 1976). Socioeconomic measures, distance measures, and objective measures of system attributes are also obtained and related to behavior measures.

The major problem with the observational research strategy is that the relationships obtained between respondent characteristics, system characteristics, attitudes, and behavior are circumstantial rather than causal. It is difficult to assess the extent to which various factors that are correlated with mode choice are actually determinants of mode choice. For example, would the upper-middle-class commuter who drives to work from a suburb where mass transit is not available use the bus even if it were available? The problem here centers on the assessment and interpretation of intercorrelations between both observed and unobserved variables in observational data. In the above example, income, residential location, mass transit availability, and attitudes toward mass transit are all interrelated. Similarly, the two most often studied variables in mode choice—travel time and travel cost of different modes—

are typically (negatively) correlated. It may well be the case that individuals independently attend to time and cost, but observational studies do not allow a clear assessment of how such variables are weighted and combined by the individual traveler in decision making and choice.

CONTROLLED EXPERIMENTAL APPROACH

In the controlled experimental approach, hypothetical travel scenarios or choice tasks are generated by manipulating selected independent variables and holding others constant or unspecified. By contrast to the revealed preference approach, the main strength of the controlled experimental approach is its ability to extract cause-and-effect relationships. For example, orthogonal designs can be used to separate the effects of factors that are ordinarily correlated in observational settings. When response measures are shown to vary reliably across systematically manipulated levels of a particular mode attribute, the researcher can measure the extent to which differences in response are due to differences in that particular attribute. Furthermore, by simultaneously manipulating several attributes in describing hypothetical transportation systems, the researcher can develop behavioral models that describe how the various factors are evaluated, weighted, and combined (Equations 2-4) to affect travelers' judgments and decisions. As will be described in more detail later, this marks the approach used by the present authors and their colleagues (Lerman & Louviere, 1978; Levin & Herring, 1981; Levin, Mosell, Lamka, Savage, & Gray, 1977; Louviere, Wilson, & Piccolo, 1979; Meyer, Levin, & Louviere, 1978).

It has been argued, however, that the process by which hypothetical transportation systems are evaluated in controlled settings is not necessarily the same as the process by which existing travel systems are evaluated in day-to-day travel decisions. Respondents' ability to respond reliably to hypothetical situations that they have never experienced—especially if these situations are extremely unrealistic—has been questioned. Studies will be cited later that mitigate this argument by demonstrating the relationship between responses to hypothetical situations and actual mode choice.

The difference between the two approaches can be summarized as follows: The observational methods are very weak in assessing causality and in developing critical tests for deciding differences between competing model forms. They are also very weak in assessing the appropriateness of the hypothesized functional form or the attributes that comprise it. They are very strong in face validity because they are calibrated to real choices. The controlled, simulated choice tasks are very strong in assessing causality and in developing critical tests for deciding differences between competing model forms. They are also strong in assessing the appropriateness of the hypothesized form and the attributes that comprise it. They are weak in face validity because they are calibrated not to real choices, only to simulated choices.

It is possible to combine elements from the two different research approaches to utilize the strengths and minimize the weaknesses of the respective approaches. The present authors are currently engaged in a project where respondents are asked questions about their current travel behavior, their reactions to various components of available transportation systems, and their reactions to a series of hypothetical mode-choice situations. These latter situations are carefully programmed to allow causal inferences about the effects of important factors in mode choice. Selection of factors and combinations of factor levels was conducted with careful consideration of existing and projected attribute levels so as to avoid unrealistic situations. A major goal of this project is to develop causal models of travel demand based on controlled experimental design, where measures of user characteristics and preferences are included as covariates, and the model's predictive ability is tested with measures of current travel behavior.

QUASI-EXPERIMENTAL DESIGN

Another approach that attempts to apply the analytic abilities of the experimental approach to naturalistic observations is the quasi-experimental design. An attempt is made to approximate a true experiment in a naturalistic setting by systematically eliminating alternative explanations of the observed phenomenon. This often involves before-and-after observations centered on an event of interest. For example, Campbell (1969) reported observations before and after a crackdown on speeding in Connecticut in 1955. The number of traffic fatalities decreased following the crackdown. However, other factors may have contributed to the decrease. A strong inference about the causal relationship between the crackdown on speeding and the reduction in fatalities was made only when it was shown that (1) several years of data both before and after the crackdown revealed a marked discontinuity in the number of traffic fatalities only following the crackdown on speeding; and (2) data from comparable states (controls) did not exhibit a similar effect.

Although other transportation researchers working in naturalistic settings have not been able to exercise the controls used by Campbell, several studies of critical events affecting travel behavior have been conducted through the use of a before-and-after design. For example,

Neveu (1977) analyzed urban travel behavior before and during the energy crisis of 1973–1974. By comparing interview data from various parts of the country before and during the crisis, the author concluded that transit ridership rose only slightly during the crisis; fuel conservation was accomplished primarily by individuals with some flexibility in travel behavior, such as those with high levels of income and auto ownership; and the availability of gasoline was a more important factor in determining travel demand during the short-term crisis than was fuel price. A recent study reported by Levin, Louviere, Meyer, and Henley (1980) showed that increases in fuel price during the preceding year had at least served to promote increased awareness of commuting costs. This study will be described in more detail later.

The different research approaches have different requirements for measuring the factors of interest. For example, the observational approach often incorporates psychological measurement or scaling techniques to measure factors, such as attitudes, that are incorporated in travel demand models. The controlled simulation approach relies on scaling techniques to measure behavioral intentions or preferences. The next section describes several psychological measurement techniques and illustrates how they have been applied in travel demand modeling.

APPLICATIONS OF PSYCHOLOGICAL MEASUREMENT

There has been considerable interest in the development of psychological measures for use in travel demand models. Many transportation researchers view measurement as a logical precursor to model building. Thus, a variety of psychological measurement models and techniques have been employed to "measure" attributes that are hypothesized to be relevant to various travel choices of interest and that have no currently accepted objective metric. In effect, this approach focuses attention on Equations 2 and 3 in our paradigm: measurement of marginal values, v, and overall values, V. These measures are then often employed directly in econometric or similar statistical procedures to predict some set of observed travel choices of interest (Equation 5). This process often involves assumptions regarding the form of the relationships in Equations 2–5, which are difficult to verify with observational data.

Quite a different conceptual view is evidenced in our own work, in which measurement and modeling are viewed as logically inseparable. In this view, one develops models of the choice and evaluation processes of interest (Equations 3 and 4) and then employs these models to deduce the measures of interest (for Equations 1 and 2).

Because there is a plethora of measurement approaches available in psychology, we focus attention on only a few of the major ones that have seen repeated application in the analysis of traveler behavior.

Semantic Differential Scaling

Semantic differential scales or bipolar adjective scales have been frequently used to measure attitudes toward transport system alternatives and attributes of these alternatives assumed relevant to traveler behavior. Examples include the work of Paine, Nash, Hille, and Brunner (1969), Stopher, Spear, and Sucher (1974), and Dobson and Tischer (1978). These studies attempted to measure beliefs about attributes of alternatives as well as attitudes towards the attributes and the alternatives, for example, "satisfaction" with attributes of alternatives and "importances" of attributes in influencing choices. The latter measures are most often used in conjunction with Fishbein-type weighted-sum attitude models. In these cases, the "importance" measures are multiplied by the "belief" and/or affect measures, and the products are summed to yield a composite attitude score. However, the numerical properties of such composite scores—where each component scale can have a different origin and unit—are basically unknown and untested.

Category Scaling

Semantic differential scaling and Likert scaling are examples of category scaling used to measure specific attributes of transportation systems (the v's in Equation 2). The present authors and their colleagues have also used category scaling procedures in conjunction with the controlled experimental research approach to model evaluations of composite multiattribute transportation systems (Equations 2 and 3). For example, respondents in the Meyer *et al.* (1978) study were asked to rate their degree of preference for car or bus for each of a number of hypothetical travel scenarios. These rating measures were used to define latent demand for various transportation alternatives and to define individual differences in the preference for different modes. Respondents in the Lerman and Louviere (1978) study were asked to estimate a numerical value for their degree of preference for each of a series of hypothetical towns described by varying populations and home-to-work distances. Responses were analyzed to show that a multiplicative relationship between the factors best describes the integration rule (Equation 3) and that the relationship between objective values and marginal utility values (Equation 2) for population and distance could be described by a power function and an exponential function, respectively. As will be described in the subsection on functional measurement, an impressive amount of evidence has been accumulated in cognitive psychology supporting the interval properties of rating scales such as those used in these studies when procedural precautions such as the use of "end anchors" and practice trials are included. Furthermore, evidence is beginning to accumulate that shows that such measures are predictive of actual behavior.

THURSTONE SCALING

The relatively few transportation studies that have employed Thurstone methods have used the method of paired comparisons. An example is Golob, Canty, and Gustafson's (1972) analysis of consumer demand for a new public transportation system (the "jitney system" or door-to-door bus service). Paired comparisons were used to establish a scale of relative preferences (i.e., V's in Equation 3) for sets of system characteristics, and this scale was then used to compare the attractiveness of alternative system designs for different population segments. In general, measures obtained with this method are affected by intercorrelations between the attributes being compared. However, Louviere and Meyer (1976) used the method of paired comparisons in conjunction with a factorial design to guarantee that the paired comparison measures would be statistically uncorrelated.

FACTOR ANALYSIS

Frequently, the judgments made by subjects on semantic differential or other scales are subjected to a factor or principal components analysis to identify the "constructs" or "dimensions" that underlie the attribute judgments (v's). Many studies have employed this measurement model because of the simple perceptual structures it provides.

Typically, factor analysis has been employed to identify clusters of related "satisfaction" measures or semantic differential judgments about attributes of travel alternatives. Examples of such applications include the work of Paine *et al.*, (1969), Horton and Reynolds (1971), Dobson and Kehoe (1974), Horton and Louviere (1974), and Koppelman and Hauser (1978). Generalizations are difficult to make because there have been virtually no replications of any research; different authors have used different sets of variables or different ways of measuring the same variables. Similarly, results have been mixed, with some authors like Koppelman and Hauser (1978) reporting good predictive ability for real behavior in split-sample tests, others not relating to real behavior at all, such as Horton and Louviere (1974).

MULTIDIMENSIONAL SCALING (MDS)

Like factor analysis, MDS attempts to identify clusters of attributes that are independent statistically and that satisfy an additive function that is marginally monotonic. Unlike factor analysis, MDS can analyze a variety of types of attribute × attribute or alternative × alternative data matrices in which the elements represent some measure of pairwise similarity between the row and column entries. The result of the analysis is a set of scores on the derived dimensions for each alternative or attribute; these scores have been used as predictor variables in an analysis of traveler behavior.

Examples of the use of this approach include studies of destination choice for shopping trips (Burnett, 1973; Cadwallader, 1975; Mackay, Olshavsky, & Sentell, 1975) and studies of transportation mode choice (Dobson, Golob, & Gustafson, 1974; Nicolaidis & Dobson, 1975). In the Dobson et al. study, MDS models were applied to paired-comparisons preference choices for transit system attributes. A vector model was used to uncover dimensions accounting for the preference choices, and derived respondent importances for the dimensions were related to the demographic and socioeconomic characteristics of the respondents via discriminant analysis. The model was then used to segment the sample according to the unique preferences of groups of respondents for the transit attributes.

As is the case with other correlational methods, it is often difficult to assess and interpret relationships observed with MDS, especially since subjectivity is introduced when identifying and defining dimensions. Nevertheless, when these methods have been used to define homogeneous market segments, the results—while not exact—can be useful to transportation planners.

ATTITUDINAL MODELING

One area in which transportation researchers have relied heavily on psychological measurement techniques to identify homogeneous population segments is attitudinal modeling of traveler behavior. Transportation researchers such as Dobson (1976), Hartgen (1973), Golob, Horowitz, and Wachs (1979), and Levin (1979) depict attitudes as *mediators* of behavior that are linked to system and user characteristics on the one hand and to traveler decisions on the other hand. By including attitudinal mediators of behavior, the implication is that travel demand models are enhanced by the inclusion of individual difference factors that shed light on the processes underlying individual decisions. This procedure, in turn, can serve to increase the policy sensitivity of the models.

DEFINITION AND MEASUREMENT OF ATTITUDES

Psychologists have provided a number of different definitions of attitudes. Thurstone (1931) defined attitude as "the affect for or against a psychological object." Allport (1935) defined an attitude as "a mental and neural state of readiness, organized through experience, exerting a directive or dynamic influence [on behavior]." Thurstone's definition is an example of a unidimensional conceptualization that stresses the affective nature of attitudes; Allport's definition is an example of a multidimensional conceptualization that includes affective, cognitive, and behavioral components.

Transportation researchers have generally adopted a multidimensional conceptualization of attitude. For example, Hartgen (1973) described three distinct components: cognition (beliefs concerning an object); affect (feelings of like or dislike toward the object); and conation (tendencies to act with respect to the object). Attitude measurement in transportation research is usually accomplished by asking respondents to rate the importance of each of a number of attributes and their level of satisfaction with that attribute for each mode (e.g., Dobson, 1976). The importance rating is said to represent the cognitive component of attitude, and the satisfaction rating is said to represent the affective component. Hartgen and Tanner (1971) defined an overall attitudinal index (analogous to V in Equation 3), which is a linear combination of importance and satisfaction ratings of qualitative system characteristics for different modes. This approach parallels Fishbein's (1967) formulation of attitudes as a linear combination of beliefs about an object and the evaluation of those beliefs.

An alternative attitude measurement technique for transportation research uses the controlled experimental approach (Levin, 1979). Individuals are asked to evaluate multiattribute systems as a whole, rather than responding to individual attributes taken out of context. By examining how ratings vary systematically over combinations of attribute levels, scaling of individual attributes (Equation 2) can be accomplished concurrently with testing algebraic formulations of how various objective characteristics are combined in evaluating transportation systems (Equation 3). The main strengths of this technique of attitude measurement are that it links attitude measures to objective system attributes, and it provides goodness-of-fit tests of alternative formulations of how various objective characteristics are combined in evaluating transportation systems (Equation 3). The main strengths of this technique of attitude measurement are that it links attitude measures to objective system attributes, and it provides goodness-of-fit tests of alternative formulations of how attributes are combined to affect attitudes. This technique, known as *functional measurement*, will be discussed in more detail in the section on psychological process theories.

<h2 style="text-align:center">ATTITUDE–BEHAVIOR RELATIONSHIP</h2>

Because most definitions of attitudes imply that attitudes exert a directive influence on behavior, they also imply that there should be a direct relationship between attitudes and behavior. However, social scientists have cautioned that empirical support for this relationship is weak and that an attitudinal measure may account for only a small proportion of the variance in overt behavior. Fishbein (1967) summarized 75 years of attitude research with the conclusion that "there is still little, if any consistent evidence supporting the hypothesis that knowledge of an individual's attitude toward some object will allow one to predict the way he will behave with respect to the object." And Wicker (1969) examined scores of previous studies dealing with the attitude–behavior relationship and concluded that attitudinal data rarely account for as much as 10% of the variance in overt behavioral measures.

According to Ajzen and Fishbein (1977) and Kiesler (1971), the relationship between a single attitudinal measure and a given behavior is likely to be low because a variety of interacting factors determine whether a person acts on his or her attitude in a given situation at a given time. These factors include interpersonal and environmental pressures for behavior and conflicting attitudes that may have different implications for the behavior. When several attitudes are relevant to some behavior, the attitude either most salient at the moment or most intensely held is the one most likely to affect behavior.

Transportation researchers may be in a better position than most social scientists to develop attitudinal models that account for overt behavior. In other areas, attitudes have often been measured for broad issues or classes of objects (e.g., racial attitudes), whereas behavior is typically directed at a specific object in a specific context. Transportation researchers can obtain evaluations of specific attribute combinations that describe current transportation systems or possible future options.

While there is need for more research to establish the strength of the attitude–behavior relationship in the context of travel demand modeling, some relevant evidence has begun to emerge. For example, Meyer *et al.* (1978), using the functional measurement technique, related mode choice to measures of preference for bus versus car (Equation 4) obtained in a series of evaluations of hypothetical mode-choice situations. The attitude measure—mean degree of preference for bus or car across situations for a given respondent—accounted for over 70% of the variance in actual mode split for the work trip for the individuals in the study, and the predictive ability was even higher when the individuals' situational constraints were incorporated into the model as a multiplier of the attitude measure. Furthermore, differences in attitude were used to cluster the respondents into three groups—a car-biased group, a bus-biased group, and an unbiased group—who were shown to weight cost and time factors differently.

The Meyer *et al.* study is only one of an increasing number of recent transportation studies to cluster or segment respondents on the basis of attitudinal measures and to show that such clusters behave differently. In another such study, Stopher and Ergün (1979) used Likert scale ratings of conceptual attributes of recreation activities as a segmentation basis for capturing differences in recreational travel behavior. Segmentation based on these attractiveness ratings produced a significant improvement in the performance of recreation activity choice models, and the differences between segments were shown to have intuitively meaningful interpretations. In a mode choice study, Dobson and Tischer (1978) collected perceptions of each mode on attributes such as comfort, convenience, and safety, using a 7-point semantic differential scale for each attribute. Perceptual groups derived from these data were readily distinguishable from each other and were highly correlated with mode choice patterns.

In these studies, attitudinal data led to market segmentation procedures that went beyond the typical socioeconomic characteristics. The ability to discriminate individuals on the basis of the strengths of their attitudes is important because, as noted earlier, attitude strength is an important determinant of whether or not a particular person will act out his or her feelings toward a particular object. This fact has major policy implications because individuals differ in their sensitivity to particular policy manipulations.

A discussion of the attitude–behavior relationship would be incomplete without an acknowledgement of the reciprocal nature of this relationship. Psychologists have long recognized that behavior can influence attitudes as well as vice versa (Festinger, 1957). In the area of travel demand modeling, Golob *et al.* (1979) developed a model that stressed the mutual interrelations among attitudes, choice constraints, and choice. The social-psychological construct *cognitive dissonance* was used to study the processes underlying mode choice. Measures of dissonance were obtained by comparing auto commuters' and bus commuters' evaluations of a variety of attributes for their own mode and the other mode. The greater the difference between users' and nonusers' ratings of a mode on a particular attribute, the greater the dissonance effect and the greater the assumed importance of that attribute. In this manner, the authors were able to show how dissonance measures could be used to identify key attributes of choice alternatives to aid in effective marketing strategies.

Measurement of Qualitative Variables

The same rating scales used to measure attitudes have allowed transportation researchers to add so-called "soft" or qualitative variables to the traditional time–cost–distance variables in their models. These qualitative variables include comfort, safety, convenience, and economy, all of which have been used to "explain" travel behavior (Hensher, McLeod, & Stanley, 1975; Levin et al., 1977; Nicolaidis, 1975; Neveu, Koppelman, & Stopher, 1978; Recker & Golob, 1976). However, all too often, the psychological scaling techniques used to measure such variables are applied uncritically, without due regard to validating operational definitions. Since these variables have the status of intervening variables, they themselves must be operationally defined or "explained" by identifying their antecedent user and system characteristics.

A study by Levin and Herring (1981) illustrates how this can be accomplished by use of the functional measurement approach. Respondents were asked to rate the relative safety, economy, and desirability of flying versus driving for each of a number of hypothetical trips described by factorially varying the factors of air fare, driving cost, distance, number of travelers, and season. Flying tended to be favored over driving on all three rating scales. Desirability ratings could be described as an additive function of all the manipulated factors. Safety ratings were a function of season and number of travelers (who could share driving responsibilities). Economy ratings were a function of air fare, driving cost, and number of travelers (who would share expenses). Because a 2:1 ratio was chosen for the levels of each of these economic factors, their effects on economy ratings were expected to be equal. Confirmation of this expectation served to support the respondents' ability to process the relevant information and to map their internal evaluations onto the required rating scales. This confirmation, in turn, supports the validity of the scaling procedures. Both safety ratings and economy ratings were positively correlated with desirability ratings, and the combined effects of safety and economy explained a higher proportion of the variance in perceived desirability than either factor by itself. The extent of the inter-relationships between the qualitative variables could be explained by the degree of overlap in the sets of antecedent factors affecting each qualitative variable.

Thus, the adaptation of psychological scaling techniques to the measurement of factors affecting travel behavior allows the inclusion of attitudinal and qualitative variables in travel demand modeling. Furthermore, the operational definitions of these variables can be validated by affirming the reliability of the effects of the objective system characteristics underlying the perceptions (ratings) of the qualitative variables. Levin *et al.* (1977) also used this approach to examine how the perceived safety of highway driving varies as a function of a variety of driving conditions and how perceived safety is related to measures of driving intention. However, in general, not enough attention has been paid to validating operational definitions of qualitative variables such as safety, comfort, and convenience.

APPLICATIONS OF PSYCHOLOGICAL PROCESS THEORY

Psychological process theories are aimed at improved understanding of behavior through an analysis of the perceptual, motivational, and learning processes underlying that behavior. These approaches are aimed at defining Equations 1–4; however, they typically concentrate on Equations 2 and 3. In travel demand modeling, the application of psychological process theories has the potential of providing better forecasting tools and increased policy sensitivity. Depending on the level at which the theory is aggregated, predictions can be made of how an individual, a group, or a subgroup will respond to a variety of travel circumstances, and planners can determine which of several policy options is most apt to produce the desired results for that individual, group, or subgroup. As illustrated in the previous section, attitudes can be incorporated into such theories as intervening links between objective system and user characteristics and measures of overt behavior. In this section, we will describe several theories and theoretical frameworks in psychology that can provide explanatory mechanisms for linking transportation attributes and user characteristics to travel behavior.

Existing theory and practice in transportation research rely heavily on the assumed validity of a given functional form (e.g., the linear-in-the-parameters form of Logit functions) relating attribute utilities to traveler choices. However, in a recent comprehensive review of research on choice behavior, Slovic, Fischhoff, and Lichtenstein (1977) noted that the field of choice behavior is moving away from the assumption that choice probability is expressible as a monotone function of the scale values or utilities of the alternatives. Recently, researchers have found it more fruitful to develop detailed, molecular concepts that describe choice in terms of information-processing phenomena. As suggested earlier in Equations 1–4, the study of traveler behavior can likewise benefit from a molecular analysis of the component processes underlying traveler perceptions, judgments, and decisions. While still at an early stage of application, the psychological process theories described in this section have contributed to better understanding of the processes underlying traveler behavior, and utility theory has provided the framework for linking process models to overt choice behavior.

UTILITY THEORY

Utility theory in economics and psychology deals with preferences for and values assigned to risky choices or gambles. The area of preferences or values assigned to riskless alternatives is clearly a subset. However, it is the riskless subset that is implicit in all the economic and psychological work in travel behavior. Basically, utility theory assumes that multiattribute alternatives may be identified according to order and equality, and that individuals are rational in their choices; that is, when one alternative dominates a second on all attributes, the individual will choose the first over the second. From these properties, we may infer indifference, transitivity, reflexivity, etc. It can be demonstrated that these notions together with various assumptions about attribute independence lead to various multilinear forms of preference or value functions. These multilinear forms correspond algebraically to the multilinear value functions that are the object of study in applications of functional and conjoint measurement.

The basic distinction that can be made is that riskless utility theory and conjoint measurement both assume that the input from subjects is of an ordinal nature. Powerful sets of axioms are then available to demonstrate that the ordinal responses may be used to deduce an interval scale for the stimuli, provided the "correct" functional form is known. Unfortunately, neither approach provides a theory of errors to guide in the rejection of false models. On the other hand, functional measurement assumes that respondents can provide their responses on an interval scale, or that the data, if not interval in level, may be monotonically transformed to be so, provided one knows the "true" model. Fortunately, functional measurement possesses an error theory to falsify models, and resort to monotone retransformation has not usually been required.

Because so much of the research in travel behavior evolved out of the notion of forecasting the *demand* for travel, much of the theory that is available is firmly rooted in economic theory, particularly the idea of utility maximization. Put briefly, we assume that the individual can assign utilities or values to a set of alternatives that have at least the properties of order and equality (preference and indifference). We assume that the individuals are perfectly transitive and reflexive and, most importantly, that they will choose that alternative to which they assign the highest value or utility (Keeney & Raiffa, 1976). In probabilistic formulations, the individual is viewed as having some probability of choosing each alternative, where probabilities are based on the relative utilities or values assigned to the various alternatives (see Equation 4).

Current econometric approaches to modeling traveler choice behavior are firmly rooted in these notions. Much recent work of a psychological nature has involved trying to link work in psychophysics, attitude measurement, and choice with econometric work on discrete choices. This work is exemplified by the present authors' research, which largely involves identifying the functional form of the utility expression used by individual travelers; the systematic relationship of individuals' utility functions with observable covariates of the individual such as age, income, auto ownership, and previous travel experiences; and the relationship of both of the foregoing to choice behavior.

FUNCTIONAL MEASUREMENT

Functional measurement, as developed by Norman Anderson (1970, 1976, 1979), represents a theoretical and methodological approach to the measurement and modeling of individual value assignments. Psychological processes are represented in the theory as the "psychophysical law" and the "psychological law." As was shown in Figure 2.1, the psychophysical law, or "valuation" process, describes how objective stimulus values are transformed into subjective scale values (Equation 2, described earlier), and the psychological law, or the "integration" process, describes how these scale values are combined into an overall judgment (Equation 3). A long history of research in cognitive psychology has shown that the psychological law can typically be described by a simple algebraic model such as adding, subtracting, averaging, or multiplying (see recent review by Anderson, 1979).

Rating scales have often been used in the application of functional measurement. The interval properties of such scales have been validated concurrently with testing a specific algebraic function describing the psychological law. This is why the term *functional measurement* has been used to describe this approach. For example, if an information integration task is constructed where an additive model is correct, if the stimulus factors have independent effects, and if the response measure is an interval scale, then the analysis of variance of the resulting responses will show no stimulus interaction. Such a result will then accomplish the following: (1) it supports the additive model; (2) it indicates that the response scale has interval properties; and (3) it yields interval scales of the stimulus variables. Analysis of variance represents a formal goodness-of-fit test (or "error theory") for distinguishing alternative model forms, with the form of interaction effects being especially crucial in this regard. (See Anderson, 1974, for a detailed description of model tests.)

The present authors and their colleagues have found the functional measurement approach particularly appealing for the development of travel demand models (Lerman & Louviere, 1978; Levin, 1977, 1979; Levin *et al.*, 1977; Louviere, 1980; Louviere *et al.*, 1979; Meyer *et al.*, 1978). The derivation of the psychological law allows transportation researchers to describe the nature of the trade-off between favorable and unfavorable transportation attributes. If attributes are combined in an additive or linear fashion, then unfavorable levels of one important factor can be compensated for by favorable levels of another important factor. If, however, a nonadditive model applies, one unfavorable factor can lead to an overall negative evaluation of an entire system. The ability to distinguish between additive and nonadditive models thus has obvious policy implications. For example, Norman and Louviere (1974) found that the stated likelihood of bus ridership was low if any of the following factors was at an unfavorable level: bus fare, distance to bus stop, and service frequency. Levin and Gray (1979) found that car pools composed of all nonacquaintances would be undesirable even when cost savings were potentially high. This finding led to suggestions for incorporating interpersonal factors into car-pool promotional programs. The psychological law also includes the desirable feature of objectively assessing the relative weights or degrees of importance of the quantitative and qualitative factors in behavior such as mode choice. Methods for accomplishing this goal are described by Levin, Kim, and Corry (1976) and Norman (1976).

The psychophysical law is also of potentially great importance to transportation researchers because it tells how the evaluation of an entire system varies over the levels of any given attribute. For example,

Meyer *et al.* (1978) found that preference ratings for those respondents who had an overall preference for car over bus varied little when daily cost differences between car and bus varied from 0 to 25¢, but preference for the car did decrease considerably when cost differences reached 75¢. Finally, the Meyer *et al.* study and the Lerman and Louviere study (1978) represent early attempts to examine the choice function (Equation 4) by showing that subjective evaluations obtained in a functional measurement study are predictive of mode choice and residential choice.

CONJOINT MEASUREMENT

Conjoint measurement is a formal measurement theory with a complete set of mathematical axioms developed by Krantz, Luce, Suppes, and Tversky (1971). When a scaling algorithm such as Kruskal's (1965) MONANOVA is added, it has been used to scale values (Equation 2) for different levels of two or more factors in a factorial experiment. In this respect, conjoint measurement is like functional measurement. However, whereas functional measurement can deal with both ordinal and interval data, conjoint measurement takes into account only ordinal information in the data. Thus, the dependent variable in studies using conjoint measurement typically consists of a ranking of stimulus inputs based on a unidimensional response criterion such as preference.

Applications of conjoint measurement include Burnett's (in press) study of destination choice for shopping trips and the Donnelly (1975) and Donnelly, Howe, and Des Champs (1976) studies of the effects of cost and service attributes on the acceptance of alternative transit programs. Donnelly *et al.* showed, for example, that preferences for programs differing in levels of service changed more with decreases in services than with increases in services when compared with a base program. The authors concluded that existing conditions are usually seen as a minimum; cutbacks or increases are seen in relation to that minimum standard.

The danger in current applications of conjoint measurement is the overreliance on goodness-of-fit measures, like STRESS, in the absence of a well-developed error theory for testing alternative model forms of the information integration process (Equation 3). If a multilinear model is the true descriptor of the judgment process, then any form of the general model that includes the main effects will probably appear to provide an excellent fit in terms of criteria such as STRESS (Dawes & Corrigan, 1974; Anderson & Shanteau, 1977). Empirical comparisons of conjoint measurement and functional measurement (e.g., Curry, Levin, & Gray, 1978) show that the marginal scale values produced by each method are nearly identical but that deviations from additivity in the utility function may be missed with conjoint measurement. The researcher using conjoint measurement often combines marginal scale values by an assumed integration rule to yield factorial cell predictions and then uses an estimation routine to develop a predictive equation. Predictions of choice behavior can be quite accurate, but inferences about the underlying psychological processes may be misleading.

RECENT DEVELOPMENTS

The research strategies and psychological measurement and modeling techniques described in this chapter have led to advances in travel demand modeling. They have provided new insights into the processes underlying a variety of traveler preferences and decisions. These include the measurement of attitudes and other qualitative factors affecting travel behavior, determination of the relative influence of qualitative and quantitative factors, the development of refined market segmentation techniques, and specification of the form of utility functions underlying travelers' preferences and choices. Furthermore, the methods we have advocated are now being extended to important problems in transportation research that have been difficult to solve with traditional methods.

New problem areas now being investigated within the authors' program of travel behavior research include a study of the relationship between actual transportation system values and their perceived counterparts (Equation 1), an analysis of the relationship between system evaluations and choices (Equation 4), and an analysis of the dynamics of travel demand.

THE PSYCHOPHYSICAL PROBLEM

Considerable attention has been given to the problem of describing how a variety of quantitative and qualitative factors combine to affect traveler judgments and decisions, and functional measurement and conjoint measurement have been applied to the problem of describing how judgments and decisions vary across levels of a given factor. However, while such approaches to the psychophysical problem are extremely useful in transforming perceived transport attributes to functional scale values on an evaluative dimension such as desirability, they leave unresolved the question of how individuals' self-estimates of the values of independent variables relate to the actual values of these variables. This question is important because even though many travel demand models use actual measures of variables such as time and cost, the traveler's *perceptions* of such variables influence behavior. A preliminary study by the present authors and their associates (reported by Levin *et al.*, 1980) illustrates how the relationship between perceived and actual values of cost and time can be investigated as a function of variables of interest in travel demand modeling.

Telephone surveys were conducted in the fall of 1978 with 36 solo car drivers, 20 car poolers, and 17 bus users. Self-reports of the time, cost, comfort, and convenience of the work trip were obtained from each respondent. On the next working day following a survey, a researcher re-created the respondent's work trip, then recorded time values, the distance measures used, car type information, and local parking fees to compute costs. Commuters in all three modal groups tended to overestimate travel time. Furthermore, the relationship between self-reports and measured travel time varied as a function of travel mode and perceived comfort. Only 10% of the car users were able to articulare dollars-and-cents cost estimates, and when they were asked to rate the relative expense of using the car versus taking a bus to work, there was a marked tendency to underestimate driving costs relative to using the bus. However, when the study was replicated a year later with 52 car drivers, 73% of the respondents were able to provide estimates of daily or weekly driving costs. While the respondents still underestimated their total (fixed plus operating) driving costs, the increased awareness was attributed to the fact that gasoline costs had nearly doubled during the period between the original study and the replicated study. These results suggest that in order to make travel demand models more responsive to the needs of policy makers, future modeling efforts should incorporate knowledge of the relationship between perceived and actual transportation system attributes (Equation 1) under those conditions likely to arise from various policy manipulations.

Choice Set Analysis

Recent progress includes the development of controlled experimental procedures for assessing individuals' choices among multiattribute alternatives. This development involves the design and analysis of what we term *double conditional experimental designs*. Double conditional designs are those in which one combines a choice set generating design with a multiattribute design for assessing trade-offs. First, one develops a set of N multiattribute alternatives (e.g., a set of bus systems described by fares, service frequencies, and walking distances to and from the stops). These N alternatives constitute the multiattribute trade-off design. Then, one creates a second 2^N design, where N is the number of alternatives (or treatment combinations) in the first design, and 2 refers to the binary state of being present or absent. This latter design generates choice sets, which are simply elements of the set of all 2^N factorial enumerations. In practice, both designs are usually structured as fractional factorial designs in order to make the experiment tractible. However, if the design is balanced so that each alternative appears an equal number of times across choice sets, then the relative frequency with which each is chosen is a ratio-scaled measure of its subjective utility.

Examples of the use of these designs are given by Louviere (1980) and by Louviere and Hensher (1980) in studies of the destination choices and air-travel-tickets choices among international travelers. Results of these and related studies indicate that this approach can develop algebraic approximations to choice processes that can forecast the probabilities of various traveler choices. Such analyses permit one to make direct inferences about Equations 1–5 in a single study. Although it is too soon to generalize, these methods offer a potential solution to the problem of directly forecasting choice probabilities.

Choice Sets and Travel Behavior Dynamics

Most applications of travel demand modeling have been "static" in the sense that model parameter differences have been investigated across individuals at a given point in time rather than across times for a given individual. As a result, the models are ungeneralizable over time, and their usefulness to transportation planners is restricted. Future research should take into account that individuals do change their preferences and choices over time as a function of a variety of exogenous factors.

One source of changing traveler preferences and choices that is amenable to analysis by the methods described in this chapter is the formation and alteration of choice sets. Most travel demand models—even those that purportedly model individual decision processes—make the implicit assumption that all individuals share identical levels of information concerning the set of available alternatives, or choice set. It is unlikely that this assumption is true, especially in light of the variable misperceptions of mode-specific cost and time values reported above. Individual differences in choice behavior may thus be a function of differences in choice set information as well as differences in preference (utility), and forecasts of travel behavior that ignore this source of variance may be prone to error.

There has been little work in the development and testing of models of choice set formation and change. The latter is particularly important in our current situation of rapidly changing fuel supplies, fuel costs, and transportation opportunities. Researchers who have addressed the problem of modeling changes in individual travel behavior over time have suggested that the choice process is an adaptive one, with variations in behavior decreasing asymptotically as a function of an individual's length of residence in an area (e.g., Burnett, 1976). However, there is little empirical evidence available to permit understanding of the factors underlying individual differences in adaptation rates and asymptotic choice levels.

A recent dissertation by Meyer (1979) illustrates how some of the methods described in this chapter can be brought to bear on this problem. A controlled laboratory study was devised to simulate spatial search (destination choice). The variables manipulated included the number of alternatives in the choice set, the mean and variance of the attractiveness of the choice set, the familiarity (number of prior observations) with a particular target choice alternative, and the mean and variance of these prior observations of the target alternative. Respondents were asked to rate how likely they would be to choose the target alternative for each of a number of different hypothetical search scenarios described by different combinations of the manipulated variables (generated by fractional factorial designs). Functional measurement procedures were used to assess the contributions of the variables and how they combine. The main findings were as follows: (1) utility assignments to the target alternative were influenced not only by the perceived mean desirability of that alternative but also by the individual's familiarity with the alternative and the amount of day-to-day variation in the attractiveness of the alternative; (2) choice behavior could be described by a "cut-off" model in which alternatives perceived as inferior are excluded from consideration; (3) utility assignment to an unfamiliar alternative depended on the perceived attractiveness of the "typical" or average alternative in the choice set; and (4) changes in utility assignment to a given alternative as a function of being imbedded in different choice sets depended on the individual's previous experiences with alternatives similar to those in the set (an "adaptation level" effect).

While Meyer's dissertation dealt with a restricted aspect of travel demand modeling (destination choice), it illustrates how experimental design procedures and rating methods from the behavioral sciences can be used to simulate changing choice sets and increasing familiarity with the attributes of choice alternatives. An obvious and desirable extension of this line of attack would be to the problem of modeling changes in mode choice as a function of changes in (perceived) fuel supply and costs. A double-barreled approach to this problem could be undertaken by applying observational as well as experimental methods. "Quasi-experimental" designs could be employed in which periodic measures of travelers' attitudes, preferences, and choices could be related over time to changes in transportation opportunities and costs. As described earlier, some short-term work of this type was conducted during the "oil crisis" of 1973–1974, but long-term stabilizing trends would be of more interest for effective transportation planning. The main problem with the quasi-experimental design is the difficulty in measuring and matching confounding variables that covary with the factors of interest. Nevertheless, results of such studies could lead to hypotheses that could be tested with more tightly controlled laboratory simulations.

At a more general level, we feel that future research should strive to reverse several current trends: (1) instead of isolated studies or "once-only" research, there must be replication over time and space; (2) rather than relying only on traditional methods, researchers should consider a variety of measurement methods and models before selecting a method of attack on a particular travel demand problem; and (3) researchers should recognize the complementarity of different approaches in meeting the multifaceted goals of travel demand modeling.

Acknowledgments

The authors wish to thank Bob Meyer, Dave Henley, Tom Eagle, and Becky Huber for their help in completing this manuscript.

REFERENCES

Ajzen, I., & Fishbein, M. Attitude–behavior relations: A theoretical analysis and review of empirical research. *Psychological Bulletin*, 1977, *84*, 888–918.

Allport, G. W. Attitudes. In C. Murchison (Ed.), *A handbook of social psychology*. Worcester, Mass.: Clark University Press, 1935, pp. 798–844.

Anderson, N. H. Information integration theory: A brief survey. In Krantz, D. H., Atkinson, R. C. Luce, R. D., and Suppes, P. (Eds.), *Contemporary developments in mathematical psychology* (Vol. 2). San Francisco: W. H. Freeman, 1974.

Anderson, N. H. Functional measurement and psychophysical judgment. *Psychological Review*, 1970, *77*, 153–170.

Anderson, N. H. How functional measurement can yield validated interval scales of mental qualities. *Journal of Applied Psychology*, 1976, *61*, 677–692.

Anderson, N. H. Introduction to cognitive algebra. Technical Report No. 85, Center for Human Information Processing, University of California, San Diego, 1979.

Anderson, N. H., & Shanteau, J. Weak inference with linear models. *Psychological Bulletin*, 1977, *84*, 1155–1170.

Ben-Akiva, M. Structure of passenger demand models. *Transportation Research Record 526*, 1974.

Burnett, K. P. Data problems in the application of conjoint measurement to recurrent urban travel. In R. G. Golledge & J. Rayner (Eds.), *Data analysis in multidimensional scaling*. Columbus: Ohio State University Press, in press.

Burnett, P. The dimensions of alternatives in spatial choice processes. *Geographical Analysis*, 1973, *5*, 181–204.

Burnett, P. Toward dynamic models of traveler behavior and point pattern of traveler origins. *Economic Geography*, 1976, *52*, 30–57.

Cadwallader, M. Behavioral model of consumer spatial decision making. *Economic Geography*, 1975, *51*, 339–349.

Campbell, D. T. Reforms as experiments. *American Psychologist*, 1969, *24*, 409–429.

Carrothers, G. A. P. An historical review of gravity and potential concepts of human interaction. *Journal of the American Institute of Planners*, 1956, *22*, 94–102.

Curry, D. J., Levin, I. P., & Gray, M. J. A comparison of additive conjoint measurement and functional measurement in a study of apartment preferences. *Technical Report #98*, Institute of Urban and Regional Research, University of Iowa, Iowa City, 1978.

Dawes, R. M., & Corrigan, B. Linear models in decision making. *Psychological Bulletin*, 1974, *81*, 95–106.

Dial, R. B. A probabilistic multipath traffic assignment model which obviates path enumeration. *Transportation Research*, 1971, *5*, 83–111.

Dobson, R. Uses and limitations of attitudinal modeling. In P. R. Stopher & A. H. Meyburg (Eds.), *Behavioral travel-demand models*. Lexington, Mass.: Lexington Books (Heath), 1976, 99–106.

Dobson, R., & Kehoe, J. F. Disaggregated behavioral views of transportation attributes. *Transportation Research Record 527*, 1974, 1–15.

Dobson, R., & Tischer, M. L. Perceptual market segmentation technique for transportation analysis. *Transportation Research Record 673*, 1978, 145–152.

Dobson, R., Golob, T. F., & Gustafson, R. L. Multidimensional scaling of consumer preferences for a public transportation system: An application of two approaches. *Socio-Economic Planning Sciences*, 1974, *8*, 23–26.

Donnelly, E. P. Formulation and evaluation of alternative state transit operating assistance programs: A quantitative preference technique. *Preliminary Research Report #90*, New York State Department of Transportation, Albany, 1975.

Donnelly, E. P., Howe, S. M., & Des Champs, J. A. Trade-off analysis: Theory and applications to transportation policy planning. *Preliminary Research Report #103*, New York State Department of Transportation, Albany, 1976.

Festinger, L. *A theory of cognitive dissonance*. Stanford, Calif.: Stanford University Press, 1957.

Fishbein, M. *Readings in attitude theory and measurement*. New York: Wiley, 1967.

Golob, T. F., Canty, E. T., & Gustafson, R. L. An analysis of consumer preferences for a public transportation system. *Transportation Research*, 1972, *6*, 81–102.

Golob, T. F., Horowitz, A. D., & Wachs, M. Attitude–behavior relationships in travel demand modeling. In D. A. Hensher & P. R. Stopher (Eds.), *Behavioural travel modelling*. London: Croom Helm, 1979, pp. 739–757.

Hartgen, D. T. The influence of attitudinal and situational variables on urban mode choice. *Preliminary Research Report #41*, New York State Department of Transportation, Albany, New York, 1973.

Hartgen, D. T., & Tanner, G. H. Investigations of the effect of traveler attitudes in a model of mode choice behavior. *Transportation Research Record 369*, 1971, 1–14.

Hauser, J. R., & Koppelman, F. S. Designing transportation services: A marketing approach. *Working Paper No. 414-16*, The Transportation Center, Northwestern University, 1976.

Hensher, D. A., McLeod, P. B., & Stanley, J. K. Usefulness of attitudinal measures in investigating the choice of travel mode. *International Journal of Transport Economics*, 1975, 2, 51–75.

Hill, D. M., & von Cube, H. G. Development of a model for forecasting travel mode choice in urban areas. *Highway Research Record 38*, 1963, 78–96.

Horowitz, J. A utility maximizing of the demand for multi-destination nonwork travel. *CTS Working Paper No. 79-9*, Cambridge, Mass., 1979.

Horton, F., & Louviere, J. J. Behavioral analysis and transportation planning: Inputs to transit planning. *Transportation*, 1974, 8, 165–181.

Horton, F., & Reynolds, D. R. Effects of urban spatial structures on individual behavior. *Economic Geography*, 1971, 49, 36–48.

Keeney, R., & Raiffa, H. *Decisions among multiple objectives: Preference and value tradeoffs.* New York: Wiley, 1976.

Kiesler, C. A. *The psychology of commitment: Experiments linking behavior to belief.* New York: Academic Press, 1971.

Koppelman, F. S., & Hauser, J. R. Destination choice behavior for non-grocery-shopping trips. *Transportation Research Record 673*, 1978, 157–165.

Krantz, D. H., Luce, R. D., Suppes, P., & Tversky, A. *Foundations of measurement: Vol. 1. Additive and polynomial representations.* New York and London: Academic Press, 1971.

Kruskal, J. B. Analysis of factorial experiments by estimating monotone transformations of the data. *Journal of the Royal Statistical Society, Series B*, 1965, 27, 251–263.

Lerman, S. R., & Louviere, J. J. Using functional measurement to identify the form of utility functions in travel demand models. *Transportation Research Record 673*, 1978, 78–86.

Levin, I. P. Information integration in transportation decisions. In M. F. Kaplan & S. Schwartz (Eds.), *Human judgment and decision processes in applied settings.* New York: Academic Press, 1977, pp. 57–81.

Levin, I. P. The development of attitudinal modelling approaches in transportation research. In D. A. Hensher & P. R. Stopher (Eds.), *Behavioural travel modelling.* London: Croom Helm, 1979, pp. 758–581.

Levin, I. P., & Gray, M. J. Evaluation of interpersonal influences in the formation and promotion of carpools. *Transportation Research Record 724*, 1979, 35–39.

Levin, I. P., & Herring, R. D. Functional measurement of qualitative variables in mode choice: Ratings of economy, safety, and desirability of flying vs. driving. *Transportation Research*, 1981, 15, 207–214.

Levin, I. P., Kim, K. J., & Corry, F. A. Invariance of the weight parameter in information integration. *Memory & Cognition*, 1976, 4, 43–47.

Levin, I. P., Mosell, M. K., Lamka, C. M., Savage, B. E., & Gray, M. J. Measurement of psychological factors and their role in travel behavior. *Transportation Research Record 649*, 1977, 1–7.

Levin, I. P., Louviere, J. J., Meyer, R. J., & Henley, D. H. Individual decision processes in mode choice. Paper presented at meetings of Transportation Research Board, January 1980, Washington, D.C.

Louviere, J. J. Applications of principles of experimental design to the modelling and prediction of judgment and choice: A functional measurement approach. Paper presented to the Meetings of the Australia Road Research Bureau, Sydney, Australia, 1980.

Louviere, J. J., & Hensher, D. A. On the design of experiments to model choice behavior: A leisure travel destination choice example. Unpublished manuscript, University of New South Wales, Sydney, Australia, 1980.

Louviere, J. J., & Meyer, R. J. A model for residential impression formation. *Geographical Analysis*, 1976, *8*, 479–486.

Louviere, J. J., Wilson, E. M., & Piccolo, J. M. Psychological modelling and measurement in travel demand: A state-of-the-art review with applications. In D. A. Hensher & P. R. Stopher (Eds.), *Behavioural travel modelling*. London: Croom Helm, 1979, pp. 713–738.

Luce, R. D. *Individual choice behavior: A theoretical analysis*. New York: Wiley, 1959.

Mackay, D. B., Olshavsky, R. W., & Sentell, G. Cognitive maps and spatial behavior of consumers. *Geographical Analysis*, 1975, *7*, 19–34.

McFadden, D. L. Conditional logit analysis of qualitative choice behavior. In P. Zarembka (Ed.), *Frontiers in economics*. New York: Academic Press, 1974, pp. 105–142.

Meyer, R. J. A behavioral model of choice set formation in destination choice. Unpublished doctoral dissertation, University of Iowa, Iowa City, 1979.

Meyer, R. J., Levin, I. P., & Louviere, J. J. Functional analysis of mode choice. *Transportation Research Record 673*, 1978, 1–7.

Neveu, A. J. The 1973–74 energy crisis: Impact on travel. *Preliminary Research Report #131*, New York State Department of Transportation, Albany, 1977.

Neveu, A. J., Koppelman, F. S., & Stopher, P. R. Perceptions of comfort, convenience, and reliability for the work trip. *Preliminary Research Report 143*, New York State Department of Transportation, Albany, 1978.

Nicolaidis, G. C. Quantification of the comfort variable. *Transportation Research*, 1975, *9*, 55–66.

Nicolaidis, G. C., & Dobson, R. Disaggregated perceptions and preferences in transportation planning. *Transportation Research*, 1975, *9*, 279–295.

Norman, K. L. A solution for weights and scale values in functional measurement. *Psychological Review*, 1976, *83*, 80–84.

Norman, K. L., & Louviere, J. J. Integration of attributes in bus transportation: Two modeling approaches. *Journal of Applied Psychology*, 1974, *59*, 753–758.

Paine, F. T., Nash, A. N., Hille, S. J., & Brunner, G. A. Consumer attitudes toward auto versus public transport alternatives. *Journal of Applied Psychology*, 1969, *53*, 472–480.

Quandt, R. E. Estimation of modal splits. *Transportation Research*, 1968, *2*, 41–50.

Recker, W. W., & Golob, T. F. An attitudinal modal choice model. *Transportation Research*, 1976, *10*, 299–310.

Restle, F. *Psychology of judgment and choice*. New York: Wiley, 1961.

Richards, M. G., & Ben-Akiva, M. E. *A disaggregate travel demand model*. Lexington, Mass.: Saxon House/Lexington Books, 1975.

Slovic, P., Fischhoff, B., & Lichtenstein, S. Behavioral decision theory. *Annual Review of Psychology*, 1977, *28*, 1–39.

Stopher, P. R., & Ergün, G. Population segmentation in urban recreation choices. Paper presented at meetings of Transportation Research Board, January 1979, Washington, D.C.

Stopher, P. R., Spear, B. D., & Sucher, P. O. Toward the development of measures of convenience for travel modes. *Transportation Research Record 527*, 1974, 16–32.

Thurstone, L. L. The measurement of social attitudes. *Journal of Abnormal and Social Psychology*, 1931, *26*, 249–269.

Watson, P. L., & Westin, R. B. Transferability of disaggregate mode choice models. *Regional Science and Urban Economics*, 1975, *5*, 227–249.

Wicker, A. W. Attitudes versus actions: The relationship of verbal and overt behavioral responses to attitude objects. *Journal of Social Issues*, 1969, *25*, 41–78.

Wilson, A. G. A statistical theory of spatial distribution models. *Transportation Research*, 1967, *1*, 253–269.

Wooton, H. J., & Pick, G. W. A model of trips generated by household. *Journal of Transport Economics and Policy*, 1967, *1*, 137–153.

3

Reinforcement Theory Strategies for Modifying Transit Ridership

PETER B. EVERETT

INTRODUCTION

The predominance of the single-occupancy private automobile as the major urban transportation mode has led to many well-recognized problems. The private car uses 27% of the nation's annual consumption of petroleum and natural gas (Sokolsky, 1979). It is the most significant contributor to urban pollution and congestion. The road systems designed to accommodate the private car have disrupted the social fabric of many neighborhoods (Leavitt, 1970), and there is good evidence that they have determined the size, shape, and character of many urban areas (Chapin, 1968). Finally, the overreliance on a single transportation mode has forced a certain component of our population (the elderly, the young, the poor, the handicapped) to be truly deprived of mobility as options other than the private car are simply not available.

Transportation problems have been traditionally dealt with by

PETER B. EVERETT • Program in Man-Environment Relations, The Pennsylvania Transportation Institute, The Pennsylvania State University, University Park, Pennsylvania 16802.

proposing and implementing capital-intensive physical–technical alternatives. These include the construction of bigger and better highways, massive subway systems, and fuel-efficient vehicles. However, in the late 1970s, policy makers came to realize that other alternatives might be less expensive and more effective in the near future and, indeed, might contribute to a resolution of urban transportation problems. These alternatives fall under the label *transportation systems management* (TSM). A recent reference to the TSM perspective is presented by Lockwood (1979). Put simply, TSM means better management of the total transportation system, with a heavy emphasis on the efficient use of existing transportation resources. In other words, the belief is that through a more efficient use of our existing automobile system, transit system, pedestrian system, bicycle system, and so forth, the problems of contemporary urban transportation will be reduced.

A major theme generated by the TSM movement is the development of strategies to change travel behavior. There is much interest in developing strategies to increase car and van pooling, bus ridership, walking and the use of bicycles. Similarly, there is interest in reducing the use of single-occupancy car travel, car travel in congested urban areas, and simply car travel altogether. The development of these travel-behavior change strategies has evolved from many perspectives and disciplines. Marketing theory and practice have suggested promotion and advertising strategies for increasing transit use (Weiglin, 1975). Economic theory and practice have suggested gasoline pricing strategies to reduce fuel purchases for private cars and parking pricing strategies to discourage intensive car travel in congested urban areas. On the other hand, economists have suggested pricing strategies for increasing car pooling and transit use. Suggestions for changing travel behavior have also emanated from psychological theory and application. Much research has focused on assessing people's attitudes toward certain traits of various transportation modes that may be discouraging their use (Recker & Stevens, 1976).

Another area of psychological theory and practice that shows promise for the task of changing travel behaviors is reinforcement theory (Skinner, 1953, 1969). It is the intent of this chapter to (1) briefly introduce the principles of reinforcement theory and present a reinforcement theory model of one type of travel behavior of interest to TSM—transit ridership; (2) discuss experimental and case study applications of reinforcement theory approaches to changing transit ridership; and (3) discuss the future of reinforcement theory applications to urban transportation problems.

THE REINFORCEMENT THEORY APPROACH

PRINCIPLES OF REINFORCEMENT THEORY

To date, the application of reinforcement theory has been quite successful in changing a variety of behaviors in diverse settings. Many of these applications have been made in clinical, educational, and correctional institutions. Recently, the application of reinforcement theory principles in a variety of work settings has increased employee productivity and reduced tardiness and absenteeism. Also, over the last four years, reinforcement theory applications have been successful in modifying behaviors related to energy consumption and environmental pollution. Before discussing the application of reinforcement theory to transportation issues, it is appropriate to review some of the basic concepts of the theory.

Two central concepts in reinforcement theory are *reinforcement* and *punishment*. Simply stated, the consequences of a given behavior influence or determine the probability of the future occurrence of that behavior. If the presentation of an event, consequent on behavior, increases the probability of the occurrence of that behavior, that event is labeled a *positive reinforcer* (it strengthens behavior, thus the term *reinforcer*). For example, if an individual completes a piece of work, such as painting a picture, and receives congratulations and/or money for the task and the frequency of painting increases, the process is called *positive reinforcement* and the praise and/or the money is labeled a *positive reinforcer*. Note that events are operationally defined by their effect on behavior. *Negative reinforcement* may also occur. If the absence or withdrawal of an event, consequent on behavior, increases the probability of the occurrence of that behavior, the event is labeled a *negative reinforcer* and the process is called *negative reinforcement*. For example, if an individual makes certain financial investments and as a consequence of doing so avoids certain taxes (i.e., invests in a tax shelter) and his/her rate of such investments increases, the absence of taxes is labeled a *negative reinforcer*. If a behavior results in the delivery of a negative reinforcer, the future probability of that behavior is usually decreased, and this is labeled a punishing consequence and a *punishment procedure*. So, in summary, reinforcers (both positive and negative reinforcers) increase the frequency of, or strengthen, behavior, while punishers decrease the frequency of, or weaken, behavior. The task of predicting and modulating behaviors has been significantly enhanced in a multitude of settings with this simple perspective (the systematic observation of behavior probabilities as a function of behavior patterns and consequent events).

Two additional concepts, the *schedule control of behavior* and *reinforcement delay*, are closely linked to the concept of reinforcement. It has been found that the probability of a reinforcer following a behavior has a significant differential effect on behavior strength. If all behaviors are followed by reinforcers, behavior strength (as measured by perseverance without reinforcement, for example) is usually at some intermediate level, whereas if only a certain proportion of behaviors is followed by reinforcers (e.g., gambling), behavior strength may be even greater. However, as the probability of reinforcement is thinned even further, behavior strength tends to dwindle rapidly. This phenomenon has been labeled the *schedule control of behavior* because the behavior is strongly controlled or influenced by the schedule (frequency) of reinforcement.

Research on reinforcement delay has demonstrated that delay has an impact on behavior similar to that of schedule control. It has been documented that the strength of behavior is significantly influenced by the temporal relationship of a consequent event following that behavior. Those events occurring most immediately after a behavior have the greatest chance of strengthening that behavior, while those temporally distant from a behavior have much less probability of influencing that response.

The concept of schedule control of behavior holds true for punishers as well as reinforcers. That is, punishers that occur at different probabilities following a behavior tend to have different impacts on the strength of the behavior. Similarly, the temporal relationship between a response and a punisher significantly affects the behavioral impact of the punisher, as does the temporal relationship between a response and a reinforcer.

Threaded throughout this discussion of the concepts of reinforcement theory are the important concepts of *target behavior* and *response contingency*. *Target behavior* refers to the specific behavior under study, on which the behavior change strategies are focused. *Response contingency* is essentially the rule or the prescription that states that when a certain target behavior occurs, a reinforcer or a punisher will follow. That is, the delivery of the reinforcing or punishing event is contingent on the occurrence of the target behavior. The dissemination of reinforcers and punishers, contingent on a certain behavior, is what makes them such salient modifiers of behavior.

A Reinforcement Theory Model of Transit Ridership

Reinforcement theory could be applied to a variety of travel behaviors (e.g., car and van pooling, walking, and bicycle riding). Furthermore, the theory could be applied simultaneously to the full spectrum of travel behaviors. However, as reinforcement theory applications to transportation are few, it would be rather superficial to deal with a wide variety of travel behaviors here. Furthermore, most of the reinforcement theory work to date has been directed at public transit. Therefore, this chapter focuses on reinforcement theory applications to public transit.

A reinforcement theory model of transit ridership is presented in Figure 1 (an earlier version of this model was presented by Everett and Hayward, 1974). Two broad classes of travel behavior are identified (using mass transit and driving a car), as are two contingent consequences of behavior (reinforcers and punishers). In each of the boxes (numbered 1 through 4), there are speculations as to the kinds of events or consequences that might *normally* follow these behaviors.

The model does have several shortcomings. First, it is static in time and space and does not account for the continual changes in behavior

CONSEQUENCES CONTINGENT ON BEHAVIOR

	REINFORCING (Positive and Negative)	PUNISHING
CAR DRIVING	1. —Short Travel Time —Prestige —Arrival/Departure Flexibility —Exhilaration —Privacy —Route Selection —Cargo Capacity —Predictability —Delayed Costs	2. —Congestion —Gas and Maintenance Costs
USING TRANSIT	3. —Freedom from car ownership responsibilities —Making friends	4. —Exposure to Weather —Discomfort —Noise —Dirt —Surly Personnel —Long Walk to Stops —Danger (Crimes) —Immediate Costs —Unpredictability —Min. Cargo Capacity —Min. Route Selection —Crowded —Min. Arrival/Departure Flexibility —Low Prestige —Long Travel Time

(BEHAVIOR (RESPONSES))

Figure 1. A reinforcement theory model of transit ridership.

and its consequences nor for changes in environmental contexts. Second, it does not incorporate the concepts of schedule of reinforcement and reinforcement delay. And third, it does not illustrate the different magnitudes or relative impacts of the various different kinds of consequences following given behaviors. The model assumes that all the consequences have roughly the same impact. Yet, in spite of these shortcomings, the model does provide a systematic framework that illustrates how the existing consequences in the environment overwhelmingly favor car driving. Furthermore, Figure 1 suggests the remedial strategies that one might institute to decrease car-driving behavior and to increase transit ridership. For example, the consequences in Boxes 1 and 4 could be reduced, or those in Boxes 2 and 3 could be increased in number to accomplish this task.

Additionally, the model demonstrates that from a practical and theoretical perspective, there are appropriate and inappropriate consequences that a decision maker can choose from. For instance, the reduction of Box 1 consequences may be politically difficult as it would entail a reduction of reinforcing events for citizens. Box 2 consequences, although favored by public-policy makers, are theoretically inappropriate to manipulate. If one chooses to decrease car driving by punishing it, and in turn to increase transit ridership, something very different may happen. Any behavior that avoids a punishing event is reinforced. However, this behavior has not been specified, so it is not known what response (e.g., transit use) might be increased. For example, a government policy may strive to suppress car driving by requiring higher taxes on gas, yet car driving may remain high because of the purchase of black-market petroleum. Punishment procedures seem to be favored as they are often easier to manage and lead to a quickly observed behavior change. Yet the unwanted behaviors (side effects?) are often not documented and may lead to problems that cancel out management efficiency.

Box 3 and 4 manipulations are the most favored. Decreasing the amount of punishment that follows transit ridership (Box 4) would be a fruitful strategy. However, the precise identification of which behaviors will be reinforced by such changes is difficult. Therefore, the consequences in Box 3 are both politically and theoretically the best to deal with. For example, increasing the number of reinforcing events that follow the use of transit requires an exact specification of which behavior will occur (e.g., bus riding, subway use) and would not evoke politically sensitive reactions to the use of punishment procedures.

As mentioned above, the model of transit ridership presented in Figure 1 needs additions that cannot be graphically represented, in order to make it more complete. First, one must not only attend to the reinforcers (both positive and negative) and punishers that are consequent on various travel behaviors but also consider the schedule of these reinforcers and punishers. For example, the reinforcing consequence of privacy has a very high probability of occurrence consequent on car driving, while privacy on mass transit is much less predictable (a very thin schedule of reinforcement), thus increasing the odds against transit ridership.

Second, one must consider delay-of-reinforcement parameters in a reinforcement theory model of transit ridership. The dollar consequences of using a private car are often deferred through a credit system, whereas an individual using a bus must pay immediately. As noted in the discussion above, immediate consequences have a greater impact on behavior than do deferred consequences. A more thorough examination of many environmental problems, such as the overuse of the private car, demonstrates even more strongly that the delay-of-reinforcement concept is a major culprit in our inability to change environmentally relevant behaviors. The immediate consequences (which, indeed, control behavior) of car driving commonly tend to favor the increase of car driving (e.g., speed of trip, prestige, privacy), whereas consequences that would have the best probability of suppressing car driving (e.g., depletion of resources, severe levels of pollution) are quite delayed, as they are several years off. Deslauriers (1975) has presented a more detailed account of the effect of delay of reinforcement parameters on travel behavior. He noted that certain modes (e.g., the private automobile and dial-a-bus) will be clearly favored over a scheduled bus as a result of the reinforcement delay inherent in the different modes.

One final comment with regard to the model (as shown in Figure 1) is appropriate. The model as presented is qualitative. It should be interesting and worthwhile to attempt to quantify the relative influences of the consequences on behavior. In other words, does the reinforcing consequence of "privacy" for car driving have an equal, less, or greater influence on behavior than "crowdedness" as a punisher for transit use? Indeed, such a quantification is the work of demand modeling. A convergence of reinforcement theory perspectives with demand modeling work would be most beneficial. Reinforcement theory would specify a general framework within which quantitative demand modeling could develop.

This brief overview of reinforcement theory and a reinforcement theory model of transit ridership provides the background for reviewing case studies and experiments that have attempted to modify transit ridership through the application of reinforcement principles.

CHANGING TRANSIT RIDERSHIP: CASE STUDIES AND EXPERIMENTS

Many programs that adhere to the principles of reinforcement theory have been implemented in an attempt to increase transit patronage or to shift ridership from the busy peak hours (morning and evening rush hours) to the off-peak. A limited number of the programs is discussed below. They tend to fall into boxes 3 and 4 of the model of transit ridership presented in Figure 1. In other words, some programs have attempted to alter ridership by reinforcing riders (Box 3 manipulations) and others by removing punishers for bus riding (Box 4 manipulations). Under each of these strategies for changing ridership (reinforcement or punishment removal for riding), case studies and experiments are discussed. The case studies are of those programs that manipulated reinforcement variables yet did not evolve from reinforcement theory. For example, marketing theory and practice, economic perspectives, and just plain old brainstorming have generated programs that manipulate variables according to reinforcement theory. The second classification, experiments, are those programs that evolved directly from reinforcement theory.

Reinforcing Transit Use

Case Studies

Many transit systems across the country have attempted to increase patronage by doling out reinforcers to individuals using transit or for behaviors allied with transit use. A sample of cities that have distributed reinforcers on a continuous reinforcement schedule is shown in Table 1.

Table 1
Continuous Reinforcement Examples

City	Program description
Minneapolis, MN	Coupon for sundae for rider of new minibus service.
Minneapolis, MN	Free zoo tickets when advance fare is purchased.
Denver, CO	Fast-food coupons distributed at promotional talks.
Indianapolis, IN	Fast-food coupons distributed to purchaser of advance bulk fares.
Worcester, MA	Free passes and savings bonds as prize to bus color-scheme designer.
Syracuse, NY	Free hamburger coupon to bulk pass customers.
Iowa City, IA	Novelty items to children who ride buses.
St. Louis, MO	Free token to those who patronize banks.

TABLE 2
SCHEDULE OF REINFORCEMENT EXAMPLES

City	Program description
Portland, OR	Bus riders draw for car and cash prizes.
Dallas, TX	Bingo contest with major prizes. Playing cards available on bus, games played on bus during off-peak hours.
Buffalo, NY	Major cash and travel prizes by drawings. Entries available on buses and from merchants.

Other cities have used variable schedules of reinforcement. Examples of some of these programs are shown in Table 2.

It is hard to evaluate many of the case studies as data are not often systematically recorded. Even if data are recorded, reports of the findings are hard to find and/or obtain. Generally, the transit systems implementing these programs deserve credit for innovation. Indeed, there are reports of very successful programs. For example, the hamburger coupons distributed to bulk pass purchasers in Syracuse increased pass sales to 86% above previous sales (*Passenger Transport,* May 16, 1975).

One major criticism of the case studies is the lack of attention to the concept of target behavior and response contingency. It is often hard to determine what behavior the transit system was trying to strengthen. For example, in Denver, food coupons were given to individuals for attending a transit promotional talk rather than for riding the bus. Similarly, in St. Louis, individuals received bus tokens for patronizing certain banks. Clearly, more effective programs for increasing transit ridership could have been designed had the issues of target behavior and response contingency been dealt with.

Experimental Study: Continuous and Variable Token Reinforcement

Several experiments, designed to change transit ridership by reinforcing riders, have evolved directly from reinforcement theory (see Everett, 1973; Everett, Hayward, & Meyers, 1974). One of these experiments (Deslauriers & Everett, 1977) is discussed here.

Deslauriers and Everett (1977) established a token reinforcement procedure on a campus bus system that served 30,000 students and 6,000 faculty and staff. Tokens were given to passengers immediately on boarding a bus. These tokens could be traded (in varying quantities) at local business establishments for a variety of goods and services. Several area merchants agreed to accept tokens in exchange for goods ranging from candy bars, to draft beer, to hamburgers, to record albums, and so

THANK YOU FOR RIDING ON THE RED STAR BUS

★ **ONE TOKEN** ★

THESE TOKENS ARE REDEEMABLE FOR ICE CREAM, BEER, PIZZA, COFFEE, CIGARETTES, MOVIES, FLOWERS, RECORDS, ETC. CONSULT THE "BUS TOKEN EXCHANGE SHEET" (AVAILABLE ON THE RED STAR BUS) FOR A COMPLETE LIST OF AVAILABLE GOODIES AND EXCHANGE RATES. TOKENS ARE VALUABLE AND EASILY EXCHANGED AT STORES LISTED ON THE "BUS TOKEN EXCHANGE SHEET."

— THANK YOU FOR BEING ECOLOGICAL —

GOOD UNTIL END OF TERM

Figure 2. A Sample Token. (Source: P. B. Everett, S. C. Hayward, & A. W. Meyers, Effects of a token reinforcement procedure on bus ridership, *Journal of Applied Behavior Analysis,* 1974, *7,* 1–9.)

forth (see Figure 2 for a sample token). The researchers reimbursed the merchants at a predetermined rate for each token collected. However, several merchants allowed the researchers to purchase the tokens at a discounted rate because of the advertising benefits of involvement in the program and the increased store traffic generated by token possessors.

In this experiment, two schedules of token reinforcement were tested: a continuous schedule of reinforcement (all the riders were reinforced) and a variable schedule of reinforcement (a certain proportion of the riders were reinforced). Basic and applied research have demonstrated that stronger behavior is often generated with schedules of reinforcement giving odds of reinforcement at something less than 100%. Hopefully, it could be demonstrated that certain schedules of reinforcement would increase ridership to levels greater than, or at least equal to, the ridership levels found under conditions of continuous reinforcement. Although such a finding would certainly be of theoretical interest, it would be of even more importance to the task of developing economically feasible reinforcement mechanisms to increase and maintain bus ridership. If only a certain proportion of bus-riding responses need be reinforced to maintain high ridership levels, then the operator of such a program would have to reimburse only a proportion of the cost of operating a continuous reinforcement procedure.

Three campus buses on the same route were used, one for the experimental bus and two controls. Several weeks of baseline data were collected on all the buses. After this period, and with appropriate media announcements, large red stars (used to discriminate the experimental bus from the control buses) were placed on one of the buses, and all passengers boarding during the next several days paid a 10¢ fare and then had a one-out-of-three chance of receiving a token (see Figure 2). After 15 days of the one-in-three odds for a token, the odds of token receipt for riding the bus were altered to 100%. This condition was held constant for several days, and then, with the appropriate media announcements, the treatment was reversed to the condition of one-in-three odds for token receipt. After several days in this last condition, the red stars were taken off the bus and baseline conditions were repeated (i.e., no reinforcement on any of the three buses).

Figure 3 depicts the results of the experiment. Of most importance, both of the reinforcement treatment conditions increased ridership to levels significantly greater than control levels. Furthermore, there were no significant differences between ridership levels obtained under the reinforcement probability schedule and the continuous reinforcement schedule. Such a finding is particularly encouraging in light of the mission of this study: to develop a more economical method of using a

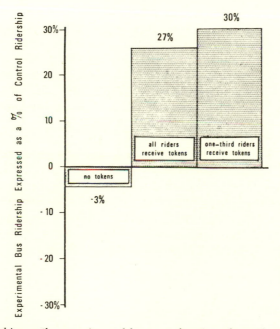

Figure 3. Ridership on the experimental bus as a function of no token reinforcement, continuous token reinforcement, and variable token reinforcement.

reinforcement procedure in a transit setting. The ridership increases attained under variable reinforcement were similar to those attained under continuous reinforcement, yet at one-third the cost. Only one-third the number of tokens were distributed, and the researchers were obligated to buy back from the merchants only that reduced number. The discount that the merchants normally passed on to the researchers as a trade-off for the marketing benefits of involvement in this program added to the relative inexpensiveness of the reinforcement procedure. If an economic analysis of the present experiment is restricted to a consideration of fare revenue and the direct cost of back-up reinforcers (i.e., merchant reimbursement), then during variable reinforcement, there was a net loss in revenue of 5%. A similar economic analysis for continuous reinforcement indicated a 75% net loss in revenue. In an applied setting, a 5% loss in revenue could easily be overcome by arranging for local merchants to give a minimal increase in their discount on the face value of the tokens exchanged at their establishments.

REMOVAL OF PUNISHMENT FOR TRANSIT USE

Case Studies

Fare payment for a transit trip and/or the requirement of "exact fare" could be viewed as punishers for transit use. Many systems have reduced fares for short periods of time (e.g., a "Nickel Day") in order to promote transit, and other systems have eliminated the fare altogether. Many of these case studies are reviewed in the booklet *Low Fare, Free Fare Transit* by Goodman and Green (1977). Some examples of free- and reduced-fare case studies are shown in Table 3.

As in the evaluation of the reinforcement case studies, it is often difficult to assess the effect of the punishment removal programs as reliable data are often not collected and/or evaluation reports are unavailable. There are, however, data on some of the experiences. Dallas reported an 80% increase in CBD ridership when their program was instituted (*Passenger Transport*, July 11, 1975). Preliminary documents report a 45–50% ridership increase in Trenton during the off-peak hours (Connor, 1979) and a 90% increase in Denver during the off-peak hours (Swan & Knight, 1979).

Experimental Studies

While the cities mentioned above should be congratulated on their innovations, only the surface has been scratched with regard to the

TABLE 3
FREE AND REDUCED FARE EXAMPLES

City	Program description
Salem, OR	Cherriot Commuter Club: Frequent riders permitted free fares.
Pittsburgh, PA	Free transit on buses with novelty markings.
Rockford, IL	Free transit tickets to new residents.
Boise, ID	Home Free Program: Merchants provide shoppers with transit tokens to return home for free.
St. Louis, MO	Free tokens to those who patronize banks.
Seattle, WA	Magic Carpet Ride: Free transit when within the Central Business District (CBD).
Madison, WI	Fare reduction during weekends. Fare removal during midday.
Denver, CO	Systemwide off-peak free transit.
Trenton, NJ	Systemwide off-peak free transit.
Dallas, TX	Free transit when within CBD.

effect of punishment removal or reduction on transit use. Many other punishers (such as transit crowding, waiting time, trip time) other than fare payment could be reduced or removed (see Figure 1). Furthermore, many additional parameters of fare reduction or removal could be explored. It was the intent of the next two experiments to do just this: explore additional parameters of fare (punishment) removal.

Free-Transit Magnitude and Expiration Date. The research question of this experiment was: "Does the amount of free transit or the number of days that free transit is available affect ridership?" (see Everett, Gurtler, & Hildebrand, in press, details). In order to factor out these variables, the following procedure was implemented. Twenty-six hundred households within two blocks of a new urban transit route (serving a university, a downtown business district, and suburban middle-income private homes and apartments) were randomly divided into four groups. Each group received a letter in the mail with a written announcement of the new route, a route map and timetable, and a packet of coupons good for free bus rides on the new route. Group 1 received 5 coupons good for the next 5 consecutive days, Group 2 received 5 coupons good for the next 15 days, Group 3 received 15 coupons good for the next 5 days, and group 4 received 15 coupons good for the next 15 days. The dependent variables were ridership increases on the new bus route and the differential rate of coupon return from Groups 1 through 4.

Figure 4 illustrates the effect the treatment had on ridership in general. Independent of the type of coupon received, ridership increased 58% above baseline levels, compared with a range of ridership increases

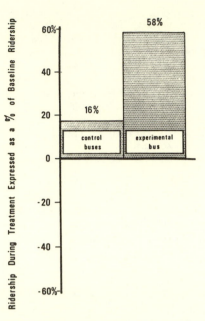

Figure 4. Ridership changes on the experimental and control buses of the experiment on free-transit magnitude and expiration date.

of 8–19% for the four control routes. The average of ridership increases was 16% for the control buses.

Figure 5 illustrates the differential impact of the various treatment conditions. The condition leading to the highest proportion of bus rides to coupons distributed was 5 coupons for 15 days. The group of households receiving 15 coupons good for 5 days exhibited the least transit use in proportion to the number of coupons they received. Results such as these are important as they give insight into the best free-ride programs to implement. If a transit system is concerned about the greatest impact per free ride, then according to this study, the distribution of a smaller number of coupons that are good for a longer time period is most appropriate. However, on an absolute basis (independent of how many coupons were distributed), the greatest number of rides was generated by the group holding the 15 coupons good for 15 days.

Contingent Free Transit.

This experiment (see Everett, Deslauriers, Newsom, & Anderson, 1978, for details) is a variant of the free transit study just discussed. As in the previous study, potential riders (individuals living along a bus route that served primarily a campus environment) were mailed coupons that were exchangeable for free bus rides. The uniqueness of this experiment was the following: more free-ride coupons were given to individuals *contingent* on their using the initial coupons.

The study was carried out in the following manner. Each subject in two treatment groups (200 subjects each) was mailed 12 coupons good for free rides on any bus of the campus bus system. These coupons were good for the next nine consecutive days. The two groups differed in the following fashion. For one group, the 12 initial coupons stated (on each coupon) that after the nine-day expiration time, each subject would receive 12 more coupons in the mail regardless of how many times he or she rode the bus during the initial nine days (control group or noncontingent free transit group). For the next group, each coupon stated that for every coupon of the initial 12 used, each subject would receive in the mail *one* additional coupon at the end of the nine days (one-for-one response-contingent free-transit group).

Figure 6 presents the results of this experiment. The contingent free-transit condition yielded a significantly greater ridership than did the noncontingent free-transit condition.

The findings of this study are important. Not only does free transit increase ridership, but the method of free-transit distribution can significantly modify ridership levels. These findings can be directly applicable to the operation of a free-transit program on a much larger scale. As opposed to a mail distribution program, it would be quite easy to contingently distribute free-transit coupons to passengers immediately on boarding a bus (in a fashion similar to distributing a transfer). Clearly,

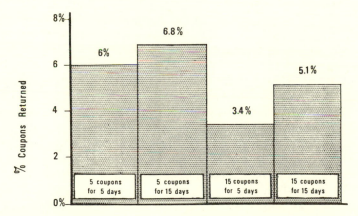

Figure 5. The percentage of the coupons returned for bus rides for the various treatment conditions of the experiment on free-transit magnitude and expiration date.

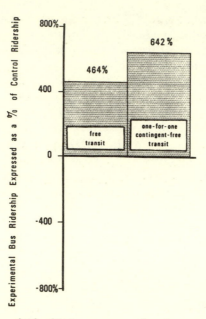

Figure 6. The percentage of ridership increases as a function ot tree transit and one-for-one contingent free-transit.

because of the concept of schedule control, many parameters of the relationship between bus-riding responses and the receipt of free-transit coupons need exploration.

DISCUSSION

GENERAL COMMENTS

At the start of this chapter, the transportation systems management (TSM) theme was introduced. It was noted that one of the major implications of TSM was the need for strategies to change travel behaviors. One of these strategies, reinforcement theory, was introduced. Then, several examples of reinforcement theory application to the task of changing one behavior of interest to TSM (transit ridership) were discussed. These applications seem to have been effective as far as they went. Yet they have not been well documented (as was the case for many of the case studies), or they were very focused or short term, or they dealt with student populations (as was the case in the experimental studies). But the future is promising. However, these applications must be made more relevant in a systemic way for the entire transportation system if they are to truly deal with the impending energy-short future. Clearly, the contingencies for our travel behavior will be changed regardless of planning. We will continue to have fuel shortages over the foreseeable future. Our choice is to plan or not to plan contingencies for our travel behavior. Our behaviors can slowly be changed to energy-efficient ones by good planning—or we can get there by many crises and shocks of realization.

The reinforcement theory focus on urban public transit has been a good place to start. This initiation has developed credibility for such applications and has enabled speculation as to the future of reinforcement theory and TSM. Some of these potential developments are discussed below.

THE FUTURE

The Immediate Future

The immediate future of reinforcement theory applications to urban transit promises to be an interesting one. The Urban Mass Transportation Administration (UMTA) is sponsoring two large-scale urban demonstrations of reinforcement theory applications. In an attempt to generalize the token reinforcement studies to a nonstudent population, the city of Spokane, Washington, implemented in 1981 a systemwide token reinforcement procedure on all of its buses for 2½ years. The program's goals are to increase off-peak transit patronage, reduce CBD vehicular traffic, and increase CBD sales. Tokens will be distributed to all passengers boarding buses during the off-peak hours. These tokens will be exchanged for discounts on goods and services provided by downtown business establishments. These businesses will support the full cost of token reimbursement in exchange for the marketing benefits of association with the program, increased customer traffic, and sales. The Spokane demonstration is a very logical "next stage" for the token reinforcement work, as it is appropriate to test whether such an approach will work in a nonuniversity setting in an economically viable format.

St. Paul and Minneapolis have been chosen by UMTA for another 2½-year reinforcement theory demonstration. This setting will provide an urban laboratory for testing many parameters (suggested by reinforcement theory) of free transit. The goal of the work is to determine the most effective and efficient means of using a short-term free-transit program either to increase ridership in general or to shift ridership to the off-peak hours. The independent variables that will be manipulated include the amount of free transit, free-transit expiration date, free-transit distribution techniques (e.g., direct mail versus employers), and rules (contingencies) for the receipt of free transit.

The free-transit demonstration in St. Paul–Minneapolis is an appropriate step to take from the case studies and experimental work discussed above. There have been sufficient urban experiences with free transit for certain times of the day (e.g., Trenton and Denver) or free transit within CBD boundaries. The experimental work has shown that many other parameters are of sufficient relevance to warrant implementation and validation in a nonuniversity setting.

Other Areas of Research

Reinforcement theory suggests several additional areas of transit research that could and should be explored. Primary among these are the determination of reinforcers and punishers for transit use, which have not been studied to date. There are many other possible reinforcers beyond fare-related ones. Service-related reinforcers certainly have an effect on user behavior. It would be appropriate to investigate ride quality, service frequency, and trip flexibility from a reinforcement perspective. Other, less tangible reinforcers are probably significant in one's choice to use transit. A top candidate for investigation would be image or prestige. Do riders feel "psychologically" lowered in social class when they board a bus, and, if so, how could this attitude be changed, or—more importantly—how could the image of oneself be increased by using transit?

Much investigation on the effect of punishment (other than fare payment) removal for transit use is also needed. Initial work by Lundberg (1976) and Slater and Watson (1980) has shown that transit vehicle conditions (e.g., crowding and trip unpredictability) are stressful. Would removal, or partial removal, of these punishers contingent on transit use significantly increase usage?

Another area of punishment inherent in transit use results from riders' inability to use current transit information aids. Lack of effective communication as to bus routes and schedules may leave an individual in the wrong part of town and without an easy return route. In addition, there is the embarrassment of making a mistake in public (i.e., in front of other riders). Indeed, Everett, Anderson, and Makranczy (1977) found that when college seniors were given typical transit maps, only 41% of objective trip-related questions could be correctly answered (see Table 4).

Research designed to determine the attributes of information systems that truly communicate how to navigate in a transit environment is scarce. This type of research would certainly be an appropriate endeavor. An additional and allied focus would be to research the relationship between transit route structure (e.g., linear or circular) and user knowledge of the system. Transit routes are often determined by rider origin–destination studies, labor contracts, fleet size, and one-way street configurations. Little, if any, concern is given to the user's perceptions of urban geography. Attention to users' urban "cognitive maps" when designing transit routes might well enhance users' ability to understand and, in turn, to use transit.

Another appealing transit research area suggested by reinforcement theory revolves around the concept of reinforcement and punishment delay. The punishing consequences of car use are often deferred through a credit system. Automobile time payments and credit purchase of gasoline disassociate the tremendous costs of car operation (estimated to be 38 cents a mile for 1980) with actual car use—thus not maximally discouraging this behavior. However, transit must be paid for immediately—with exact fare. Would payment delay (e.g., a credit system for transit use) for a bus ride increase patronage?

As this research area grows, it is most appropriate to explore joint implementations of actions from all the cells of the reinforcement theory model of transit ridership (presented in Figure 1). For example, what would be the joint effect of simultaneously removing reinforcers for car use, punishing car use, removing punishers for transit use, and reinforcing transit patronage? This is a promising question to pursue. Additionally, it would be of benefit to demonstrate the actions that are most synergistic and those that have the highest productivity levels.

It is quite obvious that the reinforcement theory perspective could

TABLE 4

PERCENTAGE OF CORRECT RESPONSES FOR EACH OF THE SEVEN OBJECTIVE
PERFORMANCE QUESTIONS FOR ALL 19 PAMPHLETS[a]

What is the name (or number) of the bus you take?	39
What time will you board the bus?	45
How much will the trip cost?	44
Will you travel on _____ Street for part of the trip?	49
What is the name of the bus stop where you will get off the bus?	53
How long will the trip take?	24
Which bus would you take for a return trip?	29
Overall performance	41

[a] Source: P. B. Everett, V. B. Anderson, and U. Makranczy. Transit route pamphlets: Do they work? *Transit Journal*, 1977, 3, 59–70.

address other transportation issues on the TSM theme (e.g., car pooling, van pooling, bicycle riding, and walking). A study by Foxx and Hake (1977) does just this. Weekly mileage in private automobiles was reduced by reinforcing low odometer readings. The theory could address each travel mode in isolation, as has been the case for the transit examples given here, or jointly. In addition to addressing behaviors related to different modes, reinforcement theory could deal with behaviors *related* to transit use. For example, what kinds of behaviors are strengthened (reinforced) in our educational system? Would it be appropriate to develop transportation education programs rather than to continue only driver education? Driver education, as well as transit and energy education, could be equal components of a transportation education program.

Two other behaviors related to transit use could also be investigated. The first is the host of behaviors leading up to transit use. Primary among these would be "waiting behaviors." Attention has been given to the reinforcers and punishers contingent on being in a transit vehicle (e.g., fare, crowding, ride quality). Yet the wait for a trip is often significantly greater in time than the trip itself. Concern about the inherent reinforcers and punishers in the waiting situation is very important, and, indeed, the potential payoff could be greater than simply focusing on the events paired only with actual vehicle entry and use.

The second behavior on which reinforcement theory should focus is that of public transit drivers. Traditionally, drivers are paid for effective vehicle operations and not customer relations. The majority of management control techniques involve punitive actions. Drivers could act as public relations people, sources of information, and general promoters of a transit system. What driver behaviors would encourage transit use, and what types of reinforcement strategies would increase and maintain these driver behaviors? These are only a few ideas for future applications of reinforcement theory to specific problems of low transit ridership and the general goals of TSM.

SUMMARY

This chapter has presented a reinforcement theory model of transit ridership. Within the framework of this model, both case studies and experimental work were reviewed. The results are quite promising, as ridership seems to be sensitive to parameters of reinforcement. As this application area is quite new, many suggestions for future work were made.

A reinforcement theory approach to the study of transit ridership shows much promise. As the area grows, it will be necessary to expand beyond transit and, simultaneously, to deal with the many and varied aspects of complex contemporary transportation systems. Furthermore, the boundaries of reinforcement theory should be flexible, and proponents of this perspective should be open to other theories of travel behavior. In complex, real world settings, an eclectic approach can only contribute to the enhancement of applied problem-solving.

REFERENCES

Chapin, F. S., Jr. Taking stock of techniques for shaping urban growth. *Journal of the American Institute of Planners,* 1968, *29,* 76–87.

Connor, D. L. *Findings of preliminary analyses of the Trenton, New Jersey off-peak fare-free transit demonstration.* U.S. Department of Transportation, 1979, NTIS 52-0001-79-1.

Deslauriers, B. C. A behavioral analysis of transportation: Some suggestions for mass transit. *High Speed Ground Transportation Journal,* 1975, *9,* 13–20.

Deslauriers, B. C., & Everett, P. B. Effects of intermittent and continuous token reinforcement on bus ridership. *Journal of Applied Psychology,* 1977, *62,* 369–375.

Everett, P. B. Use of the reinforcement procedure to increase bus ridership. *Proceedings of the 81st Annual Convention of the American Psychological Association,* 1973, *8* (Pt. 2), 891–892.

Everett, P. B., & Hayward, S. C. Behavioral technology—An essential design component of transportation systems. *High Speed Ground Transportation Journal,* 1974, *8,* 139–143.

Everett, P. B., Hayward, S. C., & Meyers, A. W. Effects of a token reinforcement procedure on bus ridership. *Journal of Applied Behavior Analysis,* 1974, *7,* 1–9.

Everett, P. B., Anderson, V. B., & Makranczy, U. Transit route pamphlets: Do they work? *Transit Journal,* 1977, *3,* 59–70.

Everett, P. B., Deslauriers, B. C., Newsom, T., & Anderson, V. B. The differential effect of two free ride dissemination procedures on bus ridership. *Transportation Research,* 1978, *12,* 1–7.

Everett, P. B., Gurtler, M. D., & Hildebrand, M. G. Free Transit: How Much—How Long? *Transportation Research,* In press.

Foxx, R. M., & Hake, D. F. Gasoline conservation: A procedure for measuring and reducing the driving of college students. *Journal of Applied Behavior Analysis,* 1977, *10,* 61–74.

Goodman, K. M., & Green, M. A. *Low fare, free fare transit.* Urban Mass Transportation Administration (UMTA), Feb. 1977, NTIS 52-0002-77-1.

Leavitt, H. *Superhighway—superhoax.* New York: Doubleday, 1970.

Lockwood, S. C. TSM planning—An emerging process. In G. E. Grey & L. A. Hoel (Eds.), *Public transportation: Planning, operations, and management.* Englewood Cliffs, N.J.: Prentice-Hall, 1979, pp. 354–381.

Lundberg, U. Urban commuting crowdedness and catecholamine secretion. *Journal of Human Stress,* 1976, *2,* 26–32.

Recker, W. W., & Stevens, R. F. Attitudinal models of modal choice: The multinomial case for selected network trips. *Transportation,* 1976, *5,* 355–375.

Skinner, B. F. *Science and human behavior.* New York: Macmillan, 1953.

Skinner, B. F. *Contingencies of reinforcement.* New York: Appleton-Century-Crofts, 1969.

Slater, J. S. & Watson, B. G. Psychological and physiological indicators of stress in various travel and commuting modes. Unpublished masters paper, The Pennsylvania State University, May, 1980.

Sokolsky, S. Energy: Case studies. In G. E. Grey & L. A. Hoel (Eds.), *Public transportation: Planning, operations, and management.* Englewood Cliffs, N.J.: Prentice-Hall, 1979. pp. 550–562.

Swan, S., & Knight, R. *Denver off-peak free fare public transit experiment (interim report).* UMTA, May 1979, NTIS 06-0010-79-1.

Weiglin, P. C. Marketing and the management attitude. *Transit Journal,* 1975, 2, 35–44.

4

Transportation and Well-Being

AN ECOLOGICAL PERSPECTIVE

DANIEL STOKOLS and RAYMOND W. NOVACO

INTRODUCTION

In large metropolitan areas of the United States, the work day routinely begins with a monumental traffic jam. Traffic congestion prevails in America primarily because commuters prefer to travel to and from work by private automobile (cf. Aangeenbrug, 1965; Catanese, 1972). In 1970, approximately 66% of the American labor force traveled to work by private car (Federal Highway Administration, 1977). Within certain metropolitan areas (e.g., Atlanta, Dallas, Detroit, Los Angeles, and Orange County, California), the proportion of automobile commuters ranged from 85% to 93%. Despite the recent surge and projected increases in the cost of fuel, the proportion of automobile commuters in the national work force is expected to be about 73% by 1990 (cf. Kain, Fauth, & Zax, 1977).

DANIEL STOKOLS and RAYMOND W. NOVACO • Program in Social Ecology, University of California, Irvine, California 92717. Preparation of this chapter and the reported research were funded by the Institute for Transportation Studies (ITS) and by the Focused Research Program in Human Stress at the University of California, Irvine. Computer funding for portions of the statistical analyses was provided by the Research Program in Human Stress at the University of California, Irvine.

What are the costs of our dependence on the automobile as a means of traveling to work? What are the relative costs of alternative travel modes? What conditions associated with transportation may have negative effects on well-being? The costs and benefits of environmental conditions and social programs typically are gauged by their immediate and economically tangible outcomes (cf. Catalano, 1979). When considering alternative modes of travel, individual commuters generally focus on the relative monetary expense, time constraints, and opportunities for privacy associated with the various modes. Government agencies tend to emphasize factors such as community levels of air pollution and fuel consumption (cf. Hartgen, 1977; Horowitz & Sheth, 1976). This emphasis on the economic and environmental consequences of personal and community travel patterns neglects a potentially important set of transportation-related outcomes, namely, the cumulative emotional, behavioral, and health consequences of travel conditions. These outcomes, while less immediate and tangible than monetary and time constraints and less conspicuous than environmental decay, nevertheless should be considered in any attempt to assess the impact of transportation environments on people.

Identifying the previously neglected impacts of transportation on health and behavior is a matter of practical as well as theoretical significance; for if the prevalence and severity of such impacts are demonstrated empirically, then a number of ameliorative strategies might be devised and implemented by transportation planners. Although research concerning the adverse behavioral and health consequences of travel conditions has been sparse, preliminary evidence suggests that these effects may be both prevalent and disruptive.

In a national survey of American workers conducted in 1977, for example, 38% of the commuters sampled reported that they experienced transportation-related problems (Quinn & Staines, 1979).[1] Among those respondents mentioning problems, about 50% cited "traffic congestion, nuisances, or inconveniences."[2] Also, 33% of the respondents characterized their travel problems as "sizable" or "great" (vs. "no problem at all," 8%, or "slight problem," 59%). In an earlier survey of Salt Lake City motorists, 12% of the men and 18% of the women sampled reported that at times, they "could gladly kill another driver" (Turner,

---

[1] We are grateful to Sandra Kirmeyer for bringing this survey to our attention.
[2] Twelve other categories of problems were mentioned by respondents. The second most frequently mentioned problem was "traffic dangers" (18.5%). Other problems cited were "travel expense" (4%), "lack of parking space" (2.5%), and "inconvenient public transit schedules" (2.1%). The least frequently mentioned category was "worker's transportation inconveniences his or her family" (.6%).

Layton, & Simons, 1975, p. 1100). Furthermore, field-experimental studies of automobile drivers have shown a significant relationship between exposure to rush-hour traffic and a variety of adverse physiological reactions, including chest pain and cardiac arrhythmia (cf. Aronow, Harris, Isbell, Rokaw, & Imparato, 1972; Taggart, Gibbons, & Somerville, 1969).

While the above studies suggest the range of behavioral and health problems associated with travel conditions, they do not provide an integrative theoretical analysis of the multiple environmental and personal underpinnings of those problems. The major objective of this chapter is to develop a systematic theoretical framework that addresses the relationships among transportation conditions and human well-being.

In the following section of the chapter, previous research on transportation and stress is reviewed. Certain limitations of this work are noted as the basis for developing an alternative conceptual and methodological approach. The next section outlines the prerequisites for an ecological analysis of transportation and well-being, and it identifies the key assumptions underlying our theoretical approach. Specifically, our analysis portrays certain conditions of transportation (e.g., traffic congestion) as environmental demands that tax the individual's adaptive capacity. The emotional, behavioral, and health consequences of these demands are assumed to be jointly determined by a complex array of circumstances existing within various domains of the individual's life situation (i.e., within one's community, transportation, residential, and work environments).

In the final section of the chapter, a longitudinal field experiment designed to assess certain predictions suggested by our analysis is summarized. The findings from the first phase of the research reveal the interactive effects of transportation conditions (e.g., length of commute, type of car) and personal attributes (e.g., residential choice, personality dispositions) on the mood, physiology, and task performance of automobile commuters. Data from the second phase of the study highlight the adaptive problems that arise in relation to commuting conditions, as well as the active efforts made by some commuters to alleviate such problems. The research and policy implications of our analysis are subsequently discussed.

PREVIOUS RESEARCH ON TRANSPORTATION AND STRESS

We will provide a selective yet representative overview of previous work concerning transportation and stress, but before examining specific studies, we will be more explicit about our principal concepts. The term *transportation* has been used to refer to diverse phenomena: the vehicle itself, alternative modes of travel, conditions within travel-related environments, and the broad network of travel facilities and services existing within a community. [3] In most research on travel conditions and traveler stress, *transportation* generally has been used to refer to the automobile mode of travel and to the immediate, intra and extravehicular conditions facing individual drivers and passengers. In a few studies, the focus has been on public transit (cf. Singer, Lundberg, & Frankenhaeuser, 1978; Taylor & Pocock, 1972) rather than on automobile travel. Our own conceptual approach does not restrict the meaning of *transportation* to automotive and/or public transit, as will become more apparent in the following section of the chapter. In the present section, however, we highlight the typical emphasis on these modes of travel in previous studies.

The term *stress* also has been associated with several diverse meanings. In general, *stress* refers to a state of imbalance within the organism that (1) is elicited by a disparity between environmental demands and the individual's capacity to cope with those demands and (2) is manifested through a variety of physiological, emotional, and behavioral responses. These responses occur as a result of the individual's exposure to excessive environmental demands, or *stressors*. Conditions of the physical environment operate as stressors to the extent that they tax or exceed the individual's adaptive resources (cf. Lazarus, 1966; Selye, 1956).

More detailed conceptualizations of stress have been developed from the medical, psychological, and sociological perspectives. From a medical perspective, stress is typically construed as a defensive bodily response to environmental demands (e.g., toxins, microbes, extreme temperature) involving specific physiological components, such as adrenal stimulation, gastrointestinal disturbances, and the shrinkage of lymphatic structures (cf. Selye, 1956, 1976). Psychological analyses place a greater emphasis on the individual's cognitive appraisal of threatening environmental conditions and personal coping resources than do medical models of stress (cf. Appley & Trumbull, 1967; Lazarus, 1966; McGrath, 1970). And sociological analyses focus on societal conditions that adversely affect the well-being of specific groups within the community (cf. Levine & Scotch, 1970; Mechanic, 1968).

The medical perspective on stress has been the predominant orienta-

---

[3]See, for example, the glossary of transportation-related terms provided by the Federal Highway Administration (1977, pp. 42–44).

tion reflected in earlier studies of transportation and stress. Our review of the literature is organized around two broad categories of research: (1) investigations of drivers' and passengers' reactions to conditions of automobile travel; and (2) studies of commuters' responses to conditions of public transit.[4] Following our review of this research, we develop an ecological framework which integrates psychological, sociological, and medical perspectives on transportation and stress.

Research on Automobile Travel and Stress

The impact of environmental demands on automobile travelers has been assessed through experimental studies of both simulated and actual driving situations. A wide array of environmental factors have been examined in this research, including road design, traffic conditions, and intravehicular levels of noise, heat, and air pollution.

Road Design and Traffic Conditions

A study by Michaels (1962) exemplifies the kind of field investigation that has been employed to assess the relationships among route characteristics, traffic conditions, and physiological arousal while driving (or immediately thereafter). The effects of road design and traffic volume (vehicles per hour) on drivers' tension responses were examined. Six male drivers, aged 17–22, were tested on four roads of differing design (e.g., urban freeways vs. arterial and primary streets). Each driver traveled the routes 12 times each during both off-peak and peak traffic hours. Tension reactions were assessed through continuous recording of the drivers' galvanic skin response (GSR) during each trip. Elevated levels of GSR (indicating driver tension) were found to be associated with routes characterized by minimal or partial (vs. complete) control of peripheral traffic access and with conditions of high traffic volume. These findings were explained in terms of the tension-promoting interferences associated with route intersections and congested traffic.

A number of other researchers have reported a significant, positive correlation between traffic volume (e.g., driving during rush hour) and increased levels of heart rate, blood pressure, and electrocardiogram irregularities (cf. Aronow et al., 1972; Hunt & May, 1968; Simonson, Baker, Burns, Keiper, Schmitt, & Stackhouse, 1968; Taggart, Gibbons, &

[4]We are unable, in this chapter, to review the extensive literature on road hazards and traffic safety. For a review of this research and a discussion of the environmental and psychosocial determinants of traffic accidents, see Forbes (1972) and Knapper and Cropley (1978,1980).

Somerville, 1969). These cardiovascular effects are especially pronounced among drivers with coronary artery disease (i.e., those having a record of angina pain and/or myocardial infarction). But even among healthy drivers, exposure to city traffic for prolonged periods (e.g., two hours) appears to be associated with a wide range of physiological imbalances, including heightened catecholamine and adrenocortical secretion (cf. Bellet, Roman, & Kostis, 1969).

Moreover, traffic situations of high complexity (e.g., negotiating dangerous curves and motorway exchanges; passing other vehicles and sudden breaking) have been found to be associated with increased heart rate and blood pressure (cf. Littler, Honour, & Sleight, 1973; Rutley & Mace, 1970; Simonson *et al.*, 1968). The relationship between the complexity of driving tasks and increased physiological arousal suggested by these field experiments has been corroborated in a number of driving simulation studies (cf. Forbes, 1972; Heimstra, 1970). Such research also has established a significant association between the complexity of simulated driving situations and impaired performance of braking and steering tasks.

Intravehicular Conditions of Noise, Heat, and Air Pollution

Drivers' reactions to high levels of noise and heat were examined in a recent simulation study by Neumann, Romansky, and Plummer (1978). Twenty-five males, aged 18–39, were tested in a driving simulator under ambient and moderately high levels of heat and noise. Participants completed two consecutive trials in the simulator, each lasting for 2¾ hours. The room temperatures and sound levels for the two trials were 76°F and 55 decibels (dBA), and 90°F and 78dBA.

A comparison of the subjects' task performance, physiology, and mood during the two trials revealed significantly high levels of stress under conditions of increased temperature and noise. Specifically, during the second trial, the subjects exhibited response decrements on both visual and auditory tasks and manifested elevations in heart rate, GSR, systolic and diastolic blood pressure, and adrenocortical secretion. Moreover, subjective ratings of discomfort and fatigue increased during the raised-temperature–high-noise trial. Because the first and second trials were not counterbalanced, however, the possibility remains that the stress reactions observed during the latter part of the experiment were prompted partly by the sheer duration of the test session (the two trials lasting a total of 5½ hours), as well as by the heightened temperature and noise during the second trial. Furthermore, the separate effects of noise and temperature were not disentangled.

The joint effects of heat and humidity on drivers were examined in a field experiment conducted by Mackie, O'Hanlon, and McCauley (1974). The participants were 10 males and 10 females, aged 25–35, who were recruited to drive two round trips between Santa Barbara and King City, California (180 miles in each direction along U.S. 101, a four-lane divided highway). One trip was made under hot and humid conditions, while the other was completed at comfortable temperature and humidity levels (90 WBGT vs. 67 WBGT, respectively).[5] The trips, counterbalanced for order, were made one week apart. Temperature and humidity were controlled via a specially equipped heater within the experimental vehicles (two full-sized 1972 Fords). The sound level was fairly constant for all trips, ranging between 64 and 68 dBA.

A trained observer accompanied the driver during each trip. The observer occupied the rear seat and was separated from the driver by a Plexiglass divider. In addition to monitoring physiological measurement devices, the observer recorded a variety of performance and subjective-report data throughout the journey. Statistical analyses indicated significant elevations in the drivers' body temperature, systolic blood pressure, heart rate, and heart rate variability while driving under conditions of high temperature and humidity. These conditions also were associated with decreased levels of self-reported alertness and central nervous system arousal (measured via electroencephalograph readings) and decrements in driving performance (e.g., greater frequencies of technical errors such as lane drift, speeding, and tailgating).

The experiment by Mackie *et al.*, like most studies of driving and stress, employed a small sample and provided no evidence for the reliability of the observers' ratings of the drivers' performance. For the most part, however, the investigation was well designed and supported the hypothesis that prolonged exposure to heat and humidity adversely affects drivers' physiology, mood, and performance.

Air pollution is an additional environmental demand to which automobile travelers are routinely exposed. Carbon monoxide (CO) is an especially toxic pollutant produced by gasoline-powered vehicles. Intravehicular levels of CO are closely related to traffic density and speed, with the highest concentrations occurring during congested, rush-hour traffic and at busy freeway interchanges (Chaney, 1978). The maximum concentrations of CO permitted by the Federal Ambient Air Quality Standards are 9 parts per million (ppm) for 8 hours and 35 ppm for 1

---

[5]The WBGT index is a weighted sum of dry bulb (DB), wet bulb (WB), and globe thermometer (GT) readings. The index reflects the combined effects of air temperature, air velocity, and relative humidity.

hour. On the Los Angeles freeways, ambient levels of CO as high as 120 ppm have been recorded during rush-hour periods (Haagen-Smit, 1966).

Laboratory experiments have demonstrated that CO concentrations corresponding to those found during heavy rush-hour traffic can impair performance on visual signal-detection tasks (Horvath, Dahms, & O'Hanlon, 1971; Halperin, McFarland, Niven, & Roughton, 1959). The adverse consequences of exposure to CO while driving may be especially pronounced among individuals with coronary artery disease (CHD), according to the findings from a field experiment conducted by Aronow *et al.* (1972). In that study, each of 10 drivers who had been diagnosed as having CHD drove a designated route for 90 minutes during rush-hour traffic in Los Angeles. On a subsequent day, the participants drove the same route but breathed pure compressed air during the trip. Analyses indicated significantly higher CO in expired air and carboxy-hemoglobin in the blood after those trips in which the drivers inhaled impure versus pure air. Moreover, tolerance for strenuous exercise decreased and complaints of angina pain increased following exposure to the freeway air.

Research on Public Transit and Stress

The relationship between conditions of public transit and commuter stress has received little empirical attention. Only two major investigations of these phenomena have been conducted: a survey of London office workers by Taylor and Pocock (1972), and a field-experimental study of train commuters in Stockholm conducted by Singer *et al.*, (1978; cf. Lundberg, 1976).

The London survey involved 1,677 male and 317 female employees, aged 30–69, who had worked at a large company for at least one year. Each respondent completed a travel questionnaire pertaining to various aspects of the commute to work (e.g., types of transit used, duration and unpleasantness of the trip) and to several personal and demographic factors (e.g., age, sex, job grade). These variables were cross-tabulated with company records of certified and uncertified absence from work. Certified absences were defined as those validated by a medical certificate.

Of the 1,994 respondents, 1,890 (95%) used some form of public transit in their journey between home and work (e.g., British Rail and London Transport trains, public buses). Also, the journeys of public transit commuters typically involved multiple stages (i.e., portions of the trip in which neither the mode of travel nor the vehicle was changed;

walks taking five or more minutes were counted as a separate stage). The average number of stages for the entire sample was 2.84. The duration of the journey ranged from 12 minutes to 2½ hours, with a median of 1 hour. The women had somewhat shorter journeys than the men.

The major finding of the survey was a significant correlation between the number of stages in the journey and the frequency of both certified and uncertified absences from work. Moreover, car users (412 respondents) had significantly higher rates of uncertified absence than did persons who did not use private transport. Also, the frequency and length of uncertified absences were significantly greater among those commuters whose work trips took longer than 1½ hours. Ratings of actual and perceived crowdedness of public transit facilities were not significantly correlated with either certified (e.g., influenza-related) or uncertified absence rates.

The field experiment conducted by Singer *et al.* involved 30 male commuters who traveled regularly between home and work along the Nynashamn–Stockholm train line. Participants were between 20 and 67 years of age and had commuted on the same train line for at least six months. All subjects rode a morning train. One group ($n = 15$) boarded the train at its first stop (Nynashamn) and the other ($n = 15$) boarded at a midpoint on the route (Vasterhaninge). The commuting times for the two groups were 79 and 43 minutes, respectively. Over a four-day period, the subjects made psychophysical judgments concerning traveling conditions on the train (e.g., perceived crowdedness), and on the third day, they provided urine specimens prior to leaving their homes and on arrival at the Stockholm station. The urine samples were analyzed for adrenalin and noradrenalin levels.

A comparison of the data from the two groups of commuters revealed several significant trends. First, subjective reports of crowdedness and discomfort increased as the train approached the Stockholm (terminal) station. Second, for both groups of commuters, urinary levels of adrenalin and noradrenalin were higher after the train ride than before it. But the increase in adrenalin secretion during the train ride was significantly greater among the short-commute (Vasterhaninge) than among the long-commute (Nynashamn) subjects. Also, in a follow-up study involving 17 of the same individuals, ratings of perceived crowding and adrenalin levels were found to be higher among both groups of commuters on a day when more passengers rode the train than on another when the train was occupied by fewer people (Lundberg, 1976). Thus, the findings reported by Singer *et al.* and Lundberg suggest that the duration of the journey may be a less crucial determinant of commuter stress than certain other conditions of travel, including the crowdedness and complexity of commuting situations (e.g., opportunities for choosing a seat on entering a train).

The Taylor and Pocock survey and the Singer *et al.* field experiment share certain methodological difficulties. Most importantly, variables that may covary with commuting distance (e.g., degree of residential choice, chronic exposure to midtown vs. suburban living environments) cannot be ruled out as alternative explanations for the observed associations between the duration and/or complexity of the commute and levels of commuter stress. Nonetheless, the findings from these studies taken together (and especially in light of Lundberg's findings regarding crowded vs. uncrowded trains) are important in suggesting certain objective and subjective conditions of travel (e.g., the number of stages in a journey; the perceived crowdedness of transportation environments) that may promote adverse emotional, physiological, and health consequences among commuters.

LIMITATIONS OF EARLIER RESEARCH ON TRANSPORTATION AND STRESS

Despite the specific methodological difficulties inherent in many of the studies discussed above (e.g., small sample sizes, questionable observer reliability, subjects' self-selection of long- vs. short-distance commuting), we believe that on the whole, the existing literature offers converging evidence for a significant link between certain conditions of automotive and public transit and the occurrence of stress reactions among travelers. At the same time, however, the available empirical evidence provides a rather incomplete basis for understanding the specific psychological and social mechanisms that mediate the relationship between transportation and well-being and for conducting programmatic research on these issues.

A major gap in the earlier research is the absence of an integrative, theoretical, framework. This is not to say that previous work has been atheoretical, for numerous studies have been guided by detailed conceptualizations of human stress and fatigue (cf. Crawford, 1961; Forbes, 1972; Simonson *et al.*, 1968). But these conceptualizations generally reflect a medical perspective on stress. Accordingly, most experimental studies of transportation and stress have focused primarily on the physical-environmental demands of travel and correlative physiological and emotional responses, while neglecting the complex interplay of physical, social, and psychological factors that determine travelers' reactions to transportation situations.

The mediating role of individual differences (e.g., drivers' experience, medical history, and sex) has been assessed in several studies (cf.

Bellet et at., 1969; Hunt & May, 1968; Mackie et al. (1974). However, the investigations by Singer et al. (1978) and Lundberg (1976) were the first to examine systematically the contribution of cognitive processes as mediators of commuters' stress reactions. Most studies have neglected to assess the interactive effects of physical, social, and psychological factors on travelers, and no systematic conceptualization of these effects has been provided by earlier work.

Consistent with a medical model of stress, earlier investigations have focused on the short-term reactions of travelers to acute environmental demands (e.g., physiological reactions resulting from excessive temperature, air pollution, or crowding), rather than on the cumulative behavioral and health consequences of chronic exposure to travel conditions. Moreover, the lack of longitudinal studies has precluded an assessment of travelers' active attempts to cope with and, in some instances, alter their exposure to unpleasant transportation situations. Lundberg's (1976) follow-up study of Stockholm commuters offers the basis for analyzing the cumulative health consequences of routine exposure to travel demands. But the focus of that research was on the short-term effects of exposure to crowded transit facilities, rather than on the possible changes in commuters' health status that may have occurred during the period between the initial and follow-up investigations.

Finally, the potential links between research on transportation and stress and long-range transportation planning have not been established. The failure to establish connections between experimental data and policy issues may be attributable, in part, to the nature of earlier theoretical and methodological approaches. Because of the focus of previous work on the short-term effects of exposure to immediate travel demands, several broader research questions that are policy-relevant have been neglected. For example, what are the social and health-related costs associated with alternative modes of commuting? And in what ways can the adverse effects of unavoidable exposure to travel constraints be reduced through transportation planning strategies (e.g., residential zoning policies, traffic management decisions)?

Considering both the contributions and shortcomings of earlier studies, we believe that an important priority for future research is the development of an ecological conceptualization of transportation and well-being. Such an analysis would (1) emphasize the multiple dimensions of transportation situations and their impact on people; (2) examine the cumulative as well as the short-term effects of transportation conditions on health and behavior; and (3) assess the ways in which people cope with prolonged exposure to travel demands. The basic elements of an ecological perspective on transportation and well-being are discussed below.

AN ECOLOGICAL ANALYSIS
OF TRANSPORTATION AND WELL-BEING

At the outset of the preceding section, we noted the diverse phenomena associated with the terms *transportation* and *stress*. Our theoretical analysis of transportation and well-being, developed in this section, builds on the preceding definitions and discussion. First, we define *transportation stressors* as conditions associated with various forms of travel and travel-related environments that evoke unpleasant and/or health-threatening reactions in the individuals exposed to them. These stress reactions include emotional, physiological, and behavioral responses. In this definition, the term *transportation* refers to the conditions associated with any mode of travel (e.g., public vs. private) and to various travel purposes (e.g., work-related vs. recreational). Moreover, transportation stressors are construed broadly to include a diversity of travel conditions, such as traffic congestion, air pollution, interpersonal conflict, and the inconveniences associated with vehicle malfunctions.

Our theoretical analysis is principally concerned with the relationship between transportation stressors and personal well-being. The term *well-being* refers to multiple dimensions of mental and physical health, including personal productivity, sense of purpose, the quality of relationships with others, and levels of physiological and emotional disorder. Although the focus of our analysis is on the individual's response to transportation conditions, our ecological orientation encompasses the impact of such conditions on organizations and whole communities. Thus, we define *transportation strains* as travel-related conditions that impair organizational or community effectiveness vis-à-vis specific performance criteria (e.g., aggregate indices of health and productivity). The effects of transportation strains on organizations and communities can occur through their impact on particular individuals (e.g., commuting-related health problems of key executives within a firm) or on large numbers of people (e.g., the public health consequences of automobile emissions). From an ecological perspective, the transportation stressors experienced by individuals operate as transportation strains to the extent that they exert a detrimental impact on organizational effectiveness or community well-being.

Basic Tenets of an Ecological Approach
to Transportation and Well-Being

The above definitions and distinctions reflect some of the major themes or emphases of an ecological perspective on environment, behavior, and well-being (cf. Altman, 1975; Barker, 1968; Bronfenbrenner, 1979; Kelly, 1968; Wicker, 1979). Our distinction between *transportation stressors and strains*, and between *personal well-being* and *organizational effectiveness*, reflects a core theme of the ecological approach, namely, the *importance of studying the links between environment and well-being at different levels of analysis*. Thus, we are concerned with the ways in which transportation conditions affect both individuals and groups of individuals. Moreover, the conditions of transportation are construed broadly to include the particular events facing individual travelers as well as communitywide circumstances that affect large sectors of the population. Certain transportation conditions are manifested simultaneously—and can be researched—at both personal and aggregate levels of analysis.

Our distinction between *specific stress reactions* and *overall well-being* reflects an additional theme of the ecological approach, namely, an *emphasis on the reciprocal influence among environments and their occupants*. Within the context of transportation, we are concerned not only with the ways in which people are affected by travel demands but also with the processes by which they actively cope with and attempt to modify these conditions. Our conceptualization of well-being, therefore, includes active modes of cognition and behavior (e.g., one's belief in and exercise of personal competence) as well as reactive modes (e.g., physiological disorders, manifestations of helplessness). Our analysis thus reflects a *transactional* rather than a linear conceptualization of the relationship between environmental conditions, on the one hand, and human behavior and well-being, on the other (cf. Lazarus & Launier, 1978; Stokols, 1978).

Our transactional view of well-being is rooted in earlier formulations of open systems theory (cf. Katz & Kahn, 1966; Maruyama, 1963; Miller, 1955; von Bertalanffy, 1950). *Open systems* have been defined as "bounded regions in space-time involving energy interchange among their parts. . . and with their environments" (Miller, 1955, p. 514). A key assumption of systems theory is that the survival and effectiveness of individuals and groups depend on their capacity to cope with environmental constraints and to accomplish their goals and activities in spite of those constraints. Thus, *personal or collective well-being essentially reflects the degree of fit (or congruence) between human goals and activities, and the environmental context in which they are pursued* (cf. French, Rodgers, & Cobb, 1974; Harrison, 1978; Michelson, 1976). Given the diversity of goals and activities that may be relevant within particular situations, the concepts of person–environment and group–environment fit are inherently multidimensional, reflecting the overall (i.e., average) level of congruence that exists between multiple goals and activities, and prevailing environmental conditions (cf. Stokols, 1979).

A fundamental feature of systems that distinguishes them from nonsystems is the interdependence of their components, and of their components and the external environment. *According to the principle of interdependence, the various ways in which people cope with environmental constraints and strive to maintain well-being are highly interrelated.* For example, an individual's reactions to the inconveniences and discomforts of a particular journey depend on several related psychological processes, including his or her personality dispositions, attitudes about the origin and destination of the trip, and resources for choosing alternative travel modes and schedules. Similarly, the relationship between transportation conditions and well-being at the community level is mediated by a host of interdependent processes, such as the spatial distribution of urban facilities and services, regional climate and topography, and the economic resources of the community.

The multiplicity of interrelated factors that affect individual and collective experiences of transportation highlights an additional emphasis of our approach, namely, *the importance of analyzing transportation and well-being from a situational or contextual perspective.* A contextual analysis requires that the relationships between specific environmental conditions and well-being be assessed within the context of particular situations and settings (cf. Bem & Funder, 1978; Magnusson, 1980). The impact of driving demands on automobile commuters, for example, may be substantially modified by their perceptions of the overall quality of their residential and employment situations. At the societal level, the implications of urban transportation conditions (e.g., widespread reliance on the automobile as the predominant commuting mode) for collective well-being must be assessed in relation to relevant aspects of the international situation at a given point in time (e.g., the availability and cost of global petroleum supplies). Furthermore, national circumstances (e.g., automobile manufacturing practices, decisions concerning the distribution of fuel, and taxation policies) and international circumstances (e.g., petroleum production and pricing) may well influence the perceptions of individuals. Reductions in the availability of fuel can lead to personal frustration and can prompt antagonistic appraisals of events in commuting situations.

From an ecological perspective, then, the relationship between transportation and well-being is construed not in terms of the isolated causal connections between independent and dependent variables but in terms of the mutually causal relationships among clusters of situationally relevant factors. An important challenge posed by our contextual approach is to identify and delineate those situations, occurring at personal and/or aggregate levels of analysis, that are of greatest theoretical and policy relevance to the study of transportation and well-being.

To summarize, we have identified five basic themes of our ecological perspective on transportation and well-being: (1) an emphasis on multiple levels of analysis; (2) the reciprocal or transactional nature of person–environment and group–environment relations; (3) the importance of person–environment and group–environment fit in determining individual and collective well-being; (4) the interdependence of adaptive and coping processes; and (5) the utility of a contextual approach in the study of environment, behavior, and well-being. These general themes provide the basis for developing more specific theoretical statements and research hypotheses. Before elaborating on the specifics of our theoretical approach, however, we first consider certain alternative directions for research that are suggested by our discussion of ecological principles. A consideration of these directions provides a backdrop for locating our specific theoretical concerns within a broader set of issues.

CONCEPTUAL FOCUSES OF RESEARCH ON TRANSPORTATION AND WELL-BEING

The ecological themes outlined above suggest several levels at which transportation and well-being can be assessed. These include the individual (i.e., single traveler), small-group (e.g., members of a car pool), organizational (e.g., private corporation), community (e.g., county transit authority), and national and international levels (e.g., the Federal or International Aviation Administration). For purposes of simplifying this discussion, we shall distinguish simply between individual and aggregate levels of analysis. If the manifestations of both *transportation conditions* and *well-being* are considered at the *individual* and *aggregate levels*, then four distinct research focuses are suggested: (1) the interplay between the specific conditions faced by an individual traveler and his or her experiences of, and efforts to cope with, those conditions; (2) the relationship between the transportation conditions faced by individuals and manifestations of organizational or community well-being; (3) the link between communitywide conditions of transportation and individual well-being; and (4) the interrelations among communitywide conditions of transportation and levels of organizational or community well-being. The intersection of these levels of analysis is depicted in Figure 1, which also presents examples of research questions corresponding to the particular focuses in the matrix.

The suggested areas of research are by no means independent. In many instances, the same (or comparable) conditions that face the individual traveler affect multitudes of others as well. Moreover, an assess-

	MANIFESTATIONS OF WELL-BEING (stress and coping processes)	
	INDIVIDUAL LEVEL	AGGREGATE LEVEL
TRANSPORTATION CONDITIONS (environmental and phenomenological circumstances)	Driver performance; subjective affect; physiological arousal; cognitive and behavioral functioning; enduring attitudes; health conditions; behavioral adaptation.	Organizational performance; turnover; absenteeism; industrial accidents; automobile accidents; prevalence of illness in community; social climate; utilization of public transit.
	Examples of Research Questions	
INDIVIDUAL LEVEL Proximate commuting events; perceptions of personal travel, residential, and job domains; mediating influences of personal attributes and resources; coping efforts enacted.	What are the effects of intravehicular conditions on driver performance? To what extent is perceived traffic congestion related to negative mood? How does residential satisfaction affect the response to commuting demands? Can residential relocation to minimize exposure to traffic beneficially affect health and performance?	Are worker absenteeism and turnover related to satisfaction with the commute? Do commuter frustrations affect worker productivity or rates of industrial accidents? What is the relationship between commuting satisfaction and organizational climate? What incentives are needed to encourage carpooling and use of public transit?
AGGREGATE LEVEL Road design; physical parameters of commuting; mode of transportation; ambient conditons in commuting environment; economic constraints; governmental programs regulating travel.	What is the relationship between traffic volume and driver tension? Does long-distance commuting result in elevated blood pressure? Do heat, humidity, and smog have adverse effects on driver performance and health? What are the attitudes of commuters toward restricted lanes on freeways? Does changing one's mode of commuting to reduce driving demands have a positive health consequence?	Is the widespread reliance on the automobile a primary cause of urban sprawl? Do highway safety improvements reduce accident rates in a cost-effective manner? Is hypertension more prevalent among automobile drivers than among those who ride buses or trains? What are the public health consequences of automobile emissions? What are the transportation requirements of the elderly, the handicapped, and the poor? Is the quality of life in a metropolitan area related to its transit resources?

Figure 1. Levels of analysis in the study of transportation and well-being and research questions suggested by the intersection of these levels.

ment of personal indices of well-being is often crucial to an understanding of communitywide, aggregate health statistics. Nonetheless, the proposed classification of research focuses suggests alternative analytical perspectives and research issues that might be emphasized in the study of transportation and well-being.

While our ecological orientation subsumes a diversity of perspectives, the scope of our theoretical analysis and research program is necessarily limited (by time, resources, and expertise) to a subset of these issues. The primary focus of our analysis is on the first and third sets of issues mentioned above, namely, the relationship between conditions faced by individuals and/or large numbers of travelers and personal well-being. We also are concerned, though less directly, with the impact of such conditions on organizational effectiveness. The fourth set of issues, concerning the interrelations between communitywide transportation conditions and community well-being, is least amenable to the conceptual framework and methodological strategies described below and thus is beyond the scope of the present analysis.

TRAVEL IMPEDANCE AND COMMUTER STRESS

Our research focuses on the behavioral and health consequences of individuals' prolonged exposure to transportation stressors. Although the studies reviewed earlier provide ample evidence that exposure to various travel demands is often associated with short-term stress reactions, they offer no direct evidence for the psychological, behavioral, and physiological residues of long-term exposure to such demands.

One category of stressors to which travelers, especially commuters, are routinely exposed is *impedance.* Sources of impedance include any circumstances (e.g., traffic congestion, traffic signals, characteristics of the vehicle) that retard or otherwise interfere with one's movement between two or more points. The degree of impedance encountered by travelers can be indexed in terms of at least two situational parameters: (1) the distance traveled between origin and destination and (2) the amount of time spent in transit between these points. Presumably, the greatest degree of impedance would result from traveling large distances slowly, whereas the least amount of impedance would arise from traveling small distances in a short amount of time.

Several areas of research, especially those relating to human aggression (cf. Berkowitz, 1965; Donnerstein & Wilson, 1976; Novaco, 1979; Rule & Nesdale, 1976) and crowding (cf. Altman, 1975; Baum & Epstein, 1978), indicate that environmental constraints can induce both physiological stress and performance deficits. Psychological analyses of stress (cf. Appley & Trumbull, 1967; Lazarus, 1966; McGrath, 1970), however, highlight the interdependence of cognitive, motivational, and physiological determinants of people's reactions to environmental demands and suggest that these reactions vary considerably across individuals.

Lazarus (1966), for example, has developed a detailed conceptualization of psychological stress emphasizing the individual's *perceived* inability to cope with *perceived* environmental demands. According to this view, a particular environmental condition (e.g., traffic congestion) is likely to prompt diverse reactions among different persons depending on their respective perceptions of the threat posed by the condition (primary appraisal) and their resources for coping with it (secondary appraisal). A variety of circumstances may affect individuals' appraisal of environmental demands and their reactions to them, including motivational factors (e.g., the desire to arrive at a meeting on time and to avoid the embarrassment of being late), cognitive factors (e.g., the unexpectedness of detours and delays along a chosen route), personality dispositions (e.g., chronic time urgency), and medical history (e.g., chronic heart disease).

The relative contribution of various environmental and personal factors to the appraisal and impact of transportation demands may vary greatly depending on the particular situation in which the traveler is involved (e.g., commuting to work vs. embarking on a vacation). In keeping with the contextual approach mentioned earlier, we assume that the potential mediators of impedance effects on well-being can be grouped in a theoretically useful manner according to the situational contexts in which they occur. An advantage of this approach is that it accounts for certain aspects of situations (e.g., their perceived quality and importance to the individual) that may moderate the relationship between situation-specific conditions and overall well-being.

Our discussion of transportation situations builds on earlier analyses of the environmental context of behavior (cf. Barker, 1968; Bronfenbrenner, 1979; Chein, 1954; Lewin, 1936; Moos, 1976; Magnusson, 1980). We first consider basic categories of behaviorally relevant situations and then delineate certain features of situations that may mediate the relationship between transportation constraints and well-being.

Categories of Situations

Our analysis incorporates two major criteria for categorizing environments: (1) the *phenomenological perspective* from which the environment is approached and (2) the *scale* or level of complexity at which it is considered. The first criterion refers to a continuum ranging from a purely physical (or objectivist) perspective to a purely perceptual (or subjectivist) one. The second criterion refers to an hierarchical ordering of environmental units reflecting their relative organizational complexity (i.e., stimuli, events, momentary situations, behavior settings, and life domains). The criteria of perspective and scale are assumed to be independent. At any level of complexity, then, the environment can be analyzed from a physical and/or perceptual perspective.

The categorization of situations in terms of phenomenological perspective is based on a distinction between the physical and the perceived environment (cf. Chein, 1954; Lewin, 1936; Magnusson, 1980; Wohlwill, 1973). Drawing upon Magnusson's distinction between actual and perceived situations, we define the *physical environment* as that portion of the geographical, architectural, biological, and sociocultural milieu that is available for sensory perception at a given point in time. The *perceived environment* is defined as the individual's perceptions and interpretations of the physical (or sociophysical) milieu. The term *perceived* refers in this discussion to both personally and collectively held impressions of an environment. Thus, the perceived environment encompasses not only the idiosyncratic impressions of a single observer but also the shared, symbolic meanings that are ascribed to the environment by a particular group (cf. Stokols, 1980; Stokols & Shumaker, 1980).

The present analysis of transportation environments adopts a "dual" perspective, emphasizing both the physical and the perceived features of situations. We are concerned, for example, not only with the physical parameters of travel impedance (e.g., the frequency and duration of one's exposure to traffic congestion) but also with the subjective severity of these conditions as perceived by the individual traveler.

The environmental contexts of human behavior can be viewed not only from different phenomenological perspectives but also at varying levels of complexity. The complexity or scale of environmental units is reflected in the diversity and intricacy of their internal elements. The least complex environmental units are stimuli and events. *Stimuli* are environmental elements (e.g., traffic signals, hornhonking) that reinforce operant behavior or function as discriminative cues for future behavior (cf. Gibson, 1960; Skinner, 1953). *Events* are chains of stimuli that appear to an observer to be causally linked (e.g., the negative consequences of being delayed by a traffic jam).

At the next highest level of complexity are *situations*, that is, clusters of stimuli and events that are functionally organized around specific goals and activities (cf. Magnusson, 1980). Magnusson distinguished between the momentary situation and the situation type. The *momentary situation* encompasses those stimuli and events that occur at a specific time (e.g., driving home from work on Pacific Coast Highway through Laguna Beach at 4:05 on January 28, 1980), within a particular *type of situation* (e.g., driving home from work along Pacific Coast Highway).

Behavior settings, as conceptualized by Barker (1968; Barker & Associates, 1978; Wicker, 1979), are regions of the physical environment that, over time, have become associated with recurring patterns of individual and collective behavior. Examples of travel-related settings are airports, bus stations, and commuter trains. In the present analysis, behavior settings are assumed to be of greater complexity than situations because of the relatively greater stability and permanence associated with the physical milieu and the social organization of the former. Moreover, several different types of situations (emphasizing interrelated, yet distinct activities) are typically associated with a particular behavior setting.

Clusters of behavior settings that are functionally linked through the shared goals of their members comprise the next most complex unit of the environment, that is, *life domains.* These contextual units pertain to different spheres of an individual's life, such as the family–residential, employment, peer–recreational, and transportation domains. Each of these domains subsumes multiple behavior settings that are functionally organized around common goals, activities, and social relationships.

Finally, the various life domains that are perceived by the individual as being relevant to personal (albeit shared) goals and activities comprise the *overall life situation* (cf. Magnusson, 1980). The life situation of a commuter, for example, might include the home, the workplace, and the commuting and recreational domains.

Psychological Properties of Environmental Domains

A basic tenet of our ecological approach is that the relationship between transportation and well-being can best be understood within the context of specific settings and environmental domains. Essentially, we assume that certain basic properties of environmental units play a crucial role in mediating the impact of context-specific stimuli and events on personal well-being. Having delineated a categorization of environmental units, it is important now to delineate concepts and measures for describing those units in ways that reflect their contribution to the enhancement or impairment of well-being.

Our effort to provide theoretically meaningful terms for describing the links between environmental contexts and well-being focuses on a crucial facet of the perceptual environment, namely, the perceived level of person–environment fit (or more simply, environmental congruence). Earlier research suggests that the overall level of congruence existing within a particular situation, setting, or domain is closely related to the well-being of participants within that context (cf. French *et al.*, 1974; Harrison, 1978; Michelson, 1976; Stokols, 1979).

As noted above, environmental congruence reflects the degree to which an individual's major goals and activities are facilitated or constrained by environmental conditions. In the present analysis, environmental congruence is construed as an intervening psychological construct that mediates the relationship between events occurring within a particular physical environment and various aspects of personal well-being, for example, a person's satisfaction with his or her commuting situation, performance level at work, and physiological stress reactions on arrival at home in the evening.

The level of environmental congruence that exists within a situation is presumed to be highly correlated with the individual's overall assessment of (and satisfaction with) the quality of that situation. Perceived situational quality depends on at least two factors: (1) *environmental controllability*, or the degree to which the individual's level of need facilitation in the situation corresponds with expected or preferred levels of outcomes; and (2) *motivational salience*, or the subjective importance of those goals and activities that are relevant within the situation. To the extent that environmental controllability is low and motivational salience is high, the likelihood of adverse emotional, behavioral, and health consequences is expected to increase (cf. Novaco, 1979; Stokols, 1979; Thibaut & Kelley, 1959).

The dimensions of environmental controllability, salience, and congruence can be assessed with respect to multiple goals and activities that are encompassed by either individual or multiple situations, settings, and domains. In the case of environmental contexts that are comprised of multiple units (e.g., the overall life situation), the overall level of congruence is indexed in terms of a composite score reflecting the average of those scores associated with the particular units (e.g., the family, employment, and transportation domains).

A key assumption in our research is that commuters' reactions to travel demands are mediated by the level of congruence (and hence the perceived quality and satisfaction) associated with those environmental contexts comprising their typical activity pattern. Chapin (1974) has defined *human activity patterns* as "the ways in which residents in metropolitan communities go about their daily affairs" (p. 23). These patterns collectively comprise the *urban activity system,* that is, "the pat-terned ways in which individuals, households, institutions, and firms pursue their day-in and day-out affairs in a metropolitan community and interact with one another in time and space" (p.23). In relation to the environmental categories introduced earlier, it should be noted that activity patterns are less encompassing than the individual's overall life situation. That is, activity patterns subsume those places and settings in which people are regularly involved on a day-to-day basis. The life situation, on the other hand, could include life domains (e.g., relation-ships with family or friends in a distant community) that are less closely associated with the daily activities of the individual. As a basis for sim-plifying our analysis of commuting and well-being, we shall focus on the major components of the commuter's activity pattern (i.e., the commut-ing, residential, and employment domains) rather than examining all facets of the commuter's life situation. Moreover, while Chapin's con-cept of the urban activity system offers a basis for describing community-level conditions and their implications for aggregate well-being, these issues are beyond the scope of our more limited analysis of the environmental contexts of individual behavior and well-being.

GENERAL PROPOSITIONS DERIVED FROM OUR THEORETICAL ANALYSIS

The preceding conceptualization of travel impedance and of the en-vironmental contexts in which it occurs suggests at least three general propositions for empirical investigation. These propositions reflect sev-eral of the ecological principles mentioned earlier.

First, we propose that the effects of routine exposure to travel im-pedance on the well-being of commuters is mediated by several interde-pendent factors, including the duration of the commute, the perceived severity of traffic congestion, and personal dispositions toward impa-tience and time urgency. This hypothesis reflects the ecological em-phasis on the interdependence of adaptive processes.

Second, we propose that prolonged exposure to travel impedance not only evokes stress reactions but also prompts active efforts among travelers to improve their commuting situations (e.g., by moving closer to work, by changing their travel schedule or route). This hypothesis reflects the ecological emphasis on the transactional nature of person-environment relations.

Third, we propose that the relationship between travel impedance and personal well-being is mediated by the perceived quality of those domains comprising the commuter's typical activity pattern. This pre-diction reflects the ecological theme of assessing personal well-being in terms of the degree of fit between an individual's goals and activities and the environmental conditions that exist within specific contexts. An important implication of this hypothesis is that the perceived costs and constraints associated with the commuting situation may be compensated for by certain desirable features of one's residential and employment situations (cf. Campbell, 1979). This process of compensatory coping may be manifested both in the commuter's subjective appraisal of the travel situation and in enhanced levels of emotional and physical well-being.

So that we might clarify the series of conceptualizations that we have thus far presented, a summary of the key ideas is contained in Figure 2. Here we illustrate the sequential linkage of our research propositions to the array of conceptual foci in transportation research, which in turn follows from the set of ecological tenets guiding our analysis.

To address the above propositions within the same investigation, we employed a longitudinal field experiment focusing, initially, on environmental and personal determinants of commuters' stress reactions and subsequently, on commuters' active efforts to cope with travel constraints. We should note that the experiment to be described was initially designed to test specific predictions derived from a psychological model of commuting stress, rather than the more general propositions suggested by the ecological framework presented above. Our development of a broader ecological framework, in fact, was prompted by certain empirical findings from the first phase of our experiment. Therefore, several of the measures incorporated in our study do not provide as specific an assessment of certain aspects of our ecological framework as, in retrospect, we would have preferred. Our assessment of person–environment fit, for example, relies on global measures of residential, commuting, and employment satisfaction, rather than on specific measures of the perceived controllability and salience of those domains. For the most part, however, we believe that the experimental design and categories of measures employed in our study are sufficiently close to the concepts developed earlier to provide the basis for a preliminary assessment of our ecological analysis.

A FIELD-EXPERIMENTAL INVESTIGATION OF TRAVEL IMPEDANCE AND COMMUTER WELL-BEING

This section provides a general overview of our research methodology and findings. A more detailed description of the research design and methodology can be found in our earlier articles (Novaco, Stokols,

BASIC THEMES OF AN ECOLOGICAL APPROACH	CONCEPTUAL FOCUSES IN RESEARCH IN TRANSPORTATION	LONGITUDINAL RESEARCH ON IMPEDANCE STRESS AND ADAPTATION
1. Study of environment–behavior relationships at different levels of analysis.	A. Transportation conditions faced by individuals and their experience of and efforts to cope with those conditions.	Focuses emphasized: A and C
2. Emphasis on reciprocal influences among environments and their occupants.	B. Transportation conditions faced by individuals and the manifestations of organizational and community well-being.	Propositions examined: 1. Effects of travel impedance are determined by interdependent factors in the commuting context, such as travel parameters, perceptions of congestion, personal dispositions, and vehicular conditions.
3. Attention to congruence between goals and the environmental arena of their pursuit.	C. Communitywide conditions of transportation and individual well-being.	2. Prolonged exposure to travel impedance evokes stress reactions and prompts coping efforts intended to improve the commuting situation.
4. Recognition of interdependence among components of the coping process.	D. Communitywide conditions of transportation and organizational and community well-being.	3. The relationship between travel impedance and personal well-being is mediated by the perceived quality of life domains in the commuter's activity pattern.
5. Recognition of the importance of a contextual perspective for understanding behavior and well-being.		

Figure 2. Basic tenets, general research focuses, and specific study propositions.

Campbell, & Stokols, 1979; Stokols, Novaco, Stokols, & Campbell, 1978).

Method

Subjects

The present study utilized a longitudinal, field-experimental design in which urban commuters, traveling varying distances between home and work, were tested during the summer of 1976 (Phase 1) and approximately 18 months later, during the winter of 1978 (Phase 2). The participants were 100 paid volunteers recruited from two large industrial firms in Irvine, California. The employees of these companies were contacted by letter and asked to indicate their willingness to participate in a study of "Commuting Patterns, Health, and Performance." From among those employees who responded affirmatively to our request for volunteers, 100 individuals were selected on the basis of the following criteria: (1) the average distance and duration of their daily commute to and from work; (2) their time of arrival at work; and (3) the number of months during which they had traveled their current commuting route.

The Phase 1 sample consisted of 61 males and 39 females, all of whom were on the day shift and had traveled the same route for more than eight months. The Phase 2 sample consisted of those individuals who had participated during Phase 1 and were still employed by the same companies 18 months later. Of the original 100 participants, 18 individuals had quit their jobs between the summer of 1976 and the winter of 1978. An attempt was made to contact these individuals, but most had left the Irvine area and could not be reached. The remaining 82 individuals, including 49 males and 33 females, agreed to participate in the second phase of the study when recontacted by phone.

Selection of Subjects for Experimental Groups

On the basis of information obtained from an initial Phase 1 screening questionnaire, the boundary criteria for three major impedance groups were derived. *Low-impedance* subjects were those falling within the bottom 25% of the distributions of commuting distance and time. This group was comprised of 27 persons who traveled less than 7.5 miles between home and workplace and spent less than 12.5 minutes on the road in either direction. *Medium-impedance* subjects fell into the middle 30% on the time and distance distributions and consisted of 22 persons traveling between 10 and 14 miles and spending approximately 17–20 minutes on the road each way. *High-impedance* subjects fell into the top 25% of the distance and time distributions and consisted of 36 persons traveling between 18 and 50 miles and spending from 30 to 75 minutes in the commute.

The above impedance groups included only those persons having correspondent positions along the distance and time distributions (i.e., low/low, medium/medium, high/high). A subset of the experimental sample displayed noncorrespondent rankings with regard to the time and distance distributions. These persons were excluded from statistical analyses involving an assessment of the three-level impedance factor, but they were included in all other analyses.

By Phase 2, the number of participants within the low-, medium-, and high-impedance conditions were 18, 19, and 26, respectively. These reduced cell frequencies are attributable to the attrition of 18 participants by Phase 2 and to the fact that 11 of the remaining 82 subjects had altered their impedance ranking through residential relocation between phases 1 and 2. All statistical analyses of the effects of impedance on repeated measures (i.e., those administered at both Phases 1 and 2) are based on the constant-impedance sample ($n = 63$ across low-, medium-, and high-impedance cells). Several of the other analyses performed at Phase 2, however, are based on the data of all 82 individuals who participated during both phases of the study.

Just prior to Phase 1, the subjects were informed of their selection by mail and were requested to complete a series of background and personality questionnaires. Included in this set of measures was the Jenkins Activity Survey for Health Prediction (JAS), a measure of the coronary-prone behavior pattern (Jenkins, Zyzanski, & Rosenman, 1971; Zyzanski & Jenkins, 1970). Within each of the three main impedance groups, the subjects were classified as either Type A or Type B on the basis of their JAS score (see Stokols *et al.*, 1978, for a description of the scoring procedure used to determine A–B classification).

In addition to the JAS, all participants completed Rotter's (1966) Internal–External Locus of Control Scale (I-E) and Novaco's (1975) Anger Inventory (AI). The incorporation of the JAS, I-E, and AI scales in the present study was based on the assumption that coronary-prone behavior, chronic internality of control, and anger might mediate commuters' reactions to travel impedance. In this chapter, we summarize certain findings relating to the JAS and the I-E. A detailed discussion of the interactive effects of I-E and impedance, and Type A behavior and impedance, can be found in Novaco *et al.* (1979) and in Stokols *et al.* (1978), respectively.

Testing Procedure

In Phase 1, subjects were contacted by phone to schedule their participation times. Each subject participated in the study for one week. During this time, they completed five daily commuting logs pertaining to the actual distances and times traveled each day and to subjective impressions of the journey (e.g., perceived congestion, air quality, and temperature inside the vehicle). These logs were completed on arrival at work and at home for the morning and afternoon commutes.

Upon arrival at work on Monday, Wednesday, and Friday, the employees drove to a testing station located in the parking lot of their company. There, each person's systolic and diastolic blood pressure were recorded using a Physiometrics SR-2 automatic blood pressure recorder. Heart rate was also measured by means of a cardiotachometer attached to the blood pressure recorder.

On Tuesday and Thursday of the testing week, the participants reported to a company conference room approximately 1½ hours after arriving at work. Here, measures of blood pressure, heart rate, and mood were again obtained. Subsequently, one or two brief tasks were administered to assess the cumulative effects of impedance on psychomotor performance and tolerance for frustration.

During the Tuesday session, the subjects performed the "perceptual reasoning" test developed by Feather (1961). The test consists of four puzzles, two of which are insoluble (Puzzles 1 and 3) and two of which are soluble (Puzzles 2 and 4). The subjects were asked to trace the lines of a diagram without lifting the pen or retracing a line. This task has been employed by Glass and Singer (1972) as a measure of frustration tolerance and has been found to be sensitive to the aftereffects of environmental stressors.

During the Thursday session, the subjects performed the digit symbol task from the Wechsler Adult Intelligence Scale (Wechsler, 1958). The task is a measure of psychomotor speed and concentration in which persons are required to copy the symbols associated with a line of digits into rows of boxes over a 90-second period. Immediately after performing this task, the subjects were administered a memory test in which they were given 30 seconds to recall the symbols associated with the nine digits of the Wechsler task.

On completion of the testing week, all subjects were provided with a summary of their daily blood pressure and heart rate readings, as well as a detailed explanation of the research procedures. All individuals were paid $10 for their participation during Phase 1.

Eighteen months after the initial testing session, all subjects were sent a letter requesting their participation in the second phase of the study. Those individuals still employed by the same companies agreed to participate and were sent a follow-up questionnaire concerning personal health status and satisfaction with employment, residential quality, and the commute between home and work. Enclosed with the questionnaire was an invitation to attend a presentation by the authors of the findings from the first phase of the study. This presentation was held in a conference room at each of the participating firms. The Jenkins Activity Survey (JAS) was readministered to all participants just prior to the authors' presentation. The participants were paid $5 for completing the Phase 2 questionnaires.

Major Categories of Dependent Measures

Several of the measures utilized in this study were administered at both Phases 1 and 2. The remainder were administered at Phase 1 or at Phase 2 only.

The repeated measures consisted of three basic categories: (1) general mood on arrival at home from work; (2) self-reported satisfaction with various life domains, including residential, employment, and community situations; and (3) attitudes regarding environmental problems and transportation management strategies. Items relating to each of these categories were contained in the background and follow-up questionnaires. In addition, a number of miscellaneous questions concerning personal and demographic issues (e.g., length of time at current residence and job; socioeconomic status; type of car owned; history of traffic accidents; alcohol consumption; exercise regimen) were administered at both phases of the study.

The mood index consisted of six bipolar scales (e.g., tense-relaxed, tired-energetic) pertaining to the individual's typical emotional state on arrival at home from work. A series of semantic differential scales also were used to assess commuters' satisfaction with their commute, residence, and job. Ratings of the commuting situation, for example, included two 7-point scales regarding the extent to which the subjects were inconvenienced by traffic congestion and satisfied with their commute. Residential satisfaction was indexed by three 7-point scales pertaining to residential crowding, desire to relocate, and overall satisfaction with current residence. In addition, the subjects were questioned about the degree of choice they had exercised in deciding where to live and the extent to which they wanted to move from their current residence because of traffic-related problems. Job satisfaction was measured by five Likert items concerning different dimensions of employment (e.g., feelings of accomplishment derived from the job; adequacy of current salary) and with two additional sets of semantic differential scales pertaining to the quality of social and physical conditions at work. Finally, the subjects' attitudes about the severity of urban environmental problems (i.e., traffic congestion, air pollution) and their agreement with potential transportation management strategies (e.g., development of company-sponsored "van pool" programs; use of traffic-metering devices on major thoroughfares) were assessed with eight 7-point scales.

Physiology and task performance were measured during Phase 1 only. Systolic and diastolic blood pressure and heart rate were measured on each day of the testing period as described earlier. The principal measures of task performance were (1) the number of attempts made by each subject on Feather's (1961) insoluble puzzles; (2) the number of boxes correctly completed on the digit symbol task; and (3) the number of symbols recalled in the digit-symbol memory task.

Additional measures administered at Phase 1 only included a nine-item mood scale completed by each commuter on arrival at work in the morning, and the five daily travel logs completed on arrival at work and at home for the morning and afternoon commutes. These logs assessed commuters' impressions of traffic conditions and provided a record of daily commuting distances and times.

Several sets of questionnaire items were administered only at Phase 2. These included an index of the frequency and severity of health problems occurring between Phases 1 and 2 (e.g., number of occasions on which various illnesses occurred; number of days hospitalized) and a measure of the frequency ("not at all"–"often") with which medication was taken in relation to chronic health problems. Also administered at Phase 2 were self-reports of activities undertaken to alter and to cope more effectively with commuting and residential situations (e.g., purchase of a new car, alteration of commuting schedule or travel mode, residential relocation, increase in the weekly rate of physical exercise between Phases 1 and 2). A related set of items assessed the availability of special features (e.g., tape deck, air conditioning) in the vehicle that served to enhance the quality of the journey between home and work and the individual's reasons for purchasing his or her current commuting vehicle. Finally, several semantic-differential scales were incorporated into the Phase 2 questionnaire to provide validity checks on our conceptualization and measurement of impedance. For instance, the subjects were asked to estimate the frequency ("very rarely"–"very often") at which they found it necessary to apply their brakes while driving between home and work and to reduce their travel speed because of constraints such as traffic signals, traffic jams, and accidents. Also, the subjects were asked to indicate the number of points in their commute at which they changed from freeways to surface streets and to estimate the percentage of their trip between home and work spent on freeways or on other major, limited-access highways.

Statistical Analyses of Phase 1 and Phase 2 Data

Those measures administered during both phases of the study were analyzed in terms of a repeated-measures analysis of variance (ANOVA) design, incorporating the factors of impedance (low, medium, and high), time (Phase 1 and Phase 2), and dimensions that were expected to mediate the effects of impedance on commuters (e.g., coronary-prone behavior, internal-external control). All repeated-measures analyses were based on the constant-impedance sample ($n=63$). In those analyses incorporating an additional factor (e.g., median split on the JAS scores), the data from subjects whose position on that factor shifted between Phases 1 and 2 (e.g., from Type A at Phase 1 to Type B at Phase 2) were excluded.

The measures administered only at Phase 1 or at Phase 2 were analyzed separately in terms of one-way (impedance) or two-way (impedance × personality factor) ANOVAs. Chi-square analyses were performed on dichotomous variables as described below.

RESULTS

The results summarized here represent only a small portion of the findings from our investigation. Our strategy in this chapter is to present a sampling of the findings that are pertinent to the three general propositions mentioned earlier. For a more detailed discussion of the Phase 1 analyses and findings, see Stokols *et al.* (1978) and Novaco *et al.* (1979)

Proposition 1: The effects of routine exposure to travel impedance on commuters' well-being is mediated through an interplay of personal and environmental factors. This hypothesis is based on at least two specific assumptions: (1) that sources of impedance operate as environmental demands that evoke adverse reactions in travelers and (2) that the impact of impedance on specific individuals is determined by both personal and situational circumstances. To test the adequacy of these assumptions, it is first necessary to assess the construct validity of the impedance factor, defined in this study by the dimensions of commuting distance and duration; and, second, to demonstrate that travel impedance is reliably associated with stress reactions.

Evidence for the construct validity of the impedance factor is presented in Table 1. The pattern of means reflected in participants' ratings of their commute indicate that at both Phases 1 and 2, higher levels of impedance were associated with greater perception of traffic congestion as an inconvenience [$F(2,54) = 5.22$, $p<.009$] and lower satisfaction with the commute [$F(2,55) = 9.86$, $p<.001$]. Also, across all impedance groups, the perception of congestion increased and commuting satisfaction decreased between Phases 1 and 2 [$F(1,54) = 7.32$, $p<.009$; and $F(1,55) = 8.52$, $p<.005$, respectively]. And on Phase 2 ratings of the commute, individuals in the high-impedance groups reported that they encountered conditions of heavy traffic and traffic jams more often than did low-impedance commuters [$F(2,57) = 14.98$, $p<.008$; $F(2,51) = 20.07$, $p<.006$, respectively]. That the above findings are attributable to travel demands rather than to subject self-selection biases across experimental groups is suggested by the lack of impedance main effects on the demographic dimensions of age, socioeconomic status (SES), education, and sex.

The focus of our analysis is on the interactive effects of travel impedance and personal factors on well-being. Before considering these effects, however, it is important to note that physical parameters of commuting appear to be independently related to heightened physiological arousal and health problems. Commuting distance, for example, was found to be significantly correlated with systolic and diastolic blood pressure at Phase 1 [$r(62) = .26$, $p<.01$, $r(62) = .25$, $p<.02$]. Also, the number of days hospitalized for various illnesses between Phases 1 and 2 was significantly related to the total number of interchanges between surface streets and expressways during the commute to work [$r(67) =$

TABLE 1
MEAN RATINGS OF THE COMMUTE DURING PHASES 1 AND 2[a]

| Impedence condition | n | Satisfaction with commute | | | | Traffic congestion as an inconvenience | | | |
| | | Phase 1 | | Phase 2 | | Phase 1 | | Phase 2 | |
		M	SD	M	SD	M	SD	M	SD
Low	18	5.94	1.20	5.64	1.22	3.18	1.94	4.35	2.09
Medium	19	5.56	1.26	4.38	1.63	4.13	2.00	4.60	2.16
High	26	4.48	1.26	4.12	1.62	4.84	1.57	5.64	1.58

[a] Both items are 7-point semantic differential scales. Larger means indicate higher scores on the attribute listed.

.55, $p<.001$]. This relationship between stages of the journey and health status parallels the findings of Taylor and Pocock (1972), discussed earlier.

The dimension of coronary-prone behavior was one of the factors incorporated in this study to assess the interactive effects of impedance and personal characteristics on well-being. Previous research indicates that Type A's typically strive harder than Type B's to avoid loss of control over their environment, but that A's are more adversely affected by highly uncontrollable situations than are B's (cf. Krantz, Glass, & Snyder, 1974). Moreover, time-urgent A's become more impatient and irritated when they are delayed by co-workers on joint decision-making tasks (Glass, 1977). Thus, we expected that among high- and medium-impedance subjects, greater stress (i.e., negative mood, performance deficits, and elevated physiological arousal) would be manifested by A's than by B's.

As indicated in Table 2, significant AB × impedance interaction effects were obtained on Phase 1 measures of systolic blood pressure [$F(2,55) = 3.34$, $p<.04$] and performance on a tolerance-for-frustration task [$F(2,56) = 5.02$, $p<.01$].[6] But contrary to our initial expectations, the pattern of means on these variables suggests that among high-impedance commuters, Type B's experienced greater stress than Type A's; and among medium-impedance commuters, A's experienced greater stress than B's.

The relatively greater job involvement and residential choice of A's vis-à-vis B's have been suggested as possible contributors to the elevated stress levels of Type B–high-impedance commuters (cf. Stokols et al., 1978). Moreover, the possible lack of fit between the impatient style of Type A's and their greater exposure to low-speed, surface street (vs. higher-speed expressway) travel under medium- versus high-impedance conditions may have contributed to the heightened stress reactions among medium-impedance A's. Our consideration of these issues in light of the findings from Phase 1 prompted us to develop a broader conceptual framework in which the interdependencies among individuals' residential, employment, and commuting situations were explicitly considered. The role of residential choice in mediating workers' reactions to their commute is discussed more fully in the ensuing discussion of our third proposition.

Proposition 2: Prolonged exposure to the demands of travel impedance prompts active efforts among commuters to improve their commuting situations. This hypothesis is based on our transactional view of person–environ-

---

[6] High-impedance subjects reported significantly greater feelings of annoyance on arrival at work than did low-impedance subjects, but the predicted AB × impedance interaction effects on indices of mood and on digit-symbol task performance were not significant.

TABLE 2
PHASE 1 BLOOD PRESSURE AND TASK PERFORMANCE LEVELS[a]

Condition	n	Systolic blood pressure		Diastolic blood pressure		Attempts on puzzles 1 & 3 (insoluble)	
		M	SD	M	SD	M	SD
Low impedance							
Type A	11	122.64	12.22	74.75	3.50	14.45	7.29
		(11.06)	(.54)	(8.36)	(.20)	(2.51)	(.65)
Type B	10	124.20	14.82	76.50	9.92	11.50	3.92
		(11.13)	(.67)	(8.73)	(.57)	(2.39)	(.33)
Medium impedance							
Type A	6	135.83	7.47	80.50	6.72	15.33	9.73
		(11.65)	(.32)	(8.97)	(.37)	(2.47)	(.88)
Type B	12	126.50	16.47	75.58	8.71	16.17	6.51
		(11.23)	(.73)	(8.68)	(.50)	(2.71)	(.38)
High impedance							
Type A	15	125.93	8.00	76.47	7.10	18.27	6.17
		(11.22)	(.36)	(8.74)	(.41)	(2.85)	(.34)
Type B	10	138.90	11.30	82.00	8.30	10.00	6.82
		(11.78)	(.48)	(9.05)	(.46)	(2.06)	(.77)

[a] Numbers in parentheses are transformed means and standard deviations. Transformations of puzzle data are logarithmic. Transformations of blood pressure are based on the square root of the original means.

ment relationships. The evidence for or against a transactional view of commuting and well-being can be assessed with relation to at least three specific questions: (1) What percentages of workers take active steps to alter or otherwise cope with their commuting situations? (2) What personal and situational attributes are predictive of coping efforts? (3) Are efforts to cope with travel constraints effective; that is, do such efforts enhance personal well-being?

To assess the prevalence of coping efforts among commuters, we asked participants at Phase 2 whether or not they had altered their travel schedule to avoid traffic congestion; altered their mode of commuting; purchased a new car; or changed their residence between Phases 1 and 2. The percentages of individuals who had engaged in these activities were 35%, 25%, 37%, and 32%, respectively ($n=82$). These figures suggest that active efforts to cope with transportation constraints are not uncommon among commuters.[7]

---

[7] An important issue that is not addressed by our research concerns the timing of coping efforts. Because we are interested in the health and behavioral effects of prolonged exposure to commuting constraints, we chose to study commuters who had been traveling the

As for the environmental and personal antecedents of coping, chi-square analyses revealed that the percentages of individuals engaging in coping activities were not significantly different across impedance groups. The findings presented in Table 3, however, suggest that individuals scoring high on a summary index of coping behavior between Phases 1 and 2 were more likely to have been dissatisfied with their commuting situation [$t(67) = 2.67$, $p<.009$] and bothered by traffic congestion at Phase 1 [perceived congestion during evening commute, $t(67) = 2.90$, $p<.005$; congestion as an inconvenience, $t(67) = 2.89$, $p<.001$]. At the same time, high scorers on the coping index were less time-urgent [$t(67) = 3.43$, $p<.001$] and exhibited lower diastolic blood pressure [$t(67) = 2.12$, $p<.038$] than low scorers. Moreover, females displayed a greater tendency to cope with commuting demands than did males under high-impedance conditions (Fishers' Exact Test = .08), and Type B individuals were more likely to cope than were Type As [$\chi^2(1) = 5.21$, $p<.02$], across all impedance conditions.

The summary index of coping behavior was derived by assigning each individual a score of 0 or 1 on three of the dimensions mentioned above, that is, alteration of commuting schedule (e.g., 0 = same schedule, 1 = altered schedule), change of travel mode,[8] and purchase of a new commuting vehicle. The dimension of residential relocation was omitted from the index since analyses included only constant-impedance subjects. In place of the relocation dimension, a fourth aspect of coping was added to the summary index, namely, whether or not the individual had increased or decreased his/her average number of exercise hours per week between Phases 1 and 2 (where 0 = decreased hours or stayed the same, and 1 = increased hours of exercise). Each person's scores on the four coping dimensions were summed and a median split was performed on the subjects' total coping scores to form the low-coping and high-coping groups.

Summary scores similarly were computed to assess overall levels of residential, commuting, and job satisfaction at Phases 1 and 2 (these

---

same route for at least eight months prior to our first testing session. This selection strategy precluded a comparison of coping efforts and health outcomes among long-term commuters versus those who had been on the route for relatively shorter (or longer) amounts of time. An important direction for future research is to examine the processes of long-term as opposed to short-term adaptation and coping with commuting constraints.

[8]The index of travel mode alteration was the total number of changes (e.g., joining a company van pool, switching from private automobile to public or corporate commuting vehicle) made by the individual. For purposes of computing the summary index of multiple coping activities, each individual's score (i.e., 0 or 1) on the mode change item was based on a median split of the mode-change total scores.

TABLE 3
DIFFERENCES BETWEEN LOW AND HIGH SCORERS ON A SUMMARY INDEX
OF COPING BEHAVIOR[a]

| Variable | Individuals scoring low on coping index ($n = 37$) | | Individuals scoring high on coping index ($n = 32$) | | | |
	M	SD	M	SD	t value	alpha
Commuting satisfaction, Phase 1	5.62	1.16	4.77	1.45	2.67	<.009
Perceived congestion during evening commute, Phase 1	4.31	1.74	5.46	1.42	−2.90	<.005
Perception of traffic congestion as an inconvenience, Phase 1	3.47	1.61	4.70	1.84	−2.89	<.005
Chronic time urgency (S factor score on JAS), Phase 1	1.24	9.33	−5.34	6.42	3.42	<.001
Diastolic blood pressure, Phase 1	77.19	7.57	73.10	8.17	2.12	<.038
Difference score (Phase 2–Phase 1 on a summary index of overall satisfaction with commuting, residential, and employment domains	−.15	2.18	1.08	2.15	−2.12	<.038

[a] Larger means indicate higher scores on the attribute listed.

scores were based on five, two, and four separate scales within the three satisfaction domains, respectively).[9] Frequency distributions and tertile splits were computed for each item, and each subject was assigned a score of 1, 2, or 3 (corresponding to low, medium, or high tertiles) on each scale. The sum of the individual item scores within each domain yielded a summary index of residential, commuting, and job satisfaction. Moreover, the sum of these domain scores yielded an index of overall satisfaction across all three domains.

By comparing each individual's levels of overall satisfaction at Phases 1 and 2, we derived a satisfaction change score based on the dif-

[9]Residential satisfaction summary scores were based on the following repeated measures: (1) the desire to change residence: (2) the reporting of commuting inconvenience as a reason for wanting to move: (3) perceived crowding in the home: (4) residential choice: and (5) residential satisfaction. The commuting satisfaction index was based on the two items listed in Table 1: (1) perception of traffic congestion as a frequent inconvenience and (2) satisfaction with the commuting process. The job satisfaction index incorporated the individual's total scores on separate sets of items pertaining to (1) ratings of the physical environment at work; (2) ratings of the social environment at work; (3) job satisfaction in general; and (4) the individual's job involvement (J factor) score on the JAS.

ference between Phase 2–Phase 1 levels of overall satisfaction. As can be seen in Table 3, high scorers on the coping index manifested higher levels of overall satisfaction by Phase 2, whereas low scorers exhibited lower levels of satisfaction at Phase 2 than at Phase 1 [$t(67) = 2.12$, $p < .038$].

Further evidence that efforts to cope with commuting constraints are effective is presented in Table 4. These data indicate that among high-impedance commuters ($n = 82$, including those who subsequently changed impedance level), 62% of the high-satisfaction individuals at Phase 2 had made efforts to alter their commuting mode (e.g., by joining or quitting car pools and van pools, and/or by substituting public transit, bicycling, or walking for prior automobile commuting) between Phases 1 and 2, while only 20% of the low-satisfaction subjects had implemented changes in their commuting mode (Fisher's Exact Test = .031).

Proposition 3: The relationship between routine exposure to travel impedance and personal well-being is mediated by the perceived quality of those domains comprising the commuter's typical activity pattern. This hypothesis reflects our emphasis on the contextual (or domain-specific) mediators of transportation and well-being. Two basic sets of analyses were employed to test the hypothesis: (1) a series of regression analyses in which Phase 1 indexes of impedance (e.g., commuting distance, self-reported frequency of braking during the commute), personality, residential choice, and job involvement were utilized to predict overall satisfaction at Phase 2, both within and across different activity domains; and (2) a series of satisfaction × impedance, repeated-measures ANOVAs performed on Phase 2 indexes of well-being, and including only those subjects whose rankings on the satisfaction and impedance dimensions had remained constant between Phases 1 and 2. In this chapter, we discuss only a subset of the regression analyses.

TABLE 4

DISTRIBUTION OF HIGH-IMPEDANCE COMMUTERS BY OVERALL SATISFACTION AT PHASE 2 AND BY ALTERATION OF COMMUTING MODE BETWEEN PHASES 1 AND 2[a]

Overall satisfaction at Phase 2	Alteration of commuting mode	
	Low scorers on index of commuting mode alteration ("low coping")	High scorers on index of commuting mode alteration ("high coping")
Low satisfaction	12	3
High satisfaction	5	8

[a] Fisher's Exact Test = .031.

In all regression equations, the dimensions of age and SES were entered at Step 1 as covariates for those criteria with which they were significantly correlated. At the next step, either commuting distance or an index of brake application during the commute was entered. The dimensions of residential choice, job involvement, and I-E were entered next in a stepwise procedure to determine whether or not these variables accounted for a significant proportion of the variance once the covariates and impedance dimension had been entered into the regression equation. All analyses were based on the constant-impedance sample.

The impedance index of distance was found to be significantly associated with overall commuting satisfaction at Phase 2, while the braking index was significantly related to the Phase 2 summary scores of overall satisfaction (across domains), commuting satisfaction, and residential satisfaction. The prediction of Phase 2 commuting satisfaction by commuting distance and Phase 1 measures of I-E, residential choice, and job involvement is summarized in Table 5. The data indicate that perceived residential choice at Phase 1 (one of the components of the residential-satisfaction summary index) did contribute significantly to the prediction of emotional well-being (i.e., overall commuting satisfaction at Phase 2), once the dimensions of SES, travel distance, and I-E had been entered into the equation.

The above findings provide partial support for a contextual analysis of transportation and well-being and are consistent with our earlier interpretation of the AB × impedance effects on physiology and performance. Specifically, they suggest that the effects of impedance on commuters depend not only on personality attributes but also on the degree of person–environment fit within various life domains.

SUMMARY AND IMPLICATIONS

We have delineated a framework for the ecological analysis of transportation and well-being and have presented a partial overview of findings from our longitudinal research in support of our central propositions. Evaluating the adequacy of our ecological perspective will surely require a more thorough analysis than we offer here. However, the reported findings are a preliminary corroboration of the theoretical scheme.

The data from our field-experimental study support our major assumptions concerning travel impedance and the mediational role of psychological (cognitive–personality) factors. The distance and time parameters of travel, indeed, reflect or index the behavioral constraint

TABLE 5

PREDICTION OF PHASE 2 COMMUTING SATISFACTION BY PHASE 1 INDEXES OF TRAVEL DISTANCE, PERSONAL CONTROL EXPECTANCIES, RESIDENTIAL CHOICE, AND JOB INVOLVEMENT[a]

Predictor variable	Step	Multiple r	Cumulative r^2	Simple r	Beta	Reliability of regression
Socioeconomic status (covariate)	1	.418	.161	.418	.418	$F(1,59) = 12.49$, $p < .001$
Distance	2	.580	.313	-.369	-.404	$F(2,58) = 14.17$, $p < .001$
External control expectancies (on I-E scale)	3	.607	.335	.220	.182	$F(3,57) = 2.87$, $p < .050$
Residential choice	4	.635	.361	.139	.198	$F(4,56) = 3.26$, $p < .025$
Job involvement (factor J on JAS)	5	.642	.358	.018	.111	n.s.

[a] Multivariate $F(4,56) = 9.46$, $p < .001$, at Step 4. Each of the univariate F's reflects the significance of the predictor variable at the step at which it was entered into the equation.

properties of commuting as a phenomenological reality. The empirical link between our operationalized conditions of impedance and the commuters' subjective evaluations of travel conditions in terms of congestion, inconvenience, dissatisfaction, and impediments to movement demonstrate that our research addresses both the physical and the perceived environment. Second, in consonance with psychological perspectives on stress, cognitive and personality factors were found to mediate the impact of routine exposure to adverse environmental conditions. To be sure, the precise nature of this mediation is multifaceted and is beyond determination by tests of statistical interaction. The complex interplay of personal and environmental factors necessitates the study of coping adaptation over time.

Our conceptualization of travel impedance, its environmental contexts, and the adaptation efforts of commuters led to the formulation of several hypotheses, each of which was supported by our findings. In general, the data suggest that (1) conditions of travel impedance are associated with stress reactions (e.g., physiological arousal, negative mood, and performance deficits), but these reactions are mediated by person variables and their reciprocal influence on environmental contexts; (2) the subjective experience of commuting as negatively toned leads to active efforts to alter or otherwise cope with commuting demands; (3) efforts to cope with commuting demands enhance perceptions of personal well-being, as reflected in levels of satisfaction across life domains; and (4) life domains are interconnected, as dimensions of satisfaction within the residential domain (e.g., residential choice) prospectively influence the effects of commuting demands on level of satisfaction within the transportation domain.

SOME QUALIFICATIONS OF OUR FINDINGS

The specific results of our research must be regarded as preliminary in view of several methodological considerations. First, we have studied a small sample of urban commuters whose characteristics may or may not be representative of commuters in other communities and employment situations. The generalizability of our findings remains to be assessed in future studies employing larger samples drawn from different geographical locations. Existing data from national surveys of commuting conditions, employment demands, and well-being (e.g., Quinn & Staines, 1979) could provide the basis for such comparisons.

Second, like earlier field studies of commuting and stress (cf. Singer et al., 1978; Lundberg, 1976), our quasi-experimental investigation poses the problem of nonrandom distribution of subjects across experimental conditions. In an effort to deal with this problem, we have attempted to control for the potentially confounding effects of demographic factors through statistical procedures. Moreover, the use of a longitudinal research design in which the effects of the experimental factors are assessed at different points in time offers a stronger basis for attributing the findings to experimental conditions than does a cross-sectional design.

One potentially confounding factor that has not been controlled in our research is the increased exposure to air pollution associated with long-distance, rush-hour commuting. Earlier studies (e.g., Aronow *et al.*, 1972; Chaney, 1978) indicate that exposure to elevated levels of carbon monoxide while traveling is associated with physiological and behavioral impairments. Although we have not accounted for these effects in our research, certain of our findings (e.g., the impedance main effects on perceived congestion) suggest that the behavioral constraints associated with travel impedance exert significant effects on well-being, above and beyond those attributable to air pollution alone. Moreover, the interaction effect among impedance and personal factors, such as Type A/Type B, argues against the explanation of stress effects as primarily due to air pollution, since there were no differences between A's and B's in the distance of the commute.

The reported study suggests several issues for future research that are both theoretically and practically important. First, while focusing on the health and behavioral consequences of automobile commuting, we have not yet examined the relative health costs associated with alternative modes of travel (e.g., car pools, van pools, and public transit vs. solo automobile commuting). Second, we have focused primarily on the relationship between commuting conditions and personal well-being while neglecting to assess the impact of transportation conditions on organizational effectiveness and community well-being. Our findings concerning the physiological, behavioral, and emotional consequences of travel impedance suggest that organizations and whole communities may be sustaining substantial "hidden" costs associated with conditions of transportation (e.g., in the form of increased disability claims, illness-related absence from work, and reduced levels of employee productivity and morale).

Behavioral Research as a Basis for Transportation Planning

The theoretical and policy implications of our findings suggest several potentially fruitful links among existing areas of research on transportation and behavior. Much of the existing literature on behavioral aspects of transportation can be grouped into two broad areas: (1) attitudinal analyses and market segmentation research aimed at increasing levels of ride sharing (e.g., by providing rapid transit facilities and corporate-sponsored commuting programs) within the community (cf. Hartgen, 1977; Horowitz & Sheth, 1976; Recker & Golub, 1976); and (2) experimental analyses and modification of transportation behavior (cf. Everett, this volume; Everett, Hayward, & Meyers, 1974; Everett, Studer, & Douglas, 1978). Our research on travel impedance and well-being (Novaco *et al.*, 1979; Stokols *et al.*, 1978) exemplifies a third, though perhaps less thoroughly examined, facet of the interface between transportation and behavior. In the remaining discussion, we suggest some potential links among these currently separate areas of investigation.

The findings from studies of transportation and well-being could provide an impetus for refining existing transportation services and a basis for encouraging individuals to make constructive changes in their commuting situations. Given that organizational personnel and community members in general may be sustaining health costs incurred through the demands of automobile driving, business corporations and government agencies might therefore be induced to provide more alternatives to the private automobile. In addition, research findings concerning the health consequences of impedance and the potential effectiveness of coping strategies for enhancing well-being illustrate the kinds of information that might be utilized in future informational and incentive-based campaigns aimed at persuading commuters to modify their travel behavior. Information regarding the health consequences of commuting patterns might increase the persuasive appeal of such campaigns, which, typically, have focused on economic and convenience factors, rather than on dimensions of physical and emotional well-being. As Everett *et al.* (1974) have speculated, physical technical advances might be accompanied by programs that address issues that are to a large extent behavioral in nature.

Our theoretical perspective incorporates the idea of environmental congruence, which refers to the degree to which a person's major goals are facilitated or constrained by environmental conditions. Previous studies of the attitudinal and behavioral underpinnings of ride sharing often reflect the assumption that increased citizen participation in collective transit is desirable. This assumption seems quite reasonable in view of the currently critical shortage of global fuel supplies. While increased levels of ride sharing may be necessary and desirable for societal well-being, virtually no research has been conducted on the health and behavioral consequences of participation in alternative forms of collective transit, particularly from the standpoint of person–environment fit.

The behavioral and health data furnished by studies of urban commuters could provide criteria for evaluating the cost effectiveness of organizational and community interventions designed to reduce rates of behavioral, emotional, and physical disorder. The identification of high-risk commuters, the provision of stress management programs and exercise facilities, changes in the structure of the work day, and transportation management strategies are among the intervention programs whose effectiveness might be enhanced by the findings from research on transportation and well-being.

Acknowledgments

We are grateful to Dr. Pete Fielding, Director of ITS-Irvine, for his continuing assistance and support throughout all phases of our research; and to the management and employees of Allergan Pharmaceuticals and Parker-Hannifin Corporation in Irvine, California, for their participation in this investigation. Also, we thank Lyn Long and Debbie Smith, of the Information Center at ITS-Irvine, for their bibliographic assistance on the literature review portion of this chapter; and Joan Campbell, Greg Jue, and Jeanne Stokols for their assistance with the collection and analysis of data pertaining to this project. We appreciate the helpful comments made by Sandra Kirmeyer on earlier versions of the chapter.

REFERENCES

Aangeenbrug, R. T. *Automobile commuting: A geographic analysis of private car use in the daily journey to work in large cities*. Ann Arbor, Mich.: University Microfilms International, 1965.

Altman, I. *The environment and social behavior: Privacy, personal space, territory and crowding*. Monterey, Calif.: Brooks-Cole, 1975.

Appley, M. H., & Trumbull, R. (Eds.), *Psychological stress*. New York: Appleton-Century-Crofts, 1967.

Aronow, W. S., Harris, C. N., Isbell, M. W., Rokaw, M. D., & Imparato, B. Effect of freeway travel on angina pectoris. *Annals of Internal Medicine*, 1972, 77, 669–676.

Barker, R. G. *Ecological psychology: Concepts and methods for studying the environment of human behavior*. Stanford, Calif.: Stanford University Press, 1968.

Barker, R. G., & Associates. *Habitats, environments, and human behavior*. San Francisco: Jossey-Bass, 1978.

Baum, A., & Epstein, J. (Eds.), *Human response to crowding*. Hillsdale, N.J.: Lawrence Erlbaum, 1978.

Bellet, S., Roman, L., & Kostis, J. The effect of automobile driving on catecholamine and adrenocortical excretion. *The American Journal of Cardiology*, 1969, 24, 365–368.

Bem, D. J., & Funder, D. C. Predicting more of the people more of the time: Assessing the personality of situations. *Psychological Review*, 1978, *85*, 485–501.

Berkowitz, L. The concept of aggressive drive: Some additional considerations. In L. Berkowitz (Ed.), *Advances in Experimental Social Psychology*, Vol. 2, New York: Academic Press, 1965, pp. 301–330.

Bronfenbrenner, U. *The ecology of human development*. Cambridge, Mass.: Harvard University Press, 1979.

Campbell, J. M. Ambient stress: A social-ecological perspective. Unpublished manuscript, Program in Social Ecology, University of California, Irvine, Nov. 1979.

Catalano, R. *Health, behavior, and the community: An ecological perspective*. New York: Pergamon Press, 1979.

Catanese, A. Models of commuting. In A. Catanese (Ed.), *New perspectives in transportation research*. Lexington, Mass.: Lexington Press, 1972.

Chaney, L. W. Carbon monoxide automobile emissions measured from the interior of a traveling automobile. *Science*, 1978, *199*, 1203–1204.

Chapin, F. S. *Human activity patterns in the city: Things people do in time and space*. New York: Wiley, 1974.

Chein, I. The environment as a determinant of behavior. *Journal of Social Psychology*, 1954, *39*, 115–127.

Crawford, A. Fatigue and driving. *Ergonomics*, 1961, *4*, 143–154.

Dohrenwend, B. S., & Dohrenwend, B. P., (Eds.), *Stressful life events*. New York: Wiley, 1974.

Donnerstein, E., & Wilson, D. W. Effects of noise and perceived control on ongoing and subsequent aggressive behavior. *Journal of Personality and Social Psychology*, 1976, *34*, 774–781.

Everett, P. B., Hayward, S. C., & Meyers, A. W. The effects of a token reinforcement procedure on bus ridership. *Journal of Applied Behavioral Analysis*, 1974, *7*, 1–10.

Everett, P. B., Studer, R. G., & Douglas, T. J. Gaming simulation to pretest operant-based community interventions: An urban transportation example. *American Journal of Community Psychology*, 1978, *6*, 327–338.

Feather, N. T. The relationship of persistence at a task to expectation of success and achievement related motives. *Journal of Abnormal and Social Psychology*, 1961, *63*, 552–561.

Federal Highway Administration. *A comparative analysis of urban transportation requirements*, Vol. 1, 2. Reports No. PB-267-788 and No. PB-267-789, U.W. Department of Transportation. Washington, D.C. Feb., March 1977, pp. 42–44, 312.

Forbes, T. W. *Human factors in highway traffic safety research*. New York: Wiley, 1972.

French, J. R. P., Rodgers, W., & Cobb, S. Adjustment as person–environment fit. In G. Coelho, D. A. Hamburgh, & J. E. Adams (Eds.), *Coping and adaptation*. New York: Basic Books, 1974, pp. 316–333.

Gibson, J. J. The concept of the stimulus in psychology. *American Psychologist*, 1960, *15*, 694–703.

Glass, D. C. *Behavior patterns, stress and coronary disease*. Hillsdale, N. J.: Lawrence Erlbaum, 1977.

Glass, D. C., & Singer, J. *Urban stress: Experiments on noise and social stressors*. New York: Academic Press, 1972.

Glass, D. C., Snyder, M. D., & Hollis, J. F. Time urgency and the Type A coronary prone behavior pattern. *Journal of Applied Social Psychology*, 1974, *4*, 125–140.

Haagen-Smit, A. J. Carbon monoxide levels in city driving. *Archives of Environmental Health*, 1966, *12*, 548–551.

Halperin, M. H., McFarland, R. A., Niven, J. I., & Roughton, F. W. The time course of the effects of carbon monoxide on visual threshholds. *Journal of Physiology,* 1959, *146,* 583–593.

Harrison, R. V. Person–environment fit and job stress. In C. C. Cooper & R. Payne (Eds.), *Stress at work.* New York: Wiley, 1978, pp. 175–205.

Hartgen, D. T. Ridesharing behavior: A review of recent findings. *Research Report No. 130,* Planning Research Unit, New York State Department of Transportation, Albany, Nov. 1977.

Heimstra, N. W. The effects of "stress fatigue" on performance in a simulated driving situation. *Ergonomics,* 1970, *3,* 209–218.

Horowitz, A. D., & Sheth, J. N. Ridesharing to work: A psychosocial analysis. *Report No. GMR-2216,* Research Laboratories, General Motors Corporation, Warren, Mich., Aug. 1976.

Horvath, S. M., Dahms, T. E., & O'Hanlon, J. F. Carbon monoxide and human vigilance: A deleterious effect of present urban concentrations. *Archives of Environmental Health,* 1971, *23,* 343–347.

Hunt, T. J., & May, P. I. A preliminary investigation into a psychological assessment of driving stress. London: Metropolitan Police, Accident Research Unit, 1968.

Jenkins, C. D. Zyzanski, S., & Rosenman, R. Progress toward validation of a computer-scored test for the Type A coronary-prone behavior pattern. *Psychosomatic Medicine,* 1971, *33,* 193–202.

Kain, J. F., Fauth, G. R., & Zax, J. *Forecasting auto ownership and mode choice for U.S. metropolitan areas.* Cambridge, Mass.: Harvard University Department of City and Regional Planning, 1977.

Katz, D. & Kahn, R. L. *The social psychology of organizations.* New York: Wiley, 1966.

Kelly, J. G. Toward an ecological conception of preventive interventions. In J. W. Carter, Jr. (Ed.), *Research contributions from psychology to community mental health.* New York: Behavioral Publications, 1968.

Knapper, C. K., & Cropley, A. J. Towards a social psychology of the traffic environment. In D. F. Burkhardt & W. H. Ittelson (Eds), *Environmental assessment of socioeconomic systems.* New York: Plenum Press, 1977, pp. 263–278.

Knapper, C. K., & Cropley, A. J. Social and interpersonal factors in driving. In G. M. Stephenson & J. Davis (Eds.), *Progress in applied social psychology,* Vol. 1. London: Wiley, 1980.

Krantz, D., Glass, D., & Snyder, M. Helplessness, stress level, and the coronary-prone behavior pattern. *Journal of Experimental Social Psychology,* 1974, *10,* 284–300.

Lazarus, R. S. *Psychological stress and the coping process.* New York: McGraw–Hill, 1966.

Lazarus, R. S., & Launier, R. Stress-related transactions between person and environment. In L. A. Pervin & M. Lewis (Eds.), *Perspectives in interactional psychology.* New York: Plenum Press, 1978, pp. 287–327.

Levine, S., & Scotch, N. (Eds.), *Social stress.* Chicago: Aldine, 1970.

Lewin, K. *Principles of topological psychology.* New York: McGraw-Hill, 1936.

Littler, W. A., Honour, A. J., & Sleight, P. Direct arterial pressure and electrocardiogram during motor car driving. *British Medical Journal,* 1973, *2,* 273–277

Lundberg, U. Urban commuting: Crowdedness and catecholamine excretion. *Journal of Human Stress,* 1976, *2,* 26–32.

Mackie, R. R., O'Hanlon, J. F., & McCauley, M. A study of heat, noise, and vibration in relation to driver performance and physiological status. Washington, D.C.: *Report #DOT 11S-801-215,* National Highway Traffic Safety Administration, Dec. 1974.

Magnusson, D. Wanted: A psychology of situations. In D. Magnusson (Ed.), *Toward a psychology of situations: An interactional perspective.* Hillsdale, N.J.: Lawrence Erlbaum, 1981.

Maruyama, M. The second cybernetics: Deviation-amplifying mutual causal processes. *American Scientist,* 1963, 164–179.

McGrath, J. E. *Social and psychological factors in stress.* New York: Holt, Rinehart & Winston, 1970.

Mechanic, D. *Medical sociology: A selective view.* New York: Free Press, 1968.

Michaels, R. M. The effect of expressway design on driver tension responses. *Public Roads,* 1962, *32,* 107–112.

Michelson, W. *Man and his urban environment: A sociological approach,* 2nd ed. Reading, Mass.: Addison-Wesley, 1976.

Miller, J. G. Toward a general theory for the behavioral sciences. *American Psychologist,* 1955, *10,* 513–531.

Moos, R. H. *The human context.* New York: Wiley, 1976.

Neumann, E. S., Romansky, M. L., & Plummer, R. W. Passenger car comfort and travel decisions. *Journal of Transport Economics and Policy,* 1978, *12,* 231–243.

Novaco, R. W. *Anger control.* Boston: Lexington Press, 1975.

Novaco, R. W. The cognitive regulation of anger and stress. In P. Kendall & S. Hollon (Eds.), *Cognitive-behavioral interventions: Theory, research, and procedures.* New York: Academic Press, 1979, pp. 241–285.

Novaco, R. W., Stokols, D., Campbell, J., & Stokols, J. Transportation, stress and community psychology. *American Journal of Community Psychology,* 1979, *4,* 361–380.

Quinn, R. P. & Staines, G. L. *The 1977 Quality of Employment Survey.* Ann Arbor: University of Michigan Survey Research Center, 1979.

Recker, W. W., & Golub, T. F. An attitudinal modal choice model. *Transportation Research,* 1976, *10,* 299–310.

Rotter, J. Generalized expectancies for internal versus external control. *Psychological Monographs,* 1966, *80* (Whole No. 609).

Rule, B. G., & Nesdale, A. R. Environmental stressors, emotional arousal, and aggression. In I. G. Sarason & C. D. Spielberger (Eds.), *Stress and anxiety,* Vol. 3. New York: Halsted Press, 1976, pp. 87–103.

Rutley, K. S., & Mace, D. G. W. Heart rate as a measure in road layout design. London: *Research Report No. RRL-LR 347,* Road Research Laboratory, British Ministry of Transportation, 1970.

Selye, H. *The stress of life.* New York: McGraw-Hill, 1956.

Selye, H. *Stress in health and disease.* Woburn, Mass.: Butterworths, 1976.

Simonson, E., Baker, C., Burns, N., Keiper, C., Schmitt, O. H., & Stackhouse, S. Cardiovascular stress (electrocardiographic changes) produced by driving an automobile. *American Heart Journal,* 1968, *75,* 125–135.

Singer, J., Lundberg, U., & Frankenhaeuser, M. Stress on the train: A study of urban commuting. In A. Baum, J. Singer, & S. Valins (Eds.), *Advances in environmental psychology,* Vol. 1. Hillsdale, N.J.: Lawrence Erlbaum, 1978, pp. 41–56.

Skinner, B. F. *Science and human behavior.* New York: Macmillan, 1953.

Stokols, D. A congruence analysis of human stress. In I. G. Sarason & C. D. Spielberger (Eds.), *Stress and anxiety,* Vol. 6. Washington, D.C.: Hemisphere Press, 1979, pp. 27–53.

Stokols, D. Environmental psychology. *Annual Review of Psychology,* 1978, *29,* 253–295.

Stokols, D. Group × place transactions: Some neglected issues in psychological research on settings. In D. Magnusson (Ed.), *Toward a psychology of situations; An interactional perspective.* Hillsdale, N.J.: Lawrence Erlbaum, 1981, 393–415.

Stokols, D., Novaco, R. W., Stokols, J., & Campbell, J. Traffic congestion, Type-A be-
    havior, and stress. *Journal of Applied Psychology*, 1978, *63*, 467–480.
Stokols, D. & Shumaker, S. A. People in places: A transactional view of settings. In J.
    Harvey (Ed.), *Cognition, social behavior, and the environment.* Hillsdale, N.J.: Lawrence
    Erlbaum, 1981, 441–488.
Taggart, P., Gibbons, D., & Somerville, W. Some effects of motor-car driving on the
    normal and abnormal heart. *British Medical Journal*, 1969 *4*, 130–134.
Taylor, P. J. & Pocock, S. J. Commuter travel and sickness absence of London office
    workers. *British Journal of Preventive and Social Medicine*, 1972, *26*, 175–172.
Thibaut, J. W., & Kelley, H. H. *The social psychology of groups.* New York: Wiley, 1959.
Turner, C. W., Layton, J. F., & Simons, L. S. Naturalistic studies of aggressive behavior:
    Aggressive stimuli, victim visibility, and horn honking. *Journal of Personality and Social
    Psychology*, 1975, *31*, 1098–1107.
von Bertalanffy, L. The theory of open systems in physics and biology. *Science*, 1950, *111*,
    23–29.
Wechsler, D. *The measurement of adult intelligence.* Baltimore: Williams & Wilkins, 1958.
Wicker, A. W. *An introduction to ecological psychology.* Monterrey, Calif.: Brooks/Cole, 1979.
Wohlwill, J. F. The environment is not in the head! In W. F. Preisser (Ed.), *Environmental
    design research*, Vol. 2. Stroudsburg, Pa.: Dowden, Hutchinson, & Ross, 1973, 166–181.
Zyzanski, S. J., & Jenkins, C. D. Basic dimensions within the coronary-prone behavior
    pattern. *Journal of Chronic Diseases*, 1970, *22*, 781–795.

5

Human Factors Engineering and Psychology in Highway Safety

RICHARD A. OLSEN

SOME DEFINITIONS

Human factors engineering or *human factors* (HF), is one of several terms used to describe the art and science of systematically designing practical systems that include human operators or users, mechanisms or information, and environmental or situational constraints. The term, unfortunately, is interpreted very loosely by both the lay public and many non-HF specialists to include more general notions. In the discussion that follows, the engineering aspects of HF will be stressed. In this context, HF is the art of applying known principles of human perception and behavior (i.e., psychology) in the development of human–machine systems, so that the capabilities and limitations of the human are fully considered in the attempt to produce an efficient system capable of achieving its assigned goals within the expected environmental and social constraints.

The distinction between psychology and HF is important. There have been arguments that two fields as different as clinical (therapeutic) psychology and experimental (scientific?) psychology should be known

RICHARD A. OLSEN • Formerly of The Pennsylvania State University. Currently at the Lockheed Missiles and Space Company, Sunnyvale, California 94086.

by different names because their theories, concerns, approaches, methods, and practitioners are often so far apart (but see Shevrin & Dickman, 1980).

The HF concern is that of an engineer looking for better solutions to practical problems. Fortunately, there is a growing concern about the application of what is known about people as they operate in various systems. There is a distinct engineering flavor to this concern, in spite of its emphasis on people. Nowhere is there a better example of the need for HF approaches than in the operation of a system of highway traffic, and the need for psychology as an input source not only remains but is becoming more important as the effects become more and more subtle in an evolving system (Munson, 1980). In a system where almost everyone over 16 expects to be able to drive a car, any hope of standard conditions and controlled variables is largely abandoned. More fundamental knowledge of how operators function is needed to influence the system development in increasingly fruitful ways.

APPLYING RESEARCH FINDINGS

The following discussion includes a brief history of traditional ideas about driver behavior and traffic safety, and reviews of the status of two more specific topics: driver fatigue and the driver's night visual environment. From these reviews, it will appear that there is little theoretical or conceptual depth in driver-safety research efforts, more because of the diversity of concerns involved in attempts to find practical solutions to problems of immense complexity than because of lack of interest or progress in research. The field is young, and sophisticated individual studies cannot be expected to produce wide-ranging results. Much of the effort is absorbed in correcting long-standing deficiencies in data bases, and political pressures have been intense at times, demanding immediate results in a very visible area of public concern. This review is intended to illustrate some of the problems that face researchers and administrators and to show where progress is being made or can be expected in the near future, provided realistic program goals and funding levels are available. Two fairly obvious extensions into accident analysis are given to illustrate how far the field must go to become an integrated science. The simple conception of driver error must give way to one encompassing many error sources within various parts of the system. Fatigue must also be discussed in more specific terms if accidents that are attributed to "fatigue" are to be made less frequent.

After the discussion of these two topics, this chapter concludes with a topic (driving and vision) about which much is known and about which much literature can be cited. Here, too, however, the application of known principles is limited by the diversity and the economic realities in the driving environments. Room for ingenuity remains, of course, and a wide variety of research can still be beneficial. The application of research results throughout our driving systems is inevitably a lengthy process.

THE TRADITIONAL THREE E'S

The tradition of the three E's in highway driving—engineering, education, and enforcement—is familiar to many Americans. In this view, a good (safe) system consists of a highway designed and maintained to the latest specifications, a driver who knows all the rules of safe driving, and an enforcement system that keeps reminding the drivers to obey all the rules. Unfortunately there is little evidence that such a system does or can work to eliminate all losses (Olsen, Helmsworth, Sweeney, & Crowley, 1980; Olsen, Haight, & Henszey, 1980).

Engineering has been effective in one outstanding instance: the interstate highway system. High design standards—including multiple lanes, merging and diverging zones, lack of intersecting traffic, good signing and marking systems, and clear areas or protective barriers on both sides of the travel lanes—have made accident rates on interstate highways much lower than on other highways. The problems are that such roads also generate more traffic than would have been attracted to slower roads, they have contributed to the decline of alternative transportation, and they have changed our living patterns in ways that probably cannot be sustained. Also, of course, it is not possible to make all roads meet interstate standards. The rural two-lane highway is indispensable and will remain the site of a large portion of fatalities (Glennon, 1979).

Education is the second E. Driver education advocates call for greater investments in traditional high-school driver training despite consistent research findings (McGuire & Kersh, 1969) that it is not effective as a means of preventing accidents: the facts point (not without considerable cloudiness) to the conclusion that drivers have about the same success in driving whether they learn from friends and relatives, a high school class, or a commercial school.

If education is a weak corrective force, enforcement—the third E—is supposed to strengthen it and keep drivers in control. Some studies of enforcement (e.g., Hauer & Cooper, 1977), show that "more is better" in terms of accident reduction and speed control, but many evaluations of increased enforcement have failed to show any real effect. Contracts from the National Highway Traffic Safety Administration (NHTSA) have begun to probe the reasons for such findings and the possibilities of countermeasures based on driver behavior (see Treat, Tumbus, McDonald, Shinar, Hume, Mayer, Stansifer, & Castellan, 1977; Summers & Harris, 1978; Lohman, Leggett, Stewart, & Campbell, 1976; Jones, Treat, & Joscelyn, 1979b; Jones, Joscelyn, Bennett, Fennessy, Komoroske, Marks, & Ruschmann, 1979a).

Enforcement, however, has an inherently negative connotation: punishment will discourage the repetition of undesired behavior. Behavioral science can be used to shape behavior, provided there is some control over rewards and punishments and the behaviors that are to be modified. In the human, presumably, a model of desired behavior can aid in structuring the interaction of the various components. However, the preconscious or habitual nature of much of driver behavior suggests that conscious models may be irrelevant after all (Olsen, 1980b).

MODELS, CONCEPTS, AND DRIVER BEHAVIOR

The traditional model of vehicle drivers is a loosely structured one based on good and evil or responsibility and the lack of it. Good drivers are courteous, respect the law, drive safely, are forgiving of the errors of other persons, and are defensive in that they anticipate the errors that other drivers or pedestrians might make and allow a safety margin to compensate for such errors. Bad drivers have accidents. Nowhere is there a systematic analysis of what behaviors constitute the desired or optimal set (e.g., see Olsen & Hostetter, 1976). Several models of ideal behavior have been proposed, but they tend to lack concrete, convincing criteria.

Enforcement success depends, to a large extent, on the general deterrent effect (Andeneas, 1974; Geerken & Gove, 1975): drivers consistently overestimate the odds of getting a citation for specific violations, such as running a red light or driving at a speed above the posted limit (Enderson, 1978; Teknekron, 1978, 1979). Conformance is less than perfect for most individuals, based on the perceived trade off between the time saved or the profit earned and the possibility of getting a ticket or being fined. Commercial drivers, especially cross-country truck drivers, typically consider fines inevitable and part of the cost of doing business (Wyckoff, 1979). This attitude is related to their relatively accurate appraisal of the chance of getting caught; the fact that repeated offenders are not seriously inconvenienced because the convictions are divided (usually illegally) among several simultaneously held driving licenses (Hagen, 1977); and consistent, strong, peer support, including citizen's band (CB) radio reporting networks.

The game-playing aspects of driving and enforcement have been neglected as a topic of study. Social and peer pressures are strong among drivers, especially commercial drivers and teen-aged males. The possibility of an accident, while not denied as a reality of driving, is sometimes ignored in the press of the "more immediate" concerns of mood, convenience, and the need to respond to other drivers. On the other hand, the cat-and-mouse games between CB users and police show some signs of abating, and the overwhelming benefits of CB communications are beginning to be realized. Nevertheless, the attitude between drivers and police is seldom conducive to reshaping behaviors or to developing a mutually useful CB information network that works to increase highway efficiency. This area would benefit from more formal studies, but there have been few to date.

Basic to the adversary condition of enforcement in driver behavior is the lack of accepted optimal behaviors; a goal-seeking system must have well-defined goals. The research findings and accident statistics have proved that seat belts and motorcycle helmets, for example, are highly cost-effective, yet at least 25 states have yielded to the desires of various groups and repealed mandatory helmet-use laws, even though such laws had temporarily reduced accident fatalities by up to 40% (National Highway Transportation Safety Administration, 1979). The seat-belt–starter interlock was another example of a good idea shot down by public pressure, though in this case, insufficient thought had been given to the details of the mechanism and implementation of the system; the backfire in public reaction hurt this aspect of public health seriously. Mandatory seat-belt laws, found repeatedly in surveys to be acceptable to or desired by about two-thirds of the U.S. population, have not been created by any state. Once more, evidence from Australia (Boughton & Milne, 1978) and Canada (Green & Sharp, 1979) overwhelmingly supports such laws, in terms of both dramatic accident-loss reductions and public acceptance. The attitude in the United States seems to be that technology (passive belts or air bags) is preferable to even gentle persuasion. Whether this attitude is pervasive or not, the political climate is such that no mandatory belt-use laws are expected in the near future.

Coercion is not entirely ruled out by the public: people believe that laws should be enforced for others, mainly for the hypothetical "bad driver" or the accident repeater. The fact is, however, that despite a long history of investigation, the accident-prone driver has not been found to be a major source of problems (Stewart & Campbell, 1972).

Drunk drivers, however, are a different matter; they exist in large numbers. The drivers who make errors, who violate laws, or who have had too much to drink and drive safely are all around us, but *we* are not among them.

The paradox presented to those looking for traffic accident countermeasures is well stated by Yankelovich, Skelly, and White (1976):

> Drivers overwhelmingly indicate a concern about the extent of unsafe driving on U.S. roads. However, a major attitudinal barrier which safer driving and safety restraint programs must overcome is the conviction among three out of four drivers that "accidents happen because other drivers are at fault." Drivers maintain this conviction despite the fact that most of them admit to taking at least minimal risks while driving. In other words, drivers blame other drivers for accidents despite the fact that they admit to taking risks themselves. (p. 6)

In a marketing study of the National Safety Council's Defensive Driving Course (DDC), Weiers (1977) noted that there was resentment of this much-publicized course, with its image as an effective, beneficial experience in the improvement of driving. DDC was considered "a corrective program for those who either do not know how to drive or for those who have had excessive violations or accidents." The respondents also expressed the view that the course was a boring repetition of facts they already knew. Some of those who took the course to become better drivers suffered because of guilt by association with those who were forced to attend for corrective reasons. Most people think they drive properly and know all they need to know; they resent the implication that they could improve, and they dislike associating with "bad" drivers. Until this widespread feeling is replaced with a receptivity to new ideas, pressures to change will be perceived as punishment.

When drivers were asked by Yankelovich *et al.* (1976) how they would classify their own driving in terms of safety or risk taking:

- 60% indicated they were "safe drivers who very occasionally find themselves driving unsafely in minor ways."
- 22% said they were the "safest drivers there are (at all times)."
- 12% reported they were "safe drivers who occasionally take major safety risks for what seems to be a good reason at the time."
- 4% said they were "drivers who take safety risks, knowing what they're doing, but more preoccupied with 'just getting where they are going.'"
- Only 2% indicated that they were "drivers who really don't know for sure what's safe and unsafe in driving."

When drivers were asked to select, from a list of seven options, the one or two courses of action that they thought would contribute most to safer driving, 51% selected "reducing the number of drunken drivers," 46% chose "stricter enforcement of existing laws," and 31% said "more and better driver education."

These opinions are clearly self-contradictory: we can't each be a good driver in a sea of bad drivers. The perception of other drivers' mistakes was almost universal (87%), but to the same degree, the attitude was fatalistic (drivers will drive as they please). Obviously, current enforcement efforts are ineffective if driver errors are so frequent, but the solution is seen as more use of existing penalties (84%). Since most drivers see themselves as behaving reasonably and the other driver as at fault in accidents, a more objective presentation of driving situations or more specific rules for determining what is correct are needed. Some outside agent seems to be essential to bringing this about. Any practical level of police enforcement activities will not suffice, and the cost and resentment generated by significant increases in enforcement activity will not be supportable for very long. Alternatives include candid TV showing common errors actually being committed (Hutchinson, Cox, & Maffet, 1969) and observers who send letters to drivers who consistently make certain errors (Ben-David, Lewin, Haliva, & Tel-nir, 1972).

The pervasive driver opinion is predictable from behavior theory. Most driving is rewarding, at least in the sense that drivers usually get where they are going without accidents or enforcement contacts. These repeated rewards are strong reasons for drivers to maintain the rewarded behaviors. They become convinced that their success is due to their much-better-than-average skill and understanding of traffic. Perhaps the constant barrage of accident information furthers this egocentric misapprehension; "If there are so many accidents and deaths, I truly must be an excellent driver because I haven't had any accidents (or none that were my fault, obviously, since I am a good driver)." Such circular reasoning will not yield to occasional traffic citations or even accidents. It might yield to strategies devised through careful research, however.

It is not completely clear that accidents are caused by specific unsafe driving acts (UDA). Each act may be seen as a common, convenient, harmless stretching of the rules, or even as a necessary act that is wrongly prohibited by the vehicle code. The driver assesses the risk— that is, the likelihood of having an accident—as being acceptably low for the perceived advantage.

One could argue that risk assessment by drivers is relatively accurate, since the frequency of accidents on a mileage basis is low. Svenson (1978) discussed the development of risk concepts in drivers in general and in those specific (hazardous) situations in which the perceived risk is unrealistically low. Näätänen and Summala (1976) also reviewed the research on drivers' risk-taking behavior and concluded that the apparent acceptance of high risk is based on the "tendency to assume . . . the continuation, in the immediate future, of the perceived event or states of affairs" (p. 156). Apparently, this optimistic attitude is developed from accumulated successful experience in cutting safety margins to an absolute minimum. The authors think that propaganda and enforcement are not effective in raising this subjective risk threshold and that environmental changes, such as the creation of the visual illusion of speed at high-risk sites, are more promising.

A FOURTH E: EXPERIMENTATION

At last, we come to the fourth E: experimentation. Much of the practice in fields related to highway use is based on tradition. "And where did this tradition come from? I'll tell you. I don't know. But it's tradition!" (from *Fiddler on the Roof*). It is clear that much current practice is not based on experimental findings, and it is also clear that some is contradicted by research. Data systems that summarize opinions reinforce errors or overgeneralizations. Even though thousands of vehicles may pass a given spot at speeds 15 mph above the limit without accidents, an accident at that speed is often reported as having been caused by speeding. If the vehicle strikes another going 15 mph below the limit, the cause is listed as excessive speed used in passing the slow vehicle. Logically, the slow vehicle was obstructing traffic flow, and it was a hazard to every other vehicle passing at the "normal" speed. Yet, tradition holds that high speed is always the cause of an accident, and low speed is safe, despite growing evidence that slow vehicles are implicated in more accidents than are fast vehicles. The severity of accidents is usually greater at higher speeds, but cause is a distinct factor that must not be lumped with severity if systematic countermeasures are to be devised.

Many aspects of enforcement and driver behavior are empirically testable. An outstanding example of good practice in this regard is the State of California. A summary of findings and activities (Kelsey, 1979) covering 84 projects completed over the last 20 years (most of them since 1974) concluded that, in spite of many "good ideas," the evidence does not support the programs as effective or worth the added cost that they would entail on a large scale. Similar programs have been "tested" by other states—often less rigorously—because program managers do not want to give up politically attractive but ineffectual programs.

Programs funded at the federal level suffer from similar tendencies. The mission-oriented programs funded by the U.S. Department of Transportation are based on the premise that the cures for most ills are known and that all we need do is find ways to implement them (but see U.S. Department of Transportation, 1979b).

There is room for much more basic and applied research on deterrence, both general and specific (through enforcement activity). Andeneas (1974), Anderson, Chiricos, and Waldo (1977), Bailey and Smith (1972), Chirocos and Waldo (1970), Erickson and Gibbs (1979), Grasmick and Appleton (1977), Ross (1973), Teevan (1976), and Zimring and Hawkins (1971), to name a few, have offered a variety of approaches in this area. General principles and useful models are being developed, though much remains to be done before the results can be usefully applied.

Drivers, business firms, and official agencies have developed a reasonably successful automobile transportation system, largely through trial and error. There have been outstanding failures, such as the automobile manufacturer that asked the public what kinds of cars they wished to have and then built them, ignoring the economic and fuel situations. High-school driver education is only now beginning to lose its only proven advantage—insurance discounts—because the actuarial loss differences are now recognized as being related to the demographic characteristics of those to whom driver education was made available, not to the education itself. There is a research base for some improvements in traffic safety, but application of this knowledge is sometimes slow.

THE SYSTEMS APPROACH AND ERROR ANALYSIS

One hears the term *systems approach* used to denote both the epitome of pretentious nonsense and the ultimate in practical design tools. The systems approach (or the cybernetic model) merely admits that any change in one component of the system can have implications throughout the system. It cautions that no change should be assumed to have local effects only, except as a simplifying assumption.

Simple assumptions may be appropriate for a superficial analysis of a system. For example, the vehicle–environment–driver system may be useful as a simple concept, but it is not of much practical use until control theory, transfer functions, differential equations, and similar sophisticated tools are employed. Because the human operator is a highly adaptive controller that changes characteristics in response to many variables, studies employing the human transfer function have not been very useful in predicting driving success. Since it has been estimated that any screening requirement that eliminated more than about 2% of the driver license applicants would not be tolerated politically, information-processing rate cannot be used as a criterion for driver selection, but it can serve as a guide to adequate designs. The task of making the highway travel system work for 98% of those who wish to drive their own vehicles is certainly a formidable challenge to both theoretical and practical professionals.

One approach to understanding system failures as the causes of highway accidents is discussed in detail by Shinar (1978). Through a detailed reconstruction of 420 accidents by in-depth multidisciplinary accident-investigation teams, the vehicle, the roadway, and the driver were studied for the certain, definite, or probable confidence levels of causation factors. For 91% of the accidents discussed by Shinar (1978), human operator deficiencies or errors were determined to be the problble or definite causes. Other studies typically find that 85%–95% of accidents are caused by driver error. While the interaction of the driver and the vehicle or the environment were recognized, 57% of the accidents were attributed solely to human error.

Error analysis is highly subjective in these cases (see Haight, Joksch, O'Day, Waller, Stutts, & Reinfurt, 1976), and as mentioned earlier, there is no single authoritative "bible" of driver behavior that defines right and wrong actions in detail. It is not at all clear that such a bible is feasible for all situations, but basic rules, beyond the Uniform Vehicle Code (UVCA, 1967), are not explicitly stated in any form.

The accident causation factors related to the driver have been defined as "human acts and failures to act in the minutes immediately preceding an accident, which increase the risk of collision beyond that which would have existed for a conscientious driver driving to a high but reasonable standard of good defensive driving practice" (Treat et al., 1977). The amount of subjectivity involved in such a definition is obvious.

In the results reported by Treat et al. (1977), about half the accidents were attributed to errors of recognition or decision errors or both. It would be quite easy to make a case for each error's being the result of the driving situation rather than the driver's deficiency. For example, improper lookout includes the driver's failure to look around the "A" pillars that support the front of the vehicle's roof. If the pillar width were less than the average distance between adult pupils as viewed from the driver's position, there would be no need to move the head to eliminate the blind spot. Excessive speed could be blamed on a roadway that looks safer than it is, or the run-off-the-road type of accident could be attributed to the lack of convincing information regarding a curve or other hazard for which reduced speed would be an obvious requirement.

The extent to which these alternative explanations of an accident are acceptable depends on the assumptions and experiences of the observer. Human errors can be traced to previous human errors in the design and use of the entire system. For example, the error analysis found in Table 1, based on a general human–machine–environment system concept,

TABLE 1
ANALYSIS FOR ULTIMATE HUMAN ERROR TYPE

1. Specification error: the objectives or tolerances on which a device or component was conceived were inappropriate, incomplete, incompatible, or otherwise in error for use in the ultimate operating environment and conditions.
2. Design error: the device or component was designed with insufficient care to fully match the specifications for the design.
3. Production error: the device or component was manufactured, assembled, or adjusted so that the delivered unit did not operate in the manner of the operating prototypes used in the design–production transition.
4. Inspection error: a detectable and correctable error was overlooked or improperly corrected in the production, installation, maintenance, or operation of a device or component.
5. Installation error: the correct device or part was installed incorrectly or incompletely, or an improper part was installed in place of the correct one.
6. Maintenance error: a device or component wore out or failed after an excessive time in use or an excessive unusual stress, or after adjustment, lubrication, or other periodic attention was not performed satisfactorily or at all.
7. Procedure error: the description of the chain of activities to be performed on or using a device or unit was incomplete or in error as it was generally understood by the persons who might carry out this kind of activity.
8. Operator error: the operator failed to carry out completely, or in proper timing or fashion, some activity that an operator with the minimal operating knowledge, skill, and efficiency specified for that position could reasonably be expected to carry out with high reliability under the circumstances at hand.
9. Supervisory error: an unqualified operator performed or failed to perform some activity that resulted in an undesirable condition because of insufficient care, poor judgment, or lack of discipline on the part of a supervisory person responsible for the activity.
10. Qualification error: the selection, training, supervision, and briefing processes to which an operator is subjected failed to ensure that the operator was, in fact, fully able to perform the tasks assigned under the range of conditions that might reasonably be expected.
11. Management error: the allocation of personnel and of facility and equipment resources resulted in insufficient information, lack of supplies, unqualified operators, unqualified supervisors, or unfilled personnel slots and made satisfactory performance of the required tasks unlikely under conditions that might reasonably be expected.

allows the driver to be excused in certain cases when other human errors have produced a system that is less controllable than it could be. Although it will be necessary to temper such error determinations with the practical consideration (cost) of reducing each type of error, the attribution of error to the driver should be seen as attribution by default rather than as a reasoned conclusion. It is true that drivers must work within an imperfect system, but it is not reasonable to punish drivers for not being perfect.

DRIVER REACTIONS TO INTERNAL STIMULI FROM FATIGUE

The driver's reaction to external stimuli via vision is discussed in a later section. The reaction to internal conditions, usually called *fatigue* or *stress*, is obviously related to interactions with the external world, though the direct effect is not observable.

The scientific literature describing fatigue and performance has not produced clear-cut terminology or methods of measuring the several phenomena commonly referred to as *fatigue*. Neither are there measures of driver performance that are widely accepted as indicative of good or poor driving ability. Without measures of performance or definitions of fatigue, it is not surprising that there are no established indicators of driver fatigue based on driver performance. The situation is complicated by the fact that both the types of operations in which drivers perform and the conditions under which they drive are so varied that drivers as a group have little in common.

Considerable ingenuity has gone into the search for objective indicators of fatigue or alertness since Musico (1921), but there is a serious lack of basic data on which to build. Olsen and Post (1978) reviewed much of the literature on this topic with regard to proposed changes in the maximum allowable duration of driving for commercial drivers. Until 1957, there was no body of literature on this subject, and the articles appearing since then either have not investigated the driving fatigue problem directly or have been piecemeal studies because small budgets required gross simplifications.

The Bureau of Motor Carrier Safety contracted for a series of studies (Harris & Mackie, 1972; Mackie & Miller, 1978), which have attempted to fill some of this gap (see also: Mackie, O'Hanlon, & McCauley, 1974). However, these reports alone cannot make up for the huge lack of knowledge about fatigue and performance in the diverse industry that employs the commercial driver.

Fatigue is a broad concept, which must be regarded as a series of distinct conditions or states that can produce undesirable results. Just as it does not make sense to talk of curing "cancer," a term that refers to perhaps 300 different diseases, it is not helpful to discuss fatigue and hours of service when at least half a dozen manifestations of temporarily reduced efficiency can be observed among drivers. If acceptable limits were devised for driving distance or time under the best conditions, the same limits would be intolerable under the worst conditions. No magic number can be determined to fit all conditions—limits must be considered guidelines in a practical sense so that they will fit human and economic realities. Of course, a limit is not meant to be a norm, though it often turns into just that under economic pressures.

The basic needs of the system are essentially productivity versus safety. Productivity can be quantified, but safety cannot be measured in accidents because of their relative rarity for any one individual and because of problems of definition. Purely monetary cost data fail to get at the real causes of accidents, and though accident likelihood may increase after some number of hours of operation, thousands of individuals routinely drive long hours without serious mishap.

There is obviously a relationship between the degree of fatigue and driving performance, but fall-asleep accidents are not uncommon during the first or second hour of driving. In fact, McFarland and Moseley (1954) stated that 60% of the "fatigue" accidents they studied occurred in the first four hours of driving. In contrast, tank crews were evaluated in a 48-hour simulation of combat, and it was concluded that their performance was not significantly reduced at the end of the 48 hours; the occasional 48-hour tour of service was therefore considered feasible (Ainsworth & Bishop, 1972).

While fatigue eventually progresses to the point at which an individual cannot perform in a manner acceptable for safe driving (Olsen, 1970), both *fatigue* and *safe driving* lack straightforward operational definitions. The problem is one of predicting at what point in a period of continuous performance the likelihood of driver errors or omissions will increase the likelihood of an accident beyond an acceptable level.

One of the major research limitations is that no formal study can require drivers to perform in actual situations for periods beyond those legally allowed. The fact that some truck operations now seem routinely to exceed legal limits (see Wyckoff, 1979) does not help the researchers much in obtaining useful data. The alternative to studying actual but illegal operations is to study unrealistic approximations to actual conditions on closed tracks or in simulations.

Defining Fatigue

The term *fatigue* has come to mean anything from a reduced work output to physiological incapacity to continue. Fatigue is generally regarded as an undesirable by-product of physical or mental activity. Two distinct forms of fatigue, acute and chronic, are recognized medically. A group of researchers, represented by Snook and Irvine (1969), has considered fatigue as it is related to activation level (Duffy, 1957). In this case, there are also two kinds of fatigue: exhaustive fatigue and a form characterized by boredom. Fatigue has also been represented as a purely subjective condition of the individual (Bartley, 1965), which is manifested in task aversion, feelings of inadequacy, and feelings of futility. This type of fatigue, if it can be shown to correlate with reduced efficiency and performance or reduced safety, is of interest as a possible mechanism for inducing the driver to voluntarily discontinue driving when that is advisable.

One notable weakness in many studies (e.g., Harris & Mackie, 1972) is the lack of explicit definitions of *fatigue*. Nine conditions seem distinct enough to merit individual consideration, even though there are overlaps in some cases. Their rates of occurrence, their sources or correlates, their effects, and their cures differ in significant ways that cannot be lumped together in a thorough discussion of the broad topic of fatigue and performance.

1. *Acute fatigue* ("tiredness")—the generalized loss of physical and mental efficiency that occurs after the passage of time. Acute fatigue is relieved by routine sleep, usually approximately 7 hours in duration.

2. *Chronic fatigue*—a pathological state from any cause, physical or emotional. The condition is not relieved by routine wake–sleep cycles and usually requires clinical intervention.

3. *Accumulated fatigue* ("weariness")—an intermediate state between acute and chronic fatigue, in which rest is temporarily not of sufficient quality or duration to relieve acute fatigue fully.

4. *Exhaustive fatigue* ("muscular fatigue" or "exhaustion")—the state of muscular or mental discomfort that accompanies extended periods of physical exertion. Exhaustion may be fully or only partially relieved by a single normal sleep cycle.

5. *Boredom* (or "monotony")—the loss of motivation or concern about continuing a routine response. Boredom is characterized by low demand, low novelty, and low information-flow rates.

6. *Loss of alertness* ("sleepiness")—the tendency or strong desire to

fall asleep. In this condition, stimuli that normally evoke a response tend to be ignored or responded to in a slower or less complete way. Sleepiness probably occurs in cycles of a few minutes to about 90 minutes in duration and may occur in any part of the normal wake–sleep cycle.

7. *Uncontrollable sleepiness* ("narcolepsy")—a condition in which there is little or none of the usual voluntary control over sleepiness. This condition makes it abnormally difficult for the individual to remain awake or alert, even when rested and highly motivated.

8. *Hypnoticlike states* ("trancelike state")—a driver may become less responsive to usual stimuli without experiencing the typical sensations of sleepiness and without eye closures. While this state may be called a trance or hypnosis by some writers, the hypnotic state is not distinguishable from waking by any known physiological measures. This state is characterized by almost automatic performance of routine tasks and disregard for other less routine tasks. Trancelike states are probably dependent on monotony, as is sleepiness, but there are few other similarities to sleep. It is in this state that the hallucinations reported so regularly by long distance drivers probably occur (Olsen, 1970).

9. *Subjective fatigue*—the driver's assessment of willingness or capacity to continue is partly a matter of habit and drive and partly a physiological and psychological limit. However, subjective fatigue is not necessarily a reliable indicator of ability to continue satisfactory operation.

Of most direct concern are the conditions of boredom and sleepiness, which depend on many transient and personal variables, such as road and traffic conditions, weather, vehicle type and condition, motivation, time pressure, food and drug intake, and personal habits and attitudes. It is likely that exhaustion is a rare occurrence, but physical activity, either before or during driving, may be helpful or detrimental to driving efficiency, depending on its extent and its scheduling.

For solo drivers, the CB radio allows contact with the outside world, which seems to be beneficial. It is also possible to make further distinctions, as McBain (1970) does, between monotony and boredom, according to which *monotony* is the stimulus situation experienced by the individual, while *boredom* refers to the individual's reaction to the situation.

Fagerstrom and Lisper (1978) reviewed the recent work on sleepiness among drivers. Sleepiness seems to have a normal distribution in the population of adults. Narcolepsy is probably caused by a neurological defect (Roberts, 1973) and is the most extreme type of involuntary sleepiness. Hypersomnia is a condition of the "sleepy normal" driver (Guilleminault, Phillips, & Dement, 1975) along a continuum from very alert to pathologically sleepy.

It is not unusual to find individuals who have problems staying awake in any common monotonous situation like driving. Fagerstrom and Lisper (1978) suggested that this propensity may warrant testing during the license application process. Testing and treatment may eventually be feasible for the screening of commercial drivers. Roberts (1973) clearly feels that such testing should be a part of the rehabilitation effort aimed at drivers who have had accidents of several types.

Case, Hulbert, and Mellinger (1970) confirmed that sleepiness is a widespread problem in drivers, and they described a few of the gadgets, drugs, and other approaches intended to help drivers stay awake. Some of these, especially drugs, may be useful in specific types of conditions, although the potential for abuse is high.

Many of the problems of fatigue are just now being investigated in rigorous ways. For example, Wertheim (1978) has strong evidence that "highway hypnosis" follows a predictable pattern and that eye movement patterns can easily be modified to reduce the occurrence of this trancelike state. It will be some time before this becomes common knowledge even if the method proves reliable.

On the subject of subjective fatigue assessments, McFarland and Moseley (1954) stated, "The driver tends to think he is doing better work, but actually his skill is getting poorer and poorer." In contrast, Cofer and Appley (1964) stated that generally fatigue is felt "long before" any decrement in performance is noted. To some extent, this is the crux of the whole debate over hours of service: drivers may tend to feel that their performance is acceptable (if not improved) after extended driving, and even if it could be demonstrated statistically or by some other scientifically sound approach that accidents were much more likely after some specific period, individual drivers would tend not to believe it and would attempt to maximize income or convenience by driving until they *felt* tired. Whether or not it is possible to ensure that an individual will take effective action in response to signs of subjective fatigue has not been determined.

PHYSIOLOGICAL CORRELATES OF FATIGUE

Researchers have been looking for measurable changes in drivers' physiology that can be used as reliable indices of fatigue. In part, they have used research on exhaustive fatigue to find guideposts. Driving seems to bring about other types of fatigue, however, some of which are more related to attitude and alertness than to the expenditure of calories.

One early study of driver physiology was performed by Jones, Flinn, and Hammond (1941) for the U.S. Public Health Service. A total of 889 truck drivers were given a battery of physiological tests. In summarizing the findings, Jones *et al*. concluded that an increased white blood cell count, increased blood pressure, and decreased heart rate tended to occur in drivers as the hours of driving increased. However, no effort was made to define these relationships quantitatively or to relate them to impaired driving performance, and none of the observed differences were subjected to statistical tests.

Burns, Baker, Simonson, and Keiper (1966) briefly reported the results of an exploratory study of EKG changes as a function of driving time and critical road situations. While they reported some effects, they gave no statistical analyses or conclusions.

Among the many attempts to find physiological correlates of fatigue are those of Dureman and Boden (1972), Lisper, Laurell, and Stening (1973), O'Hanlon (1971), and Riemersma, Sanders, Wildervanck, and Gaillard (1976), all of whom found evidence that heart rate tends to decrease with time in simulator and open-road tasks. This finding lends support to the findings of Jones *et al*. (1941) and Riemersma, Biesta, and Wildervanck (1977), who did not statistically evaluate their data. However, note that Riemersma *et al*. (1976) attributed this result to abnormally good performance at first, followed by normalization. Also, Lisper *et al*. (1973) found significant individual differences between subjects as a function of driving experience: inexperienced drivers did not show as large a decrease in heart rate; and Riemersma *et al*. (1977) discovered differential effects due to type of road and drivers' expectancy regarding the road ahead. Duggar, Epstein, Kanter, Weene, and Fox (1965), on the other hand, found no significant effects in a simulator or on the open road. Their finding agrees with the Yajima, Ikeda, Oshima, and Sugi (1976) closed-track and open-road study, for which no statistical analysis was reported. Thus, while the research does not agree on the relationship between heart rate and the amount of time on the task, there is good evidence that other factors also interact in the relationship, whatever it is.

Riemersma *et al*. (1976, 1977) found some evidence that heart rate variability may increase, and O'Hanlon (1972) reported similar findings, but he did not evaluate the data for statistical significance. Thus, this index may prove useful but requires further study.

With regard to the galvanic skin response (GSR), the findings of

Dureman and Boden (1972), Duggar *et al.* (1965), and Sussman and Morris (1970) agree that the amount of time on the task has no significant effects. The only contradictory evidence comes from Yajima *et al.* (1976), but they included no statistical support for their findings. It seems safe to conclude that GSR is not a useful measure.

Lisper *et al.* (1973) found no effects on respiration rate in an open-road task, but Yajima *et al.* (1976) found a 30–40% decrease in rate and volume, although the statistical or theoretical significance of this result was not assessed. Dureman and Boden (1972) obtained a significant decrease for subjects in one situation, but not for those in another situation involving electric shocks. Thus, no overall conclusion may be drawn.

Jones *et al.* (1941) reported an increase in blood pressure for their pre- and posttest design, but Yajima *et al.* (1976) found a decrease. Since neither study performed a statistical analysis, the best conclusion to draw is that additional research is required. The same conclusion must still be drawn with regard to the electroencephalogram (EEG) and the evoked cortical potentials (ECP), which will be discussed briefly in a later section.

Research on behavioral correlates of driver fatigue also is scanty. It is difficult to find studies that allow comparisons and generalizations, and even when such comparisons are possible, the findings are negative or inconclusive. Furthermore, it is generally unclear what relationship these measures have to driving performance. The most promising research seems to be that of Kaluger and Smith (1970), whose data on eye-movement patterns have the greatest face validity. However, this report also suffers from inadequate statistical reporting. Rackoff and Rockwell's (1975) work provides additional evidence of the utility of Kaluger and Smith's (1970) approach, indicating that eye-movement patterns may prove to be a sensitive and reliable behavioral measure. However, rather elaborate instrumentation and analysis techniques are required.

A great deal of research remains to be done on the general topic of fatigue. Of all the major performance variables that have been investigated, only steering error and direct driving-skill testing have shown any obvious value, and even these have not been explored more fully since the work of Herbert and Jaynes in 1964. In this regard, it has been suggested that a closed route containing spaced pylons, soft "pop-up" obstacles, "surprise" signals requiring braking, and similar features would provide a means of testing alertness in terms of specific skills before and after a fatigue-producing open-road drive. At least, such measures have face validity. This concept was suggested by Olsen,

Wright, Jackson, and Herendeen (1969) in a study of driver licensing and has recently been implemented (independently) by the Essex Corporation for advanced driver-training studies (Bathurst, 1979).

INFLUENCING DRIVER PERFORMANCE

The need continues for studies of performance that do not assume the presence or absence of fatigue but that concentrate on driver performance and information-processing capacities. Increased knowledge of the effects and symptoms of fatigue might be useful for individual drivers. The content of that knowledge and the methods of imparting it have not been thoroughly investigated. Rather than attempt to impose rigid rules from without, it seems more promising to aid control from within, namely, through driver judgment. It is also possible that selection tools, such as field-dependence measures (Witkin, Dyk, Faterson, Goodenough, & Karp, 1962; Loo, 1978) or sleepiness as a personality factor, might be used by employers in selecting drivers for particular kinds of driving.

Potential aids to drivers' judgment or monitors of performance could be devised to give real-time assessments of the individual's capacity to continue. While added gadgets in the vehicle may be resisted by drivers, the possible usefulness of such devices as voice-quality stress measures (Dektor, 1979) needs to be explored before this approach is summarily rejected.

A further area of potential aid is the modification of the environment to enhance driver performance. Some roadway factors may lull a driver to sleep, while others may add unreasonably to physical or mental impairment. Concepts such as atmospheric ion generation, radio alerting or CB augmentation, or on-road alerting messages have yet to be explored systematically. There appear to be many unevaluated potential ways to enhance driver safety performance, particularly since hours-of-service limitations have not been shown conclusively to be effective or enforceable (Hagen, 1977; U.S. Department of Transportation, 1979a). The nighttime visual environment, to be discussed next, has obvious relevance to alertness and the driver's ability to continue.

DRIVER REACTIONS TO EXTERNAL STIMULI IN THE VISUAL ENVIRONMENT

The previous discussion was intended to illustrate the complex and highly variable population of information processors (drivers) our system is concerned with, and some of the current areas of concern. The immediate environment of the vehicle operator is perhaps the part of the system that is easiest to optimize. The mass of data gathered from early studies in preparation for space travel (Webb, 1964), the advent of high-performance aircraft, and other military needs (Parker & West, 1973) have made it possible to eliminate many of the sources of error, confusion, and distraction that are still typically found in automobiles. Complex models of the driver's visual needs (Bhise, Farber, Saunby, Troell, Walunes, & Bernstein, 1977) have not eliminated "opera windows," which produce large blind spots for the driver. Tinted glass, which is used to reduce the load on air conditioning (by only 2% while a light-colored roof could produce a 14% savings), is widely used in cars despite its negative implications for vision under poor weather conditions or for the needs of older drivers. Improvements in auto design based on human factors are largely the result of the leadership of foreign manufacturers, rather than those in the United States, whose aerospace leaders originated the concept and gathered many of the data.

Not all improvements can be discovered by analytical means, however, and empirical tests will be essential for many improvements. For example, the logic of raising the brake light signal so that following drivers can see it in traffic is inescapable. However, the finding that one brake light signal in the center of the vehicle, just under the rear window is better than two lights is not obvious, though the high-mounted light has been shown to reduce rear-end accidents by 50% for a $5 investment (Henderson, 1980). In fact, the reason for this may be subtle: there is growing evidence that the human visual system is actually two quite separate systems. Leibowitz and Owens (1977) have suggested that the "focal" visual system (high-resolution vision, restricted to the central $2°$) and the "ambient" visual system (peripheral vision, most concerned with location, motion, and locomotion) can interact to produce unusual or dangerous results. The example these authors discussed is night driving: drivers continue to receive certain guidance cues at night from ambient vision, but many focal cues, which are used in hazard detection, are lost. Drivers, therefore, tend to drive faster than is safe. The two systems have different characteristics (Leibowitz, Rodemar, Shupert, & Dichgans, 1979), different pathways, different destinations in the brain, and different degrees of conscious awareness. The potential for the practical application of a more complete understanding of this topic is certainly high.

One of the fascinating aspects of the two visual systems is that the ambient system may operate without conscious awareness. Leibowitz and Dichgans (1977) found "blind" persons who could respond to visual inputs of which they denied being aware. Johansson (1977a,b) produced simple vertical stimuli that induced a feeling of locomotion that, when viewed with ambient vision, cannot be canceled by any degree of intellectual knowledge of the situation. When viewed with focal vision, the effect cannot be produced. There is evidence from speech perception (Forster & Govier, 1978) and from studies of subliminal perception, stabilized retinal images, binocular rivalry, and backward masking (see Shevrin & Dickman, 1980) that the definition of perception must be expanded to include all reactions to stimuli: behavioral, cognitive, or attitudinal; conscious, subconscious, unconscious, or preconscious.

THE NIGHTTIME VISUAL ENVIRONMENT

The exterior environment influencing the driver is largely the visual aspect of the roadway and its surrounding areas. Other sensations are occasionally relevant—for example, in skid control (Olsen, 1978)—but what the driver sees largely determines the response. The visual environment must be sufficiently rich and unambiguous that the expected range of drivers will be able to function, under the range of conditions which might be encountered, with reasonable chance of an acceptable outcome. The limiting conditions are generally low light levels, driver characteristics that are well below average, and precipitation or other conditions that reduce visibility.

Quantifying such entities is a complex undertaking, especially when they are complicated by glare, uncorrected vision, alcohol and drug use, the degrees of the driver's familiarity with the roadway, and so on.

The economic realities dictate that only small investments can be made in the improvement of rural roads. Low-volume rural roads— those carrying 400 vehicles per day or fewer—provide indispensable rural accessibility. About 8% of the total vehicle miles in the United States are traveled on these roads, although they constitute two-thirds of the available highway mileage (Glennon, 1979). Their accident rates are about 70% higher than those for all roads combined. The low probability of two vehicles' colliding when volumes are low is partly offset by the tendency of drivers to drive as though they will never meet another vehicle. Higher standards for low-volume roads would quickly increase the cost of maintaining them, and the balance between higher costs and higher safety is difficult to determine. Low-cost improvements are tied to how well the drivers' needs are understood and specified in objective, measurable ways.

In a summary of the cost-effectiveness of improvements made on roadways, Glennon (1979) suggested that speed signs, including warning signs on curves requiring reduced speeds, are the only roadway visibility elements that can be justified in all cases. Centerlines are added at volumes of over 300 vehicles per day, but stop signs, no-passing stripes, clear zones, wide shoulders, and guardrails are generally too expensive. Edge lines, so often mentioned by drivers as a valuable safety feature, are not even discussed because of their high cost. Sufficiency ratings of some kind are usually developed for assessing the marking of low-volume roads through site visits, since accident, volume, and hazard data do not exist. This "visit" is likely to consist of an occasional drive through the area with the observer looking for specific defects or anything unusual. The lack of general guidelines for such visits—and the fact that they are routinely made only in good, daytime weather, with no formal means for translation into nighttime or bad weather equivalents—means that any reports or recommendations for action depend on the inclination and the experience of the individual observer. There are some promising developments that may eventually make the visibility assessment more objective, but the techniques are not yet available for routine use.

What are the most critical visible features of a roadway in terms of accident prevention? The driver needs to know what is out there in order to react in the proper way at the proper time. However, these needs are relative to the level of driver performance under consideration. In their positive guidance approach, Alexander and Lunenfeld (1975) have described three such levels of driver performance: control (of direction and motion of the vehicle), guidance (deciding on the proper path and speed for the vehicle), and navigation (execution of the trip from point of origin to destination). Each level is contingent on the lower levels, so that navigation, for example, is essentially disregarded by a driver who narrowly missed a sign in the exit gore area while confused at a choice point (fails at the guidance level), and both these levels are set aside when a driver gets into a skid (fails at the control level). At the simplest level, the driver needs to know only where the lane boundaries are or where the path is in the next few hundred feet, and what obstacles are in that path or may suddenly appear there. At night in the rain, most of that information is provided by the reflection of the driver's own headlights, though other traffic and nearby land uses may present important cues. The patterns of visual energy reaching the driver depend on a multitude of variables, including the vehicle design, dirt on the windows, headlight aiming, reflectivity of objects and other surfaces, other lights, the driver's vision, and the heights of the driver's eyes and the headlights. The effects of each variable and the interactions among them defy systematic evaluation, and they do not necessarily predict the perceptual-cognitive schema that drivers might form when exposed to a complex visual environment.

DRIVER CONCEPTS AND CONSPICUITY

Each driver has a concept of the kind of driving situation being encountered. There are several conceptual levels that can be differentiated (Olsen, 1980a,b), and each level is influenced by one or more information levels. For example, the driver has a concept of *heading*, developed from visual cues, information from the vehicle, and inertial (inner-ear) cues. The driver also has a *path* concept, which involves the curves and hills that are likely to appear, and the width and other characteristics of the highway. The next higher level can be labeled the *route* concept, where the road becomes part of a network of roadways and has urban-rural and other characteristics. The highest level is the *environment* concept, which includes cultural or population characteristics that might involve hazards that are regional in character. Most persons already have these concepts, but they may be more or less inaccurate, depending on experience in driving and knowledge of the road. The highway agency is responsible for reshaping those concepts to keep the driver out of trouble. Most of this concept reshaping is done by signs and marking, but some of it is signaled by the physical structure of the surrounding world.

This world does not necessarily reveal itself at night without artificial visibility enhancement. But one does not usually add bits and pieces to a concept; rather, it is formed as a Gestalt from the context in which information is seen. That context starts with the observer's ideas or expectations and is modified when the accumulated information contradicting the original concept is great enough.

A setting with few visible features is more predictable than one with a complex visual environment. The narrow, unmarked rural roadway with foliage on all sides, on a wet, overcast, or foggy night, becomes a challenge at the most fundamental level. The cues must be conspicuous and unambiguous enough to guide even those drivers whose initial concepts of the roadway are inaccurate. Single bright spots of light from post-mounted reflectors often cannot be accurately located in space. A row of spots is clearer, but if some spots in the row are missing, the clarity of the marking is destroyed. The use of two reflectors on each post, separated vertically by a standard distance of perhaps 20 cm (8 in.), would give the driver an immediate gauge of the distance to each post, and there would be no uncertainty as to which posts were adjacent. The use of more than one color of reflectors in a row of posts is known to complicate the driver's distance-judging task, but it is still seen. Reflectors are also suspected of encouraging drivers to drive too fast in fog or rain because their high contrast provides a clear path concept, though other hazards of the route and the environment are not made obvious. In this case, a dimmer continuous cue, like center lines and edge lines, would probably be safer, though more costly because of their short lives.

While the total lack of nighttime route cues is often largely a problem of the economics of providing known visibility aids, the more complex visual environments raise the issues of human information-processing and the interpretation of visual cues. In a complex scene, the relevant cues for maintaining performance must be conspicuous. Conspicuity or conspicuousness, is a concept that is generally understood, but it is seldom possible to assign a conspicuity rating or value to an object until its setting is known. Even when information is ignored or bypassed without conscious recognition, there is a screening process by which it is classified as unimportant. Conspicuity is determined largely by the luminance contrast of the object with its immediate environment (see also Forbes, 1980). In peripheral vision, motion is likely to make an object conspicuous, though the preconscious nature of such ambient perception has already been mentioned.

The biases created by a goal-oriented behavior such as driving, however, may change the order of the conspicuity ratings of various cues considerably. Thus, the provision of visual information sources on the roadway must be concerned not only with describing the situation ahead but also with the driver's expectation of what will be there, the relative conspicuity of the visible objects, and the range of the interpretations that various road users might make of the information available. This kind of problem demands a thorough understanding of complex processing, especially since it is economically impractical to use obvious "solutions."

MODELING DRIVER INFORMATION PROCESSING

In order to provide a framework for pulling various facts, concepts, and considerations together, researchers like to build conceptual models of problem areas. A model can be highly complex and mathematical, or it may be merely a means of ensuring that all of the most important elements of a situation will be kept in mind. The EIDAC (pronounced "eye-dak") driver information processing model to be discussed here is of the simpler variety (but see Olsen, 1980a,b), though it may also have experimental implications for more sophisticated research.

The EIDAC model is based on earlier IDA model (Taylor, McGee,

Seguin, & Hostetter, 1972). IDA sequences are described in terms of the *information* the driver requires, the *decisions* to be made, and the *actions* to be taken. If one starts with the actions necessary in a situation, the decisions required for each act can be stated, and the information required for making the proper decisions becomes explicit.

For situations involving minimal delineation, the goals to be achieved may be elementary: ensure that the driver can stay on the roadway and can avoid the hazards that may be encountered. The information–decision–action sequence is still valuable, but it is incomplete. Two further concepts should be added. The EIDAC model thus consists of expectancy–information–decision–action–confirmation. Drivers unfamiliar with an area and those who have less than average driving ability (about half the population) require preparation not only for what to expect but also for the fact that something different is ahead. Other countries have used a simple sign [!] to convey this (Adasinsky, 1979). Many drivers need, in addition, assurance that the choice they have made is correct or is not correct. Drivers should be prepared for what they will encounter next, and they should be told immediately after (and even during) a maneuver that they are where they want to be or that they will need to take a corrective action because of a previous error. There are also common errors that only on-the-spot tutorial signing is likely to correct (Olsen & Hostetter, 1976). Where this kind of correction requires more signing or marking, the cost must be justified. The frequency of a need cannot be taken as the sole criterion for action, however. If a specific kind of error is made at some site by only a small percentage of drivers, the result can still be disastrous. "High-accident sites" are generally characterized by less than one collision per year.

However, one must also consider further cues for some of those in special minorities who require more information because of special conditions. For example, the tourist, the teenager, the elderly driver, the driver who has a blood alcohol level (BAL) of .05 (defined legally as sober), and the driver who is not accustomed to night driving—all fit this description.

In order to ensure that all that is economically feasible will be done to prevent driver visibility problems, we must think in terms of some worst-case driver or "design driver." Although the middle-aged male driver with a .08 or higher BAL probably has most of the characteristics of the worst case (at times constituting perhaps 20% of the drivers on some roads), there is a natural reluctance to "design roads for drunks." A more acceptable design driver is probably the 55-year-old male who drives less than 100 miles per month at night and a total of about 8,000 miles per year. Age is usually correlated with increased reaction times, increased decision times, reduced visual sensitivity and acuity, and a somewhat outmoded understanding of current laws and the newer signs and marking techniques.

The visual capabilities of older drivers can be simulated to some extent by the use of lenses that are tinted and frosted. The reduction of contrast, the reduced sensitivity to color and brightness changes, and the greater susceptibility to glare that result may help the observer appreciate the limitations of the older driver. Pastalan (1980) has provided some of this information in the form of slides which simulate impaired vision.

In spite of advances in instrumentation and improved retroflective marking materials, the degree to which the nighttime visual environment can be quantified is limited. For the purpose of sign design, visual acuity is assumed to be 4/6 (20/30), though a large portion of the driving public has no better than 4/8 (20/40) acuity in the daylight and much worse acuity at night (Leibowitz & Owens, 1975, 1977, 1978). Many other aspects of visual perception are judged subjectively in practice. The information processing and reaction capabilities required in driving must be representative of the design driver. Engineers, too familiar with the roadway, are not likely to appreciate these limitations.

Confirmation is probably the aspect of informing drivers that is least appreciated. Erratic maneuvers after a decision point may be due to the driver's uncertainty regarding the choice just made. If it is clearly correct, the maneuver is likely to be smooth; if it was clearly wrong, the driver will search for possible corrective actions at the next decision points. Where no information is available, the search will continue and may include attempts to read signs intended for the traffic in the opposite direction or other secondary information sources. A driver who doesn't know whether he is right or wrong is likely to behave in ways that are unpredictable to other drivers or that would be labeled "stupid."

IMPROVING THE VISUAL ENVIRONMENT

Several concepts that may improve the driver's visual environment, both for nighttime and for daytime driving, are discussed here to illustrate driver information needs. The first is the use of symbols for reducing the information-processing requirements and thus the frequency of erratic driving in complex freeway interchanges (Olsen, Trumbo, Serig, & Hostetter, 1981; Hostetter, Olsen et al., 1978). In this approach, a small "trail-blazer" sign is added to the usual destination or route signs so that, once a given symbol is understood to be associated with an intermediate destination (a new direction or highway number), the driver need only follow that symbol and can ignore other symbols or written legends temporarily. The symbols also may appear more frequently than regular signs because of their small size, they can be installed on the pavement to help in lane choice, and confirmation of route at each decision point is also made practical.

Another common source of erratic behavior on freeways is the missed exit. Drivers are commonly observed backing to an exit because the time and trouble required to go to the next exit and double back is excessive, or the driver feels that it would be difficult to find the same destination from a different approach. Given an authoritative indication of how to get back to a missed exit safely, the driver might not wish to take the risk of backing.

A vehicle design problem that complicates the driver's task unnecessarily is the lack of a concept of the "transparent vehicle." Window, body, and styling designs often prevent a driver from seeing through the vehicle ahead. The driver cannot be aware of other vehicles and other information sources or hazards ahead of the lead vehicle. While some vehicles, such as most heavy trucks, cannot be transparent, many that now are not could be. Optional rear-window treatments or tints are part of the problem, especially on recreation vehicles and vans, but the design of the windows and interior features of many vehicles ignores the potential benefits of providing more transparent vehicles in the traffic stream. Drivers would be better informed as to the actions they must take, as well as being more aware of the reasons for the behavior of others.

As a final example, the visual environment of the low-volume rural road, where the cost of visibility treatments is often hard to justify, can be improved if the concept of delineation is broadened. Drivers often make use of cues that were not intentionally provided for their use. For example, they can be both led and misled by tree lines and foliage. The signal from the foliage regarding the apparent but wrong path may be so strong that signs or markings must be highly conspicuous in order to overcome that message (Alexander & Lunenfeld, 1975).

Other, more novel approaches to low-cost visibility augmentation have yet to be exploited. The high likelihood that utility poles will be found adjacent to rural roadways suggests that they might be useful as delineators. While the poles are serious collision hazards themselves, it is seldom practical to place them elsewhere. Many drivers make use of the reflections from cables or wires strung between the poles as advance warning of oncoming traffic beyond hills or curves. Even well-weathered materials can provide several seconds of warning that the driver would not otherwise have. The wires could be treated to maximize this effect, and the poles could be used to support reflective devices. More efficient reflectors could also be designed for this purpose, and utility companies might install them at their own expense.

APPLYING ADVANCED CONCEPTS

The concepts discussed above are expanded in a report written for the Federal Highway Administration (Olsen, 1980b). There is also further discussion of a visual quality assessor (VQA), based on a photoscanner concept developed by Merritt, Newton, Sanderson, and Seltzer (1978) as the visual quality meter (VQM). The VQA is a hypothetical means of measuring the adequacy of the visual environment, by determining the visible contrasts of a specified level in terms of the transitional probabilities, P_t (e.g., see Brown, 1976), of the visual field relevant to driving. Information or complexity in a visual scene can be expressed as the probability that, in moving from one spatial cell to the next across the entire visible field, the luminance will change by some specified ratio or more. By aiming the device at the road, a scan of the field visible through the windshield could be obtained. The cell weightings, predetermined by the physical construction of the photo sensors, result in a single integrated luminance value for each cell. A scanning program then determines the contrasts between various cells. Where luminance value of a specific cell is very high, a glare source is suspected; where most luminances are low, a low adaptation level can be calculated and the remaining contrasts can be scaled (see Graham, 1965; Allen, O'Hanlon, McRuhr et al., 1977). The number of contrasts remaining above threshold but below disability glare levels (e.g., see Stoudt, Crowley, Gruber, Moraudi, Wolf, & McFarland, 1970; Institute of Transportation and Traffic Engineering (ITTE), 1968; DeBoer, 1973; Huculak, 1978) indicates the quantity of the available visual information. The quality is next assessed by a cumulative count of elements, along specific radial lines from the apex, for which the luminance is above the average for the entire scene, less the glare sources. Radial lines corresponding to center-line, lane-line, or edge-line delineation areas are given highest priority; those near the vanishing point and those from overhead and pavement areas are lowest. Sources with intensities much greater than the rest of the scene (glare sources) are programmed to cancel any signals from adjacent sensors. The engineering of such an instrument seems feasible with modern electronics and computer technology.

There has been recent progress on several other advances of potential value in assessing the visual environment. These include studies of eye movements and scan patterns, derivatives of electroencephalograms (EEG) called *visual evoked potentials* (VEP), and applications of modulation transfer functions (MTF). Much work has been done on specific types of visual search (e.g., Williams, 1966; Mourand & Rockwell, 1970; National Academy of Sciences, 1973; Gould & Carn, 1973; Lawson, Cassidy, & Ratches, 1978; Snyder, 1979; Akerman & Kinzly, 1979), but even in the military setting, where applied needs are foremost and the tasks are specific, the predictability of search patterns and visual search efficiency is not very good (Brown, 1976). A driver's visual search is largely restricted to edge lines, center lines, and possible hazards within about 200 feet (Mourant, Rockwell, & Rackoff, 1963, 1969; Gordon, 1966a; Shinar, McDowell, & Rockwell, 1977), although the vanishing point (VP) is the conceptual target or goal. Related to the VP is the focus of expansion—the point from which all streaming patterns of relative motion appear to issue. The focus is the only point that appears to be motionless in the environment of the moving observer, and it shifts with the curvature of the path (Gordon, 1966b; Allen *et al.*, 1977).

The data from eye movement studies give some insight as to where the eye is pointed, but the limited accuracy of the measures, the fact that "looking is not seeing," and the (partially) parallel information-processing and attention-switching or time-sharing decision–response systems, which integrate all the information into a single concept, make scan patterns and fixation times less than complete for predicting behavior. The possibility of field measurements of EEG is now real, and practical objective measures of perception, recognition, decision time, and other kinds of elusive data are now becoming available through the VEP.

The problems and applications of VEP were reviewed by Kinney (1977). Among other things, the degree of blur of an image can be measured, and fixation can be assured for vision tests that require it; blood alcohol may also be measurable via VEP. Even much earlier, workers (e.g., Williams, Morlock, Morlock, & Lubin, 1964) were able to distinguish, from EEG records, levels of attention, phases of sleep, correctness of decisions, moment of decision making, level of dark adaptation, eye closure, and similar things of interest to those involved in driver research. Technical advances in computer technology open many new possibilities. Besides such objective indices, subjective qualities such as expectancy, task relevance, uncertainty resolution, and level of attention seem to be signaled by VEP. Much of this work is being done abroad. In this country, this kind of research may have been discouraged because it smacks of "mind control" or other unpopular ideas. It should be obvious that the scientific and practical potential is great, though the United States has relatively few applied studies in this area (but see Rice, 1979, for clinical applications in assessing intelligence or developmental status).

The modulation transfer function (see Cornsweet, 1970, pp. 331–353, for an excellent introduction to the MTF concept) is another approach that has great potential. Spatial modulation—the change in luminous intensity patterns—can be described in terms of frequency and amplitude. Visual acuity can be expressed in cycles per degree (normal 4/4 or 20/20 acuity is 30 CPD). The MTF concept can replace central visual acuity as the vision criterion in driver qualification. Ability to perceive contrast in the periphery, as well as contrast sensitivity itself, could be assessed more easily with this versatile tool. It has been shown that two pilots who performed equally on tests of acuity had different response patterns to a range of spatial frequencies (Leibowitz, Post, & Ginsberg, 1979a). The pilot who responded less well on this MTF test had been involved in several incidents that would be characterized as related to poor target-detection ability.

There are also film or videotape techniques that have potential application to the assessment of the adequacy of nighttime visual environments. Cost makes most such techniques impractical for operating agencies, though a simple photographic technique in which the dark spots on a negative are counted and examined for patterns may have some potential (Olsen, 1980b). Until some of these potential tools are developed, we are limited to mostly subjective judgments of the adequacy of visual environments.

CONCLUSIONS AND FURTHER DIRECTIONS FOR RESEARCH

This has not been a review of the best research in the traffic safety field. Rather, it is an indication of the need for research, done in such a way that the more pressing problems in this complex area are attacked in realistic ways. Excellent studies are now being done on the effects of drugs on driving (e.g., see Donelson & Joscelyn, 1980), but little has been accomplished in reducing the incidence of drunken driving. Advances in measurements of component and operator reliability have made space flight possible, but drivers still go through red lights and auto brakes still fail without warning the ordinary driver.

The inertia seen in driver behavior patterns and in driver administrative processes is largely a problem for social psychologists rather than for engineers, teachers, or policemen. Selling safety has not been successful as a direct endeavor. A more fundamental understanding is needed of human error processes and of means for making statistical probabilites real to the individual driver, whose experience seems to reconfirm misconceptions periodically and to deny scientifically established (or, at least, statistical) truths. Drivers' behavior will continue to depend on what drivers feel, believe, and see, and on what they believe they can do that other drivers can or cannot do. Further understanding of how they obtain and use information, concepts, and odds (of accidents or of being arrested) and of how drivers perceive and process visual inputs is needed. Newer techniques, such as visual evoked potentials measured from the scalp, show promise of reducing the great variability characteristic of driving behavior, so that underlying processes can be assessed more directly. Similar techniques may produce practical measures of fatigue as well. The modulation transfer function is a technique that promises to correlate measures of visual capability with driver performance in a meaningful way for the first time. Microprocessors and computers could be used to make complex measures that have never before been practical, producing such things as a figure of merit for a night visual environment.

Each of these areas seems to require a new sophistication that may be possible only in generations that accept space flight and pocket computers as commonplace. Many traditional concepts are too simple for a freeway and computer society. We run the risk of forming a population that accepts new rules on authority, detached from personal experience or logical understanding, or that accepts 40,000 highway deaths in the United States annually as inevitable. There are potential technical and social means for reducing both risks; new technology, and the acceptance of changing methods that it will require, must achieve a certain degree of popularity first. The creation of better technology and the public acceptance of it are challenges to researchers both in human factors engineering and in psychology.

REFERENCES

Adasinsky, V. S. [Pedestrian facilities on rural roads.] *Automobelnye Dorogi*, 1979, 2 (567), 15 (in Russian).

Ainsworth, L. L., & Bishop, H. P. Effects of 48 hours of sustained field activity on tank crew performance. *Proceedings of the Annual Convention of the American Psychological Association*, 1972, 7(2), 625–626.

Akerman, A., III, & Kinzly, R. E. Predicting aircraft dectability. *Human Factors*, 1979, 21(3), 277–291.

Alexander, G. J., & Lunenfeld, H. *Positive guidance in traffic control*. Federal Highway Administration, Washington, D.C., April 1975.

Allen, R. W., O'Hanlon, J. F., McRuhr, D. T., *et al. Drivers' visibility requirements for roadway delineation*, Vol. 1. Final Report, DOT-FHWA-RD-77-165, 1977.

Andeneas, J. *Punishment and deterrence*. Ann Arbor: University of Michigan Press, 1974.

Anderson, L., Chiricos, T., & Waldo, G. Formal and informal sanctions: A comparison of deterrent effects. *Social Problems*, 1977, *25*, 103–116.

Bailey, W. & Smith, R. Punishment: Its severity and certainty. *Journal of Criminal Law, Criminology and Police Science*, 1972, *63*, 530–539.

Bartley, S. H. *Fatigue: Mechanism and management*. Springfield, Ill.: Charles C Thomas, 1965.

Bathurst, J. Personal communication, Essex Corporation, 1979.

Ben-David, G., Lewin, I., Haliva, Y., & Tel-Nir, N. The influence of personal communication on the driving behaviour of private motorists in Israel. *Accident Analysis and Prevention*, 1972, *4*, 269–301.

Bhise, V. D., Farber, E. I., Saunby, C. S., Troell, G. M., Walunes, J. B., & Bernstein, A. Modeling vision with headlights in a systems context. Ford Motor Company. SAE Paper 770238, 1977.

Boughton, C. J., & Milne, P. W. Occupant restraint in motor vehicles in Australia. *Proceedings of the 22nd Annual Conference*, American Association of Automotive Medicine, Ann Arbor, Michigan, 1978, 1–14.

Brown, B. Effects of background constraint on visual search times. *Ergonomics*, 1976, *19*, 441–449.

Burns, N. M., Baker, C. A., Simonson, E., & Keiper, C. Electrocardiogram changes in prolonged automobile driving. *Perceptual and Motor Skills*, 1966, *23*, 210.

Case, H. W., Hulbert, S., & Mellinger, R. L. Effects of fatigue on skills related to driving. Los Angeles: University of California Department of Engineering, Report 70-60, 1970.

Chiricos, T., & Waldo, G. Punishment and crime: An evaluation of some empirical evidence. *Social Problems*, 1970, *18*, 200–215.

Cofer, C. N., & Appley, M. H. *Motivation: Theory and research*. New York: Wiley, 1964.

Cornsweet, T. N. *Visual perception*. New York: Academic Press, 1970.

DeBoer, J. B. Quality criteria for the passing beam of motorcar headlights, 1973 (cited by Bhise *et al.*, 1977).

Dektor Counterintelligence and Security, Inc. Brochure on the psychological stress evaluator (PSE-1), Springfield, Va., 1979.

Donelson, A. C., & Joscelyn, K. B. Drug research methodology, Vol. 1–5. Final Report on DOT-HS-7-01530, 1980.

Duffy, E. The psychological significance of the concept of "arousal" or "activation." *Psychological Review*, 1957, *64*, 265–275.

Duggar, B. C., Epstein, E. N., Kanter, E. H., Weene, P., & Fox, B. H. Monitoring of wakefulness-sleepiness and performance around normal bedtime. Final Report, Cambridge, Mass.: Bio-Dynamics, Inc., 1965.

Dureman, E. I., & Boden, C. Fatigue in simulated car driving. *Ergonomics*, 1972, *15*, 299–308.

Endersen, C. Reell og applevd oppdagels-esrisiko—En studje av politiets trafikkovervaking. [Real and perceived risk of arrest—A study of traffic surveillance by the police.] Transportøkonomisk Institutt, Oslo, Norway, 1978.

Erickson, M., & Gibbs, J. On the perceived severity of legal penalties. *Journal of Criminal Law and Criminology*, 1979, *70*, 102–116.

Fagerstrom, K. O., & Lisper, H. O. Sleepy drivers: Analysis and therapy of seven cases. *Accident Analysis and Prevention*, 1978, *10*, 241–250.

Forbes, T. W. Practical aspects of conspicuity principles. Symposium on Conspicuity on the Highway, Transportation Research Board Committee on Visibility, St. Paul, June 1980.

Forster, P. M., & Govier, E. Discrimination without awareness? *Quarterly Journal of Experimental Psychology*, 1978, *30*, 289–295 (from abstract).

Geerken, M., & Gove, W. Deterrence. *Law and Society*, 1975, *9*, 497–513.

Glennon, J. C. Design and traffic control guidelines for low-volume rural roads. NCHRP Report 214, Transportation Research Board, Washington, D.C., 1979.

Gordon, D. A. Experimental isolation of the driver's visual input. *Highway Research Record 122*, 1966, 19–34. (a)

Gordon, D. A. Perceptual basis for vehicular guidance. *Public Roads*, 1966, *34*, 53–68. (b)

Gould, J. D., & Carn, R. Visual search, complex backgrounds, mental counters, and eye movements. *Perception and Psychophysics*, 1973, *14*, 125–132.

Graham, C. H. (Ed.). *Vision and visual perception*. New York: Wiley, 1965.

Grasmick, H. G., & Appleton, L. Legal punishment and social stigma: A comparison of two deterrence models. *Social Science Quarterly*, 1977, *58*, 15–28.

Green, R. N., & Sharp, G. S. Seat belt legislation. *Proceedings of the 23rd Annual Conference*, American Association for Automotive Medicine, Louisville, Ky., 1979, 18–27.

Guilleminault, C., Phillips, R., & Dement, W. C. A syndrome of hypersomnia with automatic behavior. *Electroencephalography and Clinical Neurophyiology*, 1975, *38*, 403–413. (Cited by Fagerstrom & Lisper, 1978.)

Hagen, R. E. Effectiveness of license suspension or revocation for drivers convicted of multiple driving under the influence offenses. *Report No. CAL-DMV-RSS-77-59*. Department of Motor Vehicles, Sacramento, Calif., Sept. 1977.

Haight, F. A., Joksch, H., O'Day, J., Waller, P., Stutts, J., & Reinfurt, D. Review of method for studying pre-crash factors. *Final Report*, Contract DOT-HS-4-00897, Oct. 1976 (DOT-HS-802054).

Harris, W., & Mackie, R. R. A study of the relationships among fatigue, hours of service, and safety of operations of truck and bus drivers. Goleta, Calif.: *Report No. BMCS-RD-71-2*, Human Factors Research, Inc., 1972.

Hauer, E., & Cooper, P. J. Effectiveness of selective enforcement in reducing accidents in metropliltan Toronto. *Transportation Research Record 643*, 1977, 18–22.

Henderson, R. L. NHTSA news release 45-80, U.S. Department of Transportation, Office of Driver and Pedestrian Research, Washington, D.C., May 21, 1980.

Herbert, M. J., & Jaynes, W. E. Performance decrement in vehicle driving. *Journal of Engineering Psychology*, 1964, *3*, 1–8.

Hostetter, R. S., Olsen, R. A., et al.. Color and shape coding for freeway route guidance. *Final Report* (3 vols.), Federal Highway Administration, Contract DOT-FH-11-8849, Reports FHWA-RD-78-61, 62, and 63, March 1978.

Huculak, P. The influence of glare on the detection of hazardous objects in automobile night driving. NRC/NAE Report MS-142, NRG No. 16891, Ottawa, June 1978.

Hutchinson, J. W., Cox, C. S., & Maffet, B. R. An evaluation of the effectiveness of televised, locally oriented driver re-education. *Highway Research Record 292*, 1969, 51–63.

Institute of Transportation and Traffic Engineering (ITTE). Glare and driver vision. University of California, Berkeley, *Final Report*, Contract FH-11-6549, 1968.

Johansson, G. Studies on visual perception of locomotion. *Report 206*, Department of Psychology, University of Uppsala, Sweden, 1977. (a)

Johansson, G. Visual perception of locomotion elicited and controlled by a bright spot moving in the periphery of the visual field. *Report 210*, Department of Psychology, University of Uppsala, Sweden, 1977. (b)

Jones, B. F., Flinn, R. H., & Hammond, E. C. Fatigue and hours of service of interstate truck drivers. Washington, D.C.: U.S. Public Health Service, Bulletin No. 265, 1941.

Jones, R. K., Joscelyn, K. B., Bennett, R. R., Fennessy, E. F., Komoroske, J. H., Marks, M. E., & Ruschmann, P. A. Police enforcement procedures for speeding, following too closely, and driving left of center: A review of the literature. Draft report prepared for National Highway Traffic Safety Administration Contract No. DOT-HS-8-01827. Highway Safety Research Institute, University of Michigan, Ann Arbor, 1979. (a)

Jones, R. K., Treat, J., & Joscelyn, K. A definitional study of three unsafe driving actions: Speed, following too closely, and driving left of center. Draft report prepared for National Highway Traffic Research Institute, University of Michigan, Ann Arbor, 1979. (b)

Kaluger, N. A., & Smith, G. L. Driver eye-movement patterns under conditions of prolonged driving and sleep deprivation. *Highway Research Record 336*, 1970, 92–106.

Kelsey, S. L. *A summary of findings and activities*. Department of Motor Vehicles, Sacramento, March 1979.

Kinney, J. S. Transient visually evoked potential. *Journal of the Optical Society of of America*. 1977, *67*, 1465–1474.

Lawson, W. R., Cassidy, T. W., & Ratches, J. A. A search model. U.S. Army Night Vision and Electro-Optics Lab, Ft. Belvoir, Va., June 1978.

Leibowitz, H. W., & Dichgans, J. Zwei verschiedene Sehsysteme. *Umschau in Wissenschaft und Technik*, 1977, *11*, 353–354. In Ophthalmic reports. *Review of Optometry*, 1977 (November), 16.

Leibowitz, H. W., & Owens, D. A. Anomalous myopias and the intermediate dark focus of accommodation. *Science*, 1975, *189*, 646–648.

Leibowitz, H. W., & Owens, D. A. Nighttime driving accidents and selective visual degradation. *Science*, 1977, *197*, 422–423.

Leibowitz, H. W., & Owens, D. A. New evidence for the intermediate position of relaxed accommodation. *Documenta Ophthalmologica*, 1978, *46*, 133–147.

Leibowitz, H. W., Post, R., & Ginsburg, A. The role of fine detail in visually controlled behavior. Personal communication (draft), 1979. (a)

Leibowitz, H. W., Rodemar, C. S., Shupert, H., & Duchgans, J. The independence of dynamic spatial orientation from luminance and refractive error. *Perception and Psychophysics*, 1979, *25*(2), 75–79. (b)

Lisper, H. O., Laurell, H., & Stening, G. Effects of experience of the driver on heart-rate, respiration-rate, and subsidiary reaction time in a three hour continuous driving task. *Ergonomics*, 1973, *16*, 501–506.

Lohman, L. S., Leggett, E. C., Stewart, J. R., & Campbell, B. J. Identification of unsafe driving actions and related countermeasures. Final Report, Contract DOT-HS-5-01259, National Highway Traffic Safety Administration, Dec. 1976.

Loo, R. Individual differences and the perception of traffic signs. *Human Factors*, 1978, *20*, 65–74.

Mackie, R. R., & Miller, J. C. Effects of hours of service, regularity of schedules, and cargo loading on truck and bus driver fatigue. *Final Report*, Human Factors Research, Inc., Goleta, Calif., on Contract DOT-HS-5-01142, Oct. 1978 (PB290957).

Mackie, R. R., O'Hanlon, J., McCauley, M. A study of heat, noise, and vibration in relation to driver performance and physiological status. *Final Report*, Human Factors Research, Inc., Goleta, Calif., on Contract DOT-HS-241-2-420, Dec. 1974 (PB238829).

McBain, W. N. Arousal, monotony, and accidents in line driving. *Journal of Applied Psychology*, 1970, *54*, 509–519.

McFarland, R. A., & Moseley, A. L. *Human factors in highway transport safety*. Boston: Harvard School of Public Health, 1954.

McGuire, F. L., & Kersh, R. C. *An evaluation of driver education: A study of history, philosophy, research methodology and effectiveness in the field of driver education.* Berkeley: University of California, Press, 1969.

Merritt, J. O., Newton, R. E., Sanderson, G. A., & Seltzer, M. L. Driver visibility quality: An electro-optical meter for in-vehicle measurement of modulation transfer functions. *Final Report,* Contract DOT-HS-6-D1426, Human Factors Research, Inc., April 1978.

Mourant, R. R., & Rockwell, T. H. Mapping eye-movement patterns to the visual scene in driving. An exploratory study. *Human Factors,* 1970, *12,* 81–88.

Mourant, R. R., Rockwell, T. H., & Rackoff, N. J. Drivers' eye movements and visual workload. Systems Research Group, Ohio State University, Jan. 1963.

Mourant, R. R., Rockwell, T. H., & Rackoff, N. J. Drivers' eye movements and visual workload, *Highway Research Record 292,* 1969, 1–10.

Munson, H. The right stuff may be androgyny. *Psychology Today,* 1980, *14*(1), 14–18.

Musico, B. Is a fatigue test possible? *British Journal of Psychology,* 1921, *12,* 31–46.

Näätänen, R., and Summala, H. *Road user behavior and traffic accidents.* Elsevier, N.Y., 1976.

National Academy of Sciences. *Visual search.* Symposium of Committee on Vision, Washington, D.C., 1973.

National Highway Transportation Safety Administration, *The effect of motorcycle helmet usage on head injuries, and the affect of usage laws on helmet wearing rates: A preliminary report.,* Washington, D.C., Jan. 1979.

O'Hanlon, J. R. Fatigue as estimated from concurrent performance and psychophysiological measures in prolonged driving. Goleta, Calif.: Human Factors Research, Inc., Technical Report 1712-1, 1971.

O'Hanlon, J. R. Heart rate variability. A new index of driver fatigue. Paper for Society of Automotive Engineers, SAE 720141, 1972.

Olsen, R. A. Detection of events in the visual periphery during pursuit tracing in long-term performance and in hypnotically induced fatigue. University Park, Pa.: Pennsylvania Transportation Institute, Report TTSC 7013, 1970 (also University Microfilms, University of Michigan).

Olsen, R. A. The driver as cause or victim in vehicle skidding accidents. *Accident Analysis and Prevention,* 1978, *10,* 61–67.

Olsen, R. A. Providing for visibility in night driving. Invited presentation, TRB Symposium on Conspicuity on the Highway, St. Paul, Minn. June 1980.(a)

Olsen, R. A. Quantification of the night driver's visual environment. *Final Report FHWA/ RD–80/096,* as Federal Highway Administration exchange staff member, Office of Research, U.S. Department of Transportation, Washington, D.C., Sept. 1980.(b)

Olsen, R. A., & Hostetter, R. S. Describing and shaping merging behavior of freeway drivers. *Transportation Research Record 605,* 1976, 7–13.

Olsen, R. A., & Post, D. A., Fatigue and performance. *Final Report,* American Trucking Associations, Inc., Washington, D.C., 1978.

Olsen, R. A., Wright, G. H., Jackson, T. B., & Herendeen, J. H., Jr. Preliminary design study and cost estimate for a model license testing facility for Pennsylvania motor vehicle operators. *Final Report* (TTSC 6906), March 1969.

Olsen, R. A., Helmsworth, M., Sweeney, D. G., & Crowley, K. W. Perceptions of enforcement in unsafe driving acts and driving after drinking. *Final Report* to Market Facts, Inc., under NHSA Contract, Washington, D.C., May 15, 1980.

Olsen, R. A., Haight, F. A., & Henszey, B. N. A survey of behavior, enforcement, and education relating to vehicle-pedestrian interaction in the United States. *Proceedings of the Eighth International Conference of the International Association for Accident and Traffic Medicine (IAATM),* Aarhus, Denmark, June 10–13, 1980, 50–63.

Olsen, R. A., Trumbo, D., Serig, D. I., & Hostetter, R. S. Selecting neutral symbols for temporarily assigned coding. Unpublished manuscript, 1981.

Parker, J. F., Jr., & West, V. R. (Eds.). *Bioastronautics data book*, 2nd ed. NASA SP-3006, National Aeronautics and Space Administration, Washington, D.C., 1973.

Pastalan, L. Getting out of the lab—The challenge of application. Presentation to Symposium "Aging and Human Visual Function," NAS Committee on Vision, Washington, D.C., April 1, 1980.

Rackoff, N. J., & Rockwell, T. H. Driver search and scan patterns in night driving. In "Driver Visual Needs in Night Driving." Washington, D.C., Transportation Research Board, *Special Report 156*, 1975, 53–63.

Rice, B. Brave new world of intelligence testing. *Psychology Today*, 1979, *13*(4), 27–41.

Riemersma, J. B. J., Sanders, A. F., Wildervanck, C., & Gaillard, A. W. Performance decrement during prolonged night driving. Institute for Perception, Report No. IZF 1976–14, 1976. Published in Proceedings of NATO Symposium on Vigilance II.

Riemersma, J. B. J., Biesta, P. W., & Wildervanck, C. Fatigue and stress due to prolonged driving and changing task demands. Warren, Mich.: Society of Automotive Engineers, Paper 770134, 1977.

Roberts, H. J. The role of pathologic drowsiness in traffic accidents: epidemiologic study. *Tufts Medical Alumni Bulletin*, 1973, *32*, 1–11, (cited by Fagerstrom & Lisper, 1973.)

Ross, H. L. Law, science, and accidents: The British Road Safety Act of 1967. *Journal of Legal Studies*, 1973, *2*, 1–78.

Shevrin, H., & Dickman, S. The psychological unconscious. *American Psychologist*, 1980, *35*, 421–434.

Shinar, D. *Psychology on the road*. New York: Wiley, 1978.

Shinar, D., McDowell, E. D., & Rockwell, T. H. Eye movements in curve negotiations. *Human Factors*, 1977, *19*, 63–71.

Snook, S. H., & Irvine, C. H. Psycho-physiological studies of physiological fatigue criteria. *Human Factors*, 1969, *11*, 291–300.

Snyder, H. L. (Ed.). Visual search and eye movements. Special Issue of *Human Factors*, 1979, *21*, 257–383.

Stewart, J. R., & Campbell, B. T. The statistical association between past and future accidents and violations. Highway Safety Research Center, University of North Carolina, Chapel Hill, 1972.

Stoudt, H. W., Crowley, T. J., Gruber, B, Moraudi, A. J., Wolf, E., & McFarland, R. A. Glare and driver vision. Harvard University, Final Report, Contract FH-11-6904, Jan. 1970.

Summers, L. G., & Harris, D. H. The general deterrence of driving while intoxicated. *Final report*, Vol. 1. Contract DOT-HS-6-01456, National Traffic Safety Administration, Jan. 1978.

Sussman, E. D., & Morris, D. F. An investigation of factors affecting driver alertness. Buffalo, N.Y.: Cornell Aeronautical Laboratory, Technical Report VJ-2849-B-1, 1970.

Svenson, O. Risks of road transportation in a psychological perspective. *Accident Analysis and Prevention*, 1978, *10*, 267–280.

Taylor, J. I., McGee, H. W., Seguin, E. L., & Hostetter, R. S. Roadway delineation systems. NCHRP Report 130, Highway Research Board, Washington, D.C., 1972.

Teevan, J. J. Subjective perception of deterrence. *Journal of Research in Crime and Deliquency*, 1976, *13*, 155–164.

Teknekron. 1978 Survey of public perceptions on highway safety. *Final Report*, Contract No. DOT-HS-6-01424, Teknekron Research, Inc., McLean, Va., 1978.

Teknekron. 1979 Survey of public perceptions on highway safety. *Final Report*, Contract No. DOT-HS-6-01424. Teknekron Research, Inc., McLean, Va., 1979.

Treat, J. R., Tumbus, N. S., McDonald, S. T., Shinar, D., Hume, R. D., Mayer, R. E., Stansifer, R. L., & Castellan, N. J. Tri-level study of the causes of traffic accidents. *Final Report*, Contract No. DOT-HS-034-3-535, National Highway Traffic Safety Administration, 1977.

Uniform Vehicle Code Annotated (UVCA). *Uniform vehicle code: Rules of the road with statutory annotations*. National Committee on Uniform Traffic Laws and Ordinances, Washington, D.C., 1967 (with supplement).

U.S. Department of Transportation. Proposed plan for highway safety research, development and demonstration (Section 403 of Title 23, USC) fiscal years 1980-1984. National Highway Traffic Safety Administration, Washington, D.C., DOT-HS-804-031, March 30, 1979. (b)

U.S. Department of Transportation and American Association of Motor Vehicle Administrators. Involvement of suspended/revoked drivers in traffic crashes. Washington, D.C., 1979. (a)

Webb, P. (Ed.). *Bioastronautics data book*. NASA SP-3006, National Aeronautics and Space Administration, Washington, D.C., 1964.

Weiers, R. M. An experimental study of the defensive driving course. *Transportation Research Record 629*, 1977, 56-62.

Wertheim, A. H. Explaining highway hypnosis: Experimental evidence for the role of eye movements. *Accident Analysis and Prevention*, 1978, *10*, 111-130.

Williams, H. L., Morlock, H. C., Morlock, J. V., & Lubin, A. Auditory evoked responses and the EEG stages of sleep. *Annals of the New York Academy of Science*, 1964, *112*(1), 172-179.

Williams, L. C. Target conspicuity and visual search. *Human Factors*, 1966, *8*, 80-92.

Witkin, H. A., Dyk, R. B., Faterson, H. G., Goodenough, D. R., & Karp, S. A. *Psychological differentiation: Studies of development*. New York: Wiley, 1962.

Wyckoff, D. D. *Truck drivers in America*. Lexington, Mass. Lexington Books, 1979.

Yajima, K., Ikeda, K., Oshima, M., & Sugi, T. Fatigue in automobile drivers due to long time driving. Warren, Mich.: Society of Automotive Engineers, Paper 760050, 1976.

Yankelovich, Skelly & White, Inc. A summary report of drivers attitudes toward restraints for greater safety in the operation of an automobile. Motor Vehicle Manufacturers Association, Detroit, 1976.

Zimring, F., & Hawkins, G. The legal threat as an instrument of social change. *Journal of Social Issues*, 1971, *27*, 33-38.

6

The Social Cost of Urban Transportation

LYNN G. LLEWELLYN

INTRODUCTION

Not far from Union Station, and the multimillion dollar Visitor Center erected in celebration of the Bicentennial, sits an old but stately building—an anachronism now largely unused and visibly isolated from more modern structures that testify to the rapid redevelopment of Northeast Washington, D.C. At its peak in early 1976, Saint Joseph's nursing home sheltered 168 elderly poor, most of whom were over 85 years of age; another 350 men and women were on the waiting list maintained by the Little Sisters of the Poor. Unfortunately, two years earlier, the District of Columbia government had begun construction on a six-lane highway overpass only a few feet from the main entrance of the home. In part, the rationale for building the overpass was to improve the access to the Visitor Center and to ease the traffic congestion that would surely accompany the invasion of tourists for the Bicentennial festivities.

Although a public hearing was held before construction commenced, no one bothered to inform the sisters. Only later were they told about a preliminary environmental assessment, which indicated that the overpass was deemed to have "no adverse effects." As it turned out,

LYNN G. LLEWELLYN • Division of Program Plans, U.S. Fish and Wildlife Service, Department of the Interior, Washington, D.C. 20240.

nothing could have been farther from the truth. The first of many misfortunes to befall St. Joseph's was the displacement and relocation of all the local merchants, on whom the residents depended for basic necessities. Later, when heavy equipment moved into the area to renovate a nearby underpass, the patients were beset with dust, fumes, vibration, and ear-splitting noise. Over a period of time, cracks started to appear in the building, and rats fleeing the nearby construction site invaded the home. A water main burst after being struck by a bulldozer, leaving St. Joseph's without water for several days; a similar accident left the building temporarily without lights on the first and second floors. Robberies and fire setting increased markedly in the vicinity. The overpass, which was designed to accommodate an estimated traffic flow of 2,200 vehicles per hour, was erected only 10 feet from the infirmary window; and patients who would not go outside the building for fear of being robbed also became fearful that cars would careen off the overpass and into their rooms.

Noise was especially bad. Normal conversations were frequently impossible, hindering patient care. During peak construction periods, staff reports such as the following were not uncommon:

> Last week... some of the sisters were with a resident who was in his last hours. The priest was there and began offering the prayers of the dying. The sisters were on the opposite side of the bed but we couldn't answer the prayers because the noise... was too much. We were trying to comfort the dying but we couldn't even say our prayers.[1]

It is interesting to note that in 1976, Washington, D.C., was cited as the only major metropolitan area with a shortage of more than 750 intermediate nursing care beds for the elderly; nevertheless, once the overpass opened, the situation quickly became intolerable, and the sisters were forced to move after 105 years of continuous service to the community. Some of the elderly patients were subsequently relocated to Richmond, Virginia, and Baltimore, Maryland, and appeared to be doing reasonably well; others, forced to return to impoverished environments, were described as "desperately unhappy" at the time of writing. Ironically, the Union Station's Visitor Center, which was responsible at least indirectly for the sisters' departure, attracted few tourists during the Bicentennial and is now regarded as a monumental "white elephant." Following a well-publicized demonstration at the Visitor Center to

---

[1]The description of events that culminated in the dislocation of St. Joseph's elderly patients is based largely on informal interviews conducted with staff of the Little Sisters of the Poor in 1976 and again in 1980.

dramatize the plight of the city's homeless, a bill was introduced in early 1980 authorizing millions of dollars more to restore the Visitor Center to its former function—that of a train depot.

The highway improvement project that uprooted the Little Sisters of the Poor was small when compared with construction on a new freeway, or a rapid-rail mass transit system; nonetheless, even relatively minor actions can have far-reaching consequences. What occurred to the patients of St. Joseph's is illustrative of the way people's lives are sometimes affected by well-intentioned transportation projects. Few actions of this sort are undertaken without some harmful side effects, and these social costs are often borne by those individuals in society—minorities, the poor, the elderly, and, in some circumstances, school-age children—who are the least well equipped to cope with adversity. The present chapter represents an attempt to integrate selected findings from the research literature that exemplify some of the major adverse social impacts of public works projects, many of which were either not anticipated or simply ignored by decision makers. Indeed, despite a decade of continued strong public concern about the environment and the quality of life (Mitchell, 1979), government agencies continue to make questionable transportation decisions in light of the data that are currently available to them.

SOCIAL IMPACTS AND IMPACT ASSESSMENT

THE NATURE OF SOCIAL IMPACTS

Social impact can be defined as any real or perceived change in human interaction potential that might be attributed to the implementation of specific programs or policies, or the anticipation of such actions. Simply stated, social impacts are the effects on people—the way they live, work, play, and relate to one another—resulting from the choice of a particular course of action. Our primary concern here is the consequences of decisions governing the planning, construction, and operation of transportation facilities. Of necessity, the types of transportation projects considered here are limited to new and improved highways, airports, and rapid rail.

Social impacts can occur at any time during the life of a transportation project. For example, there are "anticipatory effects," such as land speculation, that occur when a project is still in the planning stage. Another example is the general attitude of landlords, who, when faced with the long-term prospect of losing an apartment house to right-of-way acquisition preceding road construction, refuse to make repairs requested by tenants. Sometimes, the entire character of a neighborhood may change as buildings fall into disrepair and are gradually abandoned long before the first bulldozer arrives on the scene. It matters little that the project may later be terminated for economic or political reasons; the damage has already been done. Keep in mind that highway projects frequently take a minimum of 10 years from planning to completion, and some have taken considerably longer.

Construction-related impacts are often immediate and readily discernable. The physical intrusion of heavy machinery accompanied by noise, vibration, dust, and fumes assumes great importance to citizens living near the project. Small businesses, in particular, suffer during construction; many lose substantial clientele when access is impeded by excavation work or other physical obstacles. Some businesses simply don't survive or are forced to relocate after years of service in the community (Abt Associates, 1979). More subtle but often more critical are changes in social-service delivery systems during construction. Police, fire, and emergency medical teams must sometimes cope with limited access to neighborhoods. A few seconds added to vehicle response time can spell the difference between life and death.

Finally, there are social consequences that accrue after the completion of a project, sometimes many years later. Again, several examples might be useful. Occasionally, highways and rapid rail systems become physical barriers, isolating one section of the community from another. While barriers may simply result in travel inconvenience for automobile users, it is the person who must walk who is most seriously affected: access to community facilities, safety of schoolchildren, disruption of visiting or friendship patterns—all are legitimate concerns of local residents. To cite another example, new transportation facilities may completely change the aesthetics of an area by physically dominating the surroundings, or by greatly increasing traffic congestion in once peaceful neighborhoods. Land use change—loss of open space, increased development, urban sprawl—constitutes a common but often poorly anticipated consequence of locating highway interchanges, subway terminals, and new airports (Llewellyn, Bunten, Goodman, Hare, Mach, & Swisher, 1975).

The examples just mentioned are by no means exhaustive; rather, they are meant to illustrate the range of adverse effects that may accrue from a transportation project. It can be seen that some negative impacts are short-lived and, at worst, a nuisance; others, such as noise, may potentially impair an individual's ability to learn or to cope effectively in society; still others, as in the case of the forced dislocation of certain elderly people, may precipitate grief, depression, and even early death.

The Wellsprings of Social Impact Assessment

Social impact assessment (SIA) can be described as a process used for predicting and evaluating the social consequences of policies, programs, or individual projects sufficiently early in the planning stage to prevent people from being harmed. As Wolf (1977) stated:

> Social impact assessment is a newly emerging field of interdisciplinary knowledge and application. The analytic problem... is nothing less than that of estimating and appraising the conditions of a society organized and changed by large scale applications of high technology.... Unlike the more familiar "evaluation research" which gauges the effectiveness of public programs already in operation, the task for SIA is *anticipatory* research. (p.3)

Some SIA practitioners have argued that *impacts* should be regarded as a neutral concept. In other words, impacts can be either positive or negative; hence, social impact assessment should objectively weigh good outcomes against the bad. While this is a valid criticism, as Wolf pointed out, there is the risk that the final "balance sheet" will simply be a tally of plus and minus entries; and regardless of the severity of certain impacts, the temptation will always be there to let one cancel out the other. Looking back at the misfortunes of St. Joseph's nursing home, it is difficult to see how the benefits of "improved access" to Union Station could outweigh the hardships that had to be endured by the elderly patients of the Little Sisters of the Poor. Thus, to prevent or at least to minimize the occurrence of dysfunctional consequences must be regarded as one of the primary objectives of any social impact assessment.

Two articles by Wolf (1974, 1977) provide an extensive history of social impact assessment, tracing its origins in the context of other developing fields of interest in the late 1960s and early 1970s such as social accounting, evaluation research, technology assessment, and quality of life. As Wolf (1977) also noted, however, the effects of public works and other major projects had captured the attention of social scientists years earlier. In the transportation arena, highways, in particular, first became the focus of research with the advent of the interstate highway system. As originally conceived in 1944, and later approved by law in 1956, the interstate highway system would crisscross the length and breadth of the United States, linking most major population centers. The total cost of the entire 41,000-mile system was projected as $27 billion, making it the largest public works program ever undertaken. By 1970, when the system was two-thirds completed, the cost had already soared to $40 billion. Nonetheless, despite rapidly escalating costs, many of the early studies of highway effects were little more than attempts to facilitate further construction; most could be characterized as public relations efforts designed to overcome local antagonism (Horwood, Zellner, & Ludwig, 1965).

One exception to this trend was the research of Ian McHarg (1969). His early work on the environmental and social consequences of public works projects is as fresh today as it was over a decade ago:

> In highway design, the problem is reduced to the simplest and most commonplace terms: traffic, volume, design speed, capacity.... These considerations are married to a thoroughly spurious cost–benefit formula and the consequences of this institutionalized myopia are seen in the scars upon the land and in the cities.... Give us your beautiful rivers and valleys, and we will destroy them.... Give us your cities, their historic areas and buildings, their precious parks, cohesive neighborhoods, and we will rend them.... Urban freeways cut white swaths through black neighborhoods but this is not discrimination, it matters little whether they are black or white, rich or poor— although black and poor is easier. (p. 31)

McHarg went on to describe other considerations that should be included in any decision about highway route selection, and he illustrated how these variables could be addressed in a series of commonsense map transparencies. As McHarg noted: "The best route is the one that provides the maximum social benefit at the least social cost" (p.32).

Another springboard for social impact assessment was the urban violence of the late 1960s. Interestingly, Leavitt (1970) considered poor freeway planning a causative agent in several urban disorders:

> Freeways isolate nonauto owners, as happened in the Watts district of Los Angeles, where the ghetto area was sealed off by highways. Freeways take living quarters, tightening up an already overburdened housing supply... destroying established neighborhoods.... Michigan Governor George Romney told a Senate committee shortly before his appointment as Secretary of Housing and Urban Development that freeway construction in Detroit was a major cause of that city's 1967 riot. (p. 5)

Perhaps the most critical events in the evolution of social impact assessment were the rapid growth of the environmental movement and congressional passage of the National Environmental Policy Act of 1969 (Llewellyn & Peiser, 1973). Among other things, the purpose of the NEPA was to declare a national policy that would encourage productive and enjoyable harmony between man and his environment and would promote efforts to prevent or eliminate damage to the environment and stimulate human health and welfare. When the NEPA was signed into law on January 1, 1970, social impact assessment as a unified area of interest had discovered a home, albeit by the back door.

Section 102(2)(C) of the NEPA is the most controversial feature of the act. This section, inserted specifically in the NEPA to give it some teeth, establishes the requirement of environmental impact statements

(EISs). Such statements provide the opportunity for full disclosure of all the significant effects of a proposed action, permit the communication of information about environmental impacts to concerned citizens, and improve the analysis and comparison of alternative courses of action (Blisset, 1975).

The environmental-impact-statement process served as a model for social impact assessment, but more importantly as an opening wedge to ensure that some measure of attention would be focused on the consequences of federal actions that were not narrowly defined as "environmental." While some agencies normally regarded social impacts as part of the NEPA process, others considered their inclusion a bastardization of the original intent of the act. In the Second Court of Appeals ruling on the case of *Hanly* v. *Mitchell* (1972), the issue was clarified somewhat:

> The National Environmental Policy Act contains no exhaustive list of so-called "environmental considerations," but without exceptions its aims extend beyond water and air pollution.... the Act must be construed to include protection of the quality of life for city residents. Noise, traffic, overburdened mass transportation systems, crime, congestion and even availability of drugs all affect the "urban environment." (p. 22)

In 1979, the Council on Environmental Quality published revised regulations for implementing the procedural provisions of the NEPA. The guidelines indicate that agencies must consider factors such as growth-inducing effects or anything else that might precipitate changes in land-use patterns, population density, or growth rate. Also included—regardless of whether the impacts are considered direct, indirect or cumulative—are aesthetic, historic, cultural, economic, social, and health effects. With respect to the controversial concept *human environment*, the guidelines indicate that the term includes the natural and physical environment and the relationship of people with that environment. The definition goes on to state, however, that

> this means that economic or social effects are not intended by themselves to require preparation of an environmental impact statement. When an environmental impact statement is prepared and economic or social and natural or physical environmental effects are interrelated, then the environmental impact statement will discuss all of these effects on the human environment. (Council on Environmental Quality, 1979, p.791)

In essence, the Council on Environmental Quality guidelines put increased emphasis on the importance of social effects, but only in those instances where possible environmental consequences of federal actions dictate the preparation of impact statements.

At this point, it might be useful to mention briefly two additional variations of the NEPA process recently promulgated by presidential executive order. The first of these was detailed in Circular No. A-116 (Executive Office of the President, 1978) and called for preparation of urban and community impact analyses by executive branch agencies. The purpose of the analyses is to identify the likely consequences of proposed major program and policy initiatives for cities, counties, and other communities. Among the impacts that agencies are required to consider are effects on employment, population size and composition, income, and "other" factors such as neighborhood stability, housing, quality of public services, urban sprawl, environmental quality, and cost of living. One important difference between the requirements of the circular and those of the NEPA is that urban and community impact analyses are not required on individual projects. Thus, for the construction of an airport or a highway segment, the instructions would not apply; however, should there be a resumption of the supersonic transport program in this country, a strong argument could be made for the need to prepare urban and community impact analyses.

In contrast to the previously mentioned circular, which clearly spells out "social" considerations, Executive Order 12114 is less than explicit on this issue. The order directs federal agencies involved in international activities to adopt regulations requiring abbreviated analysis of the foreign environmental impacts of their actions. According to the Environmental Law Institute (1979), the substance of the executive order includes nothing about "social or socioeconomic impacts" in contrast to the current interpretation of the NEPA.

It should be apparent by this time that regulations regarding the completion of social impact assessments—when they must be done, what types of impacts should be included, and whether or not the assessments are legally binding—are hopelessly muddled. Interviews with a cross section of the state highway and transportation departments in 1974 (Llewellyn *et al.*, 1975) suggested reluctance on the part of many officials to go beyond those items that are specifically mentioned in the NEPA guidelines drafted by the Council on Environmental Quality. Indirect evidence that such a policy was being followed by many agencies appeared in a summary volume of the Institute of Ecology's Environmental Impact Statement Project. The report concluded that information on social effects was one of the primary deficiencies in most agency environmental-impact statements (Winder & Allen, 1975).

PROCEDURAL STEPS IN SOCIAL IMPACT ASSESSMENT

Although there are no rigorous standards for how a social impact assessment should be conducted and for what should be included in a comprehensive assessment, some general guidelines have evolved, in part from the NEPA process and from the experience of practitioners. The procedural steps are outlined below (see Connor, 1978; Wolf, 1980):

Scoping. This so-called preassessment defines the limits of the assessment, determines priorities, and establishes time horizons for completion of the assessment.

Problem Identification. Policy goals and planning objectives are formulated, interested and affected publics are identified, and community needs and concerns are surveyed.

Formulation of Alternatives. Reasonable alternatives based on citizen needs and concerns are defined, and identifiable economic and environmental consequences are examined for potential social effects.

Profiling. A thorough description of the community (including any historical conflicts with agency projects) is compiled containing information on the local economy, government, education, social services, and community organization and composition.

Projecting. Based on existing trends and experiences of similar communities, estimates are made of what changes might occur with or without the project.

Assessing. Analyses are conducted (with the assistance of the public) of those things that are likely to change—for examples, forced relocation, noise levels, recreation opportunities—if different alternatives are selected.

Evaluating. In this step, each alternative and the changes that are likely to occur are compared according to how much better or worse off various affected publics are likely to be, and a preferred alternative is identified.

Mitigating. Unavoidable adverse impacts are reviewed, and procedures are identified that might minimize or offset potentially harmful consequences for various publics.

Monitoring. Actual effects are compared with predicted impacts, and to the extent possible, procedures are adjusted in cases where consequences are severe or unacceptable for affected citizens.

It should be stressed that the procedural steps in social impact assessment constitute a theoretical standard that is seldom achieved in practice. Often, agency assessments are short-circuited on the basis of political decisions, or because of time and resource (manpower and dollar) constraints. Consider "monitoring," for example. Monitoring implies that agency officials will periodically assess conditions in affected communities and make adjustments in design or operating procedures to rectify unanticipated negative impacts. Frequently, this critical step never takes place, or if it does, it is only because citizen activists take on the monitoring burden themselves. Even then, it may become necessary to take the offending agency to court—or at least to threaten a class-action suit—before any adjustments are made.

In one recent case with which the writer is familiar, a proposed section of the Washington Metropolitan Area Transit Authority (Metro) rapid rail system, if completed according to plans, would have effectively blocked passage for residents of a black neighborhood in Rockville, Maryland. To be more specific, one of the few roads leading into the community crossed over existing railroad track that was also to be used as Metro rail right-of-way; however, because the proposed above-ground alignment would have necessitated closing the road to fence off the "power" rail, the community was faced with a serious access problem and, more importantly, the prospect of becoming a physically isolated ghetto. It was only after a lengthy battle (at one time, testimony alluding to the problem appeared to have been purposely dropped from the transcript of a 1974 public hearing) that a group of irate citizens, with the assistance of local newspaper editorials and social science data, was able to force much-needed changes in location and design features. These included the construction of a pedestrian bridge over the Metro rail facility and the modification of local roads to facilitate the movement of automobile traffic in and out of the community.

Two additional court cases involving citizen monitoring of transportation impacts are worthy of a brief note. In the first case, the owner of a small bookshop sued the Metropolitan Atlanta Rapid Transit Authority on the grounds that construction on a nearby transit station had impeded customer access to her business. The plaintiff also complained that the construction noise discouraged patrons and that the sound levels exceeded those specified in the Department of Transportation's environmental impact statement, a violation of the NEPA. The case (*Noe v. Metropolitan Atlanta Rapid Transit Authority*) was dismissed by the U.S. District Court for the Northern District of Georgia. Lawyers for the Department of Transportation argued successfully that an EIS is a planning document, not a contract (Environmental Law Institute, 1980a).

The ruling in a second, similar case (*Red Line Alert* v. *Adams*) involving a dispute over the use of subway construction methods different from those specified in the EIS provides a succinct rationale for the proper interpretation of the NEPA. In this instance, the court ruled that the defendants would have to bear the burden of establishing that blasting—rather than mechanical tunneling methods, which were the basis of project approval—would fall within "the general noise parameters" specified in the EIS (Environmental Law Institute, 1980b). However, the court refused to enjoin the project as requested by a group of concerned citizens pending completion of a supplementary EIS:

> The scope of this court's review of agency decisions under NEPA is very narrow, particularly where an environmental impact statement . . . has in fact been filed. The theory of NEPA is that before an action is taken, the responsible agency must consider the impact of this action on the environment and consider practical alternatives with an eye to the minimization of adverse impact on the environment. Once the responsible agency has developed the minimum level of data, and given it fair consideration, it has satisfied the requirements of the law. . . . The court's function is only to insure that the responsible agencies have taken a "hard look" at relevant environmental factors. . . . The court cannot consider arguments addressed to the wisdom of the agency decision if the procedural requirements of NEPA have been complied with. (10 ELR 20315)

Clearly, the significance of this decision should not be overlooked. In effect, it substantially weakens the value of monitoring projects once construction is well under way.

COMMUNITY-BASED SOCIAL IMPACT ASSESSMENT

One of the interesting developments in the NEPA process is the number of communities that are turning to academic institutions or private consultants for help in preparing impact assessments to counterbalance what they consider superficial and sometimes erroneous agency assessments. Most have been carried out with very limited budgets, and results have been mixed. Ward and Suedfeld (1973) conducted a study to determine how students would react to recorded highway noise. The study was done in response to plans to extend State Route 18 through New Brunswick, New Jersey, a portion of which would come very close to the dormitories of Rutgers University. To simulate the expected traffic noise, loudspeakers were place outside the buildings and recordings were played for three days. The findings showed that noise levels (65–70 decibels during daylight hours, and 55–60 at night) had an inhibitory effect on dormitory interaction and classroom behavior. Some of the observed changes included less attention to classroom proceedings and decreased classroom participation on the part of students, and a trend toward greater dependence by instructors on lecturing and less on group discussion or soliciting student opinions. Student reaction to the noise was described as very hostile, and at times almost violent: speaker cables were severed more than once, and some students threatened to destroy the equipment if it were ever left unguarded.

Weinstein (1976) provided some additional information on the results. He stated that the findings were virtually ignored by the consulting firm hired by the New Jersey Department of Transportation to do its

impact study. In fact, the agency EIS referred to the hostility and preju-
dicial attitude of the participants in the study; hence, the simulation was
rejected as irrelevant to the decision.

Another recent example of a community-based social impact assessment is that of Friedman (1978). More than 20 years ago, the North
Carolina Department of Transportation began planning for an expressway through the city of Durham as a means of linking two interstate highways. By the mid-1960s, highway construction had already
uprooted a large and historic black community, including many
minority-owned businesses. According to Friedman, a further extension
of the expressway (following the proposed route) would go directly
through the center of another stable black community, destroying most
of the homes and displacing most of the long-term residents. Friedman's
social impact assessment, performed under the aegis of the Duke University Center for the Study of the Family and the State, was divided
into two parts. The first contained a description of the community and a
historical sketch detailing how the Crest Street community evolved. The
second section was based on interviews with 80 households, a figure
encompassing slightly over one-third of the Crest Street community.
Among the topics covered in the second portion of the statement are
residence patterns, family structure, household composition, employment and household income, transportation (largely walking), education, and attitudes toward the community.

Friedman's data indicated that the community began as a settlement
of black farmers and sharecroppers on the outskirts of Durham. Crest
Street remains a closely knit, low-income community abounding in gar-
dens, ample space for children to play, and a century-old church, which
serves as the focal point for neighborhood activity. The elderly persons
in the community are a special concern of the church groups. Almost a
third of the residents have lived there for over 50 years; and a majority of
these are over the age of 65, most residing with or very near family
members. Almost half the residents belong to three-generation families,
and an even larger number have at least one relative living in the community. Friedman found that the community kinship network was important both emotionally and economically. Working parents often left
their children to be cared for by retired relatives, who thereby provided a
service that the parents could not otherwise afford; at the same time,
caring for the children gave meaning to the lives of the elderly. Older
community residents were, in turn, cared for by younger relatives in
their own homes.

The attitudinal portion of the statement underscored the emphasis
that community residents placed on interrelationships with friends,
neighbors, and relatives. The respondents also stressed the locational

aspects of community living: proximity to schools, jobs, hospital facilities, and the church. Many were also bewildered and fearful about the pending loss of their homes: "people have no place to go." One summed up her feelings by saying, "I'd like to keep it, everybody know everybody, everybody kin, hate to see it depart... I don't own property, but I'd like to do all I could to keep it" (Friedman, 1978, p. 22).

Friedman's data were featured in a report filed in testimony before the Durham City Council. One of the conclusions argued forcefully that

> construction of the highway would require relocating many of the neighborhood's residents and destroy the functioning of its kinship ties. The dispersal of extended family members would disrupt their ability to provide important daily services to one another and harm the functioning of community-based mutual-aid networks. (Stack & Holt, 1979, p. 3)

At the time of this writing, the fate of the community had not been decided.

TWO SOCIAL COSTS: FORCED RELOCATION AND NOISE

In this section, the focus changes from social impact assessments *per se* to two prominent consequences of modern urban transportation: displacement and forced relocation, and community noise. Both of these dysfunctional effects have been repeatedly cited in some of the anecdotal material discussed thus far, and with good reason. In a recent effort to provide the Federal Highway Administration with information about the general severity of different categories of social impacts, a delphi procedure was used to obtain rankings from nine social scientists with considerable experience in the transportation field. Consensus was found to be quite high after just two iterations of the procedure. Displacement and relocation of residents and transportation noise were considered among the most critical social costs and the most deserving of agency attention (Llewellyn, Goodman, & Hare, 1981). The discussion that follows is an attempt to synthesize some of the major research findings in these two areas, with special attention devoted to effects on vulnerable population groups.

DISPLACEMENT AND FORCED RELOCATION

Loss of Community

Displacement and relocation of families and small business is becoming increasingly recognized as one of the more harmful consequences of major public-works projects. Until the early 1960s relocation research concentrated primarily on the problems associated with urban renewal. What little was known about transportation-related displacement and relocation stemmed from *ex post facto* research on highway right-of-way acquisition; much of the literature consisted of case studies of specific urban highway projects emphasizing property replacement experiences of homeowners and private businesses (e.g., Adkins & Eichmann, 1961). The bulk of these investigations concluded that displaced homeowners and businessmen were fairly treated from the standpoint of financial compensation. More often than not, the benefits of relocation were highlighted: displaced owners frequently upgraded their new residences or properties, improving not only their personal situation but also the community tax base (Llewellyn *et al.*, 1981).

One of the early investigations to recognize the psychological effects of involuntary relocation was Fried's (1963) landmark study of working-class residents of Boston's West End. However, with the exception of Kemp (1965) and Fellman (1970), few researchers in the tranportation field displayed much interest in Fried's results until the publication of *Future Shock* (Toffler, 1970). Toffler's brief discussion of "mournful movers," which underscores Fried's commentary on grief for a lost place, drew increased attention to the consequences of relocation, particularly from those outside academia. Temporarily, at least, researchers studying the displacement and relocation effects associated with freeway construction began to show greater concern about nonmonetary factors in the relocation experience. Some of the more important contributions to the literature, including Fried's investigation, are discussed in the remainder of this section.

Fried's (1963) study was based on the hypothesis that any severe loss can instigate fragmentation of routines, relationships, and expectations and frequently implies an alteration in the world of physically available objects and spatially oriented action. Data from interviews conducted before relocation were compared with a "depth-of-grief" index derived from follow-up interviews approximately two years after relocation. Fried found that some individuals were happy with the change and felt no real sense of loss. However, over 25% of the 250 women who were given postrelocation interviews indicated that they still felt depressed two years later; another 20% reported depression lasting anywhere from six months to two years after the relocation experience. Approximately 38% of the men who were interviewed also showed long-term grief reactions. Fried's data also indicated a strong correlation between prior orientation to the West End neighborhood and the strength of the grief reaction. That is, the more one liked living in the West End and considered it "home," and the greater the familiarity with the community, the stronger the sense of grief. Length of residency was also positively correlated with grief, but not as strongly as some of the other factors.

In essence, the postrelocation experiences of many of Fried's interviewees had supported pessimistic prelocation expectations. Despite wide variability in both postrelocation adjustment and in the depth and quality of the loss experience, there were widespread feelings of depression and helplessness, as well as a tendency to idealize the lost place.

Much of the information available on transportation-related displacement and relocation is based on studies performed in conjunction with new highway construction. Some of these studies appear to support Fried's earlier findings, but others do not. In their study of a community threatened by beltway construction, Fellman and Brandt (1970), identified two relatively distinct groups residing in Brookline–Elm. The first group was largely students, unmarried adults, and childless couples; group members were upwardly mobile and had no strong ties to the area. A second and larger group—primarily married couples with adult children, widows and widowers, and people living in three-generational households—had strong social and emotional ties to the neighborhood. Many of this second group were members of extended families who had close friends within walking distance. Interviews conducted with this group indicated that more than 60% were "confused, upset, or distraught." Among their primary concerns were disruption of the neighborhood and the problem of relocating extended families.

Colony (1972) found further evidence of substantial differences between those satisfied with the relocation experience and those who were not. The results of interviews conducted with 228 persons displaced by Interstate 90 in Cleveland showed that unfavorable attitudes toward relocation tended to attenuate with time, and that the rate of attenuation was directly related to income and educational attainment. Colony also found, however, that unfavorable attitudes were much more resistant to change among the elderly and among those who had resided longer at their prerelocation addresses. Relocated families were about six times as likely to have made no new friends if the head of household was over 60 than were families where the head of household was 30 years old or younger. Interestingly, if the head of household earned less than $100/ week, the probability was three times as great that families had made no new friends compared with households where the head made more than that amount. Colony concluded that monetary compensation (i.e., relocation allowances and rent supplements) could not in itself relieve the psychic burden that had to be shouldered by those having to relocate.

Another investigation of historical interest is that of Mogey, Donahue, and Wiersma (1971) who studied involuntary relocation of households displaced by highway construction. Consistent with the results of subsequent studies, Mogey *et al.* found that displaced residents were much less likely to interact with friends and relatives following relocation and were somewhat less satisfied with new neighbors and neighborhoods. A later study by Burkhardt, Boyd, and Martin (1976) focused on the experiences of persons relocated in six cities; 390 respondents were interviewed prior to the relocation experience, and 190 of the original were interviewed afterwards. Although the interviewees were generally positive about various aspects of the relocation program and liked their new homes in contrast to their former homes, factors related specifically to neighborhood interaction following relocation were generally unsatisfactory:

1. "Neighboring" declined; the mean number of visitations dropped, and perhaps more significantly, neighborly assistance occurred considerably less frequently.

2. Use of neighborhood facilities diminished.

3. Participation in neighborhood organizations declined; there was no marked change in the proportion of individuals who belonged to neighborhood-oriented clubs, but the number of clubs participated in diminished.

4. The new neighborhood was less likely to be regarded as the best place to live (identification with the neighborhood declined).

5. The number of persons who reported having "no friends" in the new neighborhood rose dramatically, while the number reporting that all or most of their friends resided in the neighborhood showed a predictable decline.

Impact on the Elderly

A study by Key (1967) of families displaced by urban renewal and highway projects is revealing in its assessment of the impact on the elderly. Key's general conclusion was that forced relocation did not substantially harm the general population. However, he went on to say that

> Older people suffer more, objectively and subjectively, from both forced and voluntary moving.... Subjectively, one cannot replace memories and years of involvement with places and people. Objectively, the elderly have few remaining years in which to adapt and to replace the sights, sounds, and people from which they are separated by a move....
>
> Before the bulldozers came, many elderly males who lived in the area were fond of gathering on the steps of the Topeka Post Office. There they watched the sights and sounds of the city swirl around them while they

commented, chatted, and reminisced. For them, this served the purpose of the old village store. Now dispersed, with poor means of transportation, it is hard to recreate that social grouping which seemingly meant so much. (p. 278–279)

Two studies (Buffington, Meuth, Schafer, Pledger, & Bullion, 1974; Perfater & Allen, 1976) of more recent vintage are worth mentioning. The Buffington *et al.* study of 165 people displaced by Texas highway construction showed no statistically significant relationship between age and initial reaction to displacement. Moreover, approximately 60% of the sample were mildly or very pleased with the relocation experience, while only 25% were mildly or very upset. Buffington did find, however, that less than half of those individuals who were property owners prior to being displaced were subsequently pleased with relocation. Perhaps more to the point was the finding that elderly persons with low incomes and people who had occupied their original dwellings for at least 20 years were more likely to be upset after relocation than younger, short-term residents with higher incomes.

Perfater and Allen's (1976) study of 494 relocated Virginia residents showed that about as many people (roughly 35%) preferred their new neighborhoods after relocation as preferred their old ones. Of the latter group, old friends and access to various conveniences were most often cited as reasons for preferring the old neighborhood. Although Perfater and Allen reported no significant relationships between age of respondents, or length of time in original dwellings, and preference for the old versus the new neighborhood, nonetheless, the findings appear to be generally consistent with those previously reported. Longer-term residents of the old neighborhood were more likely to (1) identify psychological rather than economic impacts of relocation as being their dominant concerns; (2) express apprehension about the relocation process; and (3) maintain negative attitudes toward the treatment they received from the state Department of Highways and Transportation and toward the relocation program. With respect to the elderly, Perfater and Allen's data did suggest greater apprehension about displacement; and following relocation, this group made fewer friends in the new neighborhood. The investigators also found indirect evidence (obtained from unsolicited comments) of a possible link between the relocation experience and the premature death of an elderly spouse. Some of the remarks made by the interviewees are quite revealing:

"I lost my husband by death due to his worrying about where we were going and in moving our property. . . .

"My husband had suffered two or three heart attacks prior to contact by the highway department. I feel relocation killed him. . . ."

It is interesting to compare the comments of elderly relocatees in the Perfater and Allen study with those obtained by Johnson and Burdge (1974). In their investigation of involuntary relocation precipitated by Kentucky reservoir development, Johnson and Burdge described how the shock associated with displacement and the abrupt change in life-styles contributed to the death of several rural elderly:

> "Three old people died because they had to leave their homes. . . . Some old people died before they were moved out, thought they might encoun-ter . . . problems. . . .
> "All we can say is that its been all bad and destroyed people's lives. Just want to forget the whole thing. . . .
> "Everyone suffered so much because of it, lots of friends have gotten sick over it, some died."

Generally speaking, with the exception of anecdotal data, most of the information available on the relationship between forced relocation and early death among the elderly has been obtained from settings where transportation considerations were not involved. Separate studies by Pastalan (1973,1976) are a case in point. His earlier work indicated that the mortality rate of elderly persons involuntarily moved from one institutional location to another was significantly greater than the rate for persons who were not relocated. As Archea and Margulis (1979) noted, the rate of mortality was directly related to the amount of cognitive and physical decline and to the degree of environmental change. Moreover, Pastalan's data also suggest that approximately one-third of the deaths may have occurred in response to the expectation of moving, a finding consistent with the comments of relocated individuals interviewed by Perfater and Allen (1976) and Johnson and Burdge (1974). Pastalan's (1976) study of nursing home patients who were part of Pennsylvania's Relocation Program indicated that age, prognosis, and mental status at the time of relocation were the strongest predictors of mortality. The data also suggest that the length of the move and the patient's postmove attitude (i.e., reported deaths were higher among those who rejected rather than accepted relocation) were associated with mortality.

In a recent summary article of events predicting death for the el-derly, Rowland (1977), made the following observation:

> Thus the available research leads to two divergent views on the relationship between physical health status and relocation effects. One view would de-scribe relocation as a process producing declines in all elderly: Those in relatively good health get sick, and those who are severely physically im-paired become sicker and are likely to die. The other view . . . proposes that relocation has differential effects depending on the initial condition of the elderly person, that is, relocation may hasten decline in aged persons who

are already seriously physically impaired, but for those who are relatively well physically, health is not adversely affected and may even be benefited by the change in scenery. Further research is needed to determine whether an interaction exists between health status and relocation effects. (p. 362)

Rowland suggested that elderly people with impaired mental functioning and those who are undergoing depression may be especially vulnerable to death after relocation; however, it is often difficult to partial out these factors since they frequently coincide with poor physical health.

In another excellent survey of the literature, Kasl (1974) stated that there is sufficient evidence to indict the manner in which government agencies have handled displacement and relocation resulting from highway construction and other public works projects in established communities.

COMMUNITY NOISE

Overview

In the 1911 edition of *The Devil's Dictionary*, satirist Ambrose Bierce defined noise as "a stench in the ear ... the chief product and authenticating sign of civilization" (Bierce, 1958, p. 91). All things considered, Bierce's definition is probably as good as many in use today. Defining noise in a satisfactory way is no easy task, as Langdon (1975) noted; indeed, many authorities simply refer to it as "sound unwanted by the hearer."

Increasing public dissatisfaction with the cacophony of urban living was underscored in the President's 1979 Message to Congress on Environmental Priorities and Programs (Council on Environmental Quality, 1979). Mr. Carter's message cited the results of several recent surveys sponsored by the federal government or national organizations, which, collectively, supported the need for new initiatives to reduce the impact of community noise. For example, the findings of the Annual Housing Survey conducted by the U.S. Department of Housing and Urban Development indicated that noise was more frequently mentioned than crime as an "undesirable characteristic of neighborhoods"; in fact, noise ranked second only to crime as a reason for moving out of a neighborhood. Another survey performed for the National League of Cities showed that noise pollution was considered equal to water and air pollution as a significant environmental problem.

A third study mentioned in the president's environmental message was the Urban Noise Survey (U.S. Environmental Protection Agency,

1977). Utilizing both telephone and interpersonal interviews, the survey showed that sounds associated with automobiles, trucks, and motorcycles constitute the most pervasive sources of annoying noise exposure in urban America. Among the public at large, the results indicated widespread annoyance with noise, interference with conversation and disturbed sleep. The study also showed a strong relationship between reported annoyance and population density and an inverse relationship between annoyance and socioeconomic level. The report concluded that

> noise exposure, like other forms of environmental pollution, does not affect all segments of society equally. It is not that the ears of the high socioeconomic level respondents are more or less sensitive than those of other segments of society; they simply can afford to live in quieter neighborhoods. The fact that neighborhood satisfaction is inversely related to noise exposure but directly related to income and socioeconomic level suggests that quiet is a valuable attribute of neighborhoods... , those who are highly annoyed are not at all confused about this issue; most of the highly annoyed found their neighborhoods noisy and not especially pleasant to live in, were thinking of moving, and spontaneously mentioned noise as the least liked aspect of their neighborhoods. (p. 78)

Langdon (1975) appears to have arrived at a similar conclusion. While he believes that the public as a whole is uniformly affected by noise, in the sense of suffering annoyance, differences between the social classes tend to be masked by "the greater capacity of the more privileged to obtain acoustic comfort and the tendency among the underprivileged to accept generally lower standards of environmental amenity" (p.50).

In the remainder of this section, the focus is on transportation-related noise: its relationship to reported annoyance, complaints, and some of the more insidious aftereffects that are beginning to surface in the research literature. It should be stressed that the literature on noise, like that on displacement and relocation, is far too extensive to permit more than a brief glimpse at selected findings. Nonetheless, it is hoped that the significance of the problem, if not its breadth, will become apparent to the reader.

Annoyance and Individual Differences

According to Langdon (1975):

> Noise from road traffic may be regarded as more or less continuous sound which fluctuates from hour to hour over the day in a more or less regular fashion and from moment to moment with the passage of individual vehicles.

This kind of noise is obviously very different from that produced by aircraft or railways, both of which can generate higher peak levels but are intermittent in character. A more important difference is that traffic noise is
generated from the entire network of roads forming the matrix of an urban
environment. So, while aircraft noise nuisance is confined to the environs of a
few airports or their stacking points road noise will make itself felt to a
greater or lesser degree everywhere. (p. 27)

One of the early studies that examined the relationship between
noise annoyance and citizen complaints was that of McKennell (1970).
The reported investigation was one of several studies on aircraft noise
performed in Great Britain. McKennell defined a complaint as any formal, public reaction such as writing officials, signing petitions, and joining protest groups; annoyance, on the other hand, was considered a
general, subjective response or attitudinal reaction to noise.

Using a Gutman scale based on the number of different types of
disturbances (e.g., sleep, conversation) which annoyed the respondent,
McKennell found great individual variation in annoyance, and most of
the variation was independent of noise exposure. Among his findings
were the following:

1. There was a small group of people who were annoyed at the
smallest levels of noise exposure.

2. Most annoyed people were found not at the highest levels of
noise exposure but at several levels below.

3. Recent history—that is, noise exposure within the last two or
three weeks—was a good predictor of annoyance.

4. Individual reaction to noise appeared to be directly related to
overall "environmental adjustment"; that is, the more things (other than
noise) that a respondent disliked about current living conditions, the
more likely the person was to score high on the aircraft annoyance scale.

With respect to the complainants, McKennell found that almost all
of this group were annoyed, but they represented only a small percentage of those equally annoyed but uncomplaining; and like their annoyed
counterparts who did not complain, they came from all strata of noise
exposure. Moreover, such variables as occupational level, education,
organizational membership, and political activity, which were not
highly correlated with degree of annoyance, were strongly associated
with complaints. According to McKennell, complainants were typically
members of the "articulate, politically active middle class."

Guski (1977) has provided evidence of a different sort with respect
to some of the underlying factors in spontaneous noise complaints. In
the Federal Republic of Germany, there exists in several cities a well-
publicized telephone service for handling complaints on noise and other

environmental matters. Between the time the service was established in 1973 and October 1975, about 1,400 noise-related complaints were content-analyzed by a team of psychologists. The results were strikingly similar to survey findings reported in the United States. Almost three-fourths of the complaints were about intermittent noise, and most of these concerned noise occurring on a daily basis. Traffic noise generated by far the most complaints; moving road traffic—particularly trucks and, to a lesser degree, aircraft—accounted for most of the calls by irate citizens. It is interesting to note that in those cases where a second type of nuisance was reported in addition to noise, most often these reports were of unpleasant odors (e.g., engine exhaust). Among the effects that complainants attributed to noise were loss of sleep, concern about physical health, interference with relaxation, disruption of communications, and decreased satisfaction with overall living conditions. Guski also concluded that psychological factors—attitudes toward the noise source, the personality characteristics of the complainants, and stressful situations reported by callers—were often more important determinants of the amount of annoyance than the physical noise stimulus.

In his recent article summarizing the results of surveys on noise annoyance, Schultz (1978) found some remarkable consistency in the reaction of subjects to noise despite wide variations in study location and methodology. Six studies that he reviewed were concerned with aircraft noise, four with road and street noise, and one with noise emanating from railroads. Schultz first converted all the noise ratings into a common unit of measure—the day–night average sound level (L_{dn})—and then made independent judgments as to which scores should be considered "highly annoyed." Schultz feels that the mean of the "clustering surveys" represents the best available estimate of the community annoyance resulting from traffic noise of all kinds. It is interesting to note that, if the value of 55 L_{dn} (decibels) suggested by the U.S. Environmental Protection Agency were adopted, nationwide, as the standard of acceptable noise exposure, then the percentage of the population highly annoyed by traffic noise would be less than 10%. As Schultz indicated, however, only about 10% of the urban areas in the United States can currently meet that standard; in fact, approximately 75% of the U.S. urban population is already exposed to higher levels than the proposed standard. By raising the acceptable level to 70 L_{dn}, almost 90% of urban sites would be within the standard; at the same time, unfortunately, somewhere between 25% and 40% of the population would be "highly annoyed by noise or seriously disturbed in important activities" (Schultz, 1978, p. 389). It seems clear that an extension of Schultz's findings would provide decision makers the opportunity to make trade-offs between noise standards and subjective noise effects (that is, a predetermined percentage of the community that will be highly annoyed by noise).

Two investigations by Weinstein (1978, 1980) have added substantially to our knowledge of the effects that individual differences play in reactions to noise. In one longitudinal study (Weinstein, 1978), entering college freshmen were asked to complete a self-report on noise sensitivity before arriving on campus. The subjects were then divided into two subgroups, noise-sensitive and noise-insensitive, on the basis of their scores. Both groups filled out reports of dormitory noise disturbance shortly after they arrived on campus, and again seven months later. As might be expected, noise-sensitive subjects were considerably more bothered by noise and became progressively so during the ensuing months. No significant change was noted among noise-insensitive students. Of more interest, however, were the findings that noise-sensitive students had a stronger desire for privacy, fewer social skills, and significantly less intellectual ability than their noise-insensitive counterparts. Although the study is concerned with dormitory noise, not transportation related noise, the results do suggest that "its biggest impact is apparently on students already hampered by less academic ability" (p. 465). Translating these findings to the urban setting, it seems likely that those children who must spend their formative years in an intellectually impoverished environment are also those who can least afford the distraction of noise emanating from sources such as poorly planned freeways, which, at one time, were explicitly targeted for poorer neighborhoods (Llewellyn, 1974).

Additional research by Weinstein (1980) argues strongly for the importance of individual variation in response to noise and, more specifically, the tendency to make critical or negative judgments. As Weinstein suggested, these "critical tendencies" influence a broad spectrum of judgments about the environment and not simply noise alone. Weinstein took the position that it is the "critical-uncritical" dimension, more than noise exposure, that suggests why some people find little fault with air quality, amount of privacy, community services, etc., while others are generally negative.

In 1977, Weinstein conducted a survey in a physically homogeneous neighborhood approximately three months before the opening of an interstate highway. The 163 adults who were interviewed resided within 140 meters of the roadbed. The results of the survey indicated that a respondent's position on the critical-uncritical dimension accounted for approximately 32% of the variance in annoyance reactions to existing noise sources. Seven months later (four months after the highway opened and traffic volume had climbed to approximately 67,000 vehicles per day), 131 of the same individuals were reinterviewed about their reaction to the noise emanating from the freeway. A strong correlation was found between scores on the critical–uncritical dimension and highway noise annoyance. Weinstein concluded that approximately 20–30% of the variance in noise annoyance measures could be explained by "critical tendencies."

As Weinstein noted, "the ability to predict these effects [the annoyance and behavioral interference] is the criterion by which physical indices of noise exposure are judged" (p. 4). Heretofore, response curves based on grouped data facilitated the setting of noise standards because the proportion of people likely to be "highly annoyed" could be predicted; however, little could be said about which persons were likely to be annoyed. The value of Weinstein's critical-uncritical dimension is that it does appear to have some measure of predictive validity with respect to the reactions of specific individuals. How this new tool will be used and the extent to which it can be applied to site-specific problem solving where noise is at issue remain to be seen.

Effects of Transportation Noise on School-Age Children

Two recent studies (Cohen, Glass, & Singer, 1973; Bronzaft & McCarthy, 1975) have not received the attention from transportation decision-makers that they so richly deserve. Both were conducted in natural settings and underscore the insidious consequences of transportation noise on children's reading achievement.

The Cohen et al. (1973) investigation was one of a series of seminal studies on urban stressors published in the early 1970s; it was also one of the first investigations to demonstrate in a nonlaboratory setting that noise has a maladaptive influence on behavior. Based on laboratory data (Glass & Singer, 1972) that showed that the unpredictability of noise and the perceived inability to control it were instrumental in the manifestation of certain behavioral aftereffects, the investigators hypothesized that exposure to chronic traffic noise might contribute to learning deficits. Elementary-school children living in a 32-floor apartment complex overlooking a busy Manhattan expressway were given tests for auditory discrimination, reading level, and task performance. Noise measured at the base of the apartment was found to be moderately loud (84 dBA), but it gradually faded with each successive floor. Thus, a positive correlation was predicted between apartment floor and children's auditory discrimination, and between auditory discrimination and scores on reading achievement tests. Moreover, Cohen et al. felt that the longer a child had lived in the building and had been exposed to uncontrollable freeway noise, the more likely it was that both relevant and irrelevant sounds would be filtered out of awareness; hence, length of residence was expected to influence the correlation between noise and auditory discrimination. As predicted, the results showed that (1) auditory discrimination was indeed crucial to reading achievement; (2) floor level was inversely related to the ability to make auditory discriminations; and (3) duration of noise exposure appeared to impair auditory discrimination. The investigators concluded that

> despite seeming adaptation, perhaps even because of it, prolonged exposure to high-intensity traffic noise is related to deleterious aftereffects. (p. 421)

Summing up their work in a popular magazine article, the authors stated:

> The research reported here suggests there are four factors of importance in determining the effects of noise on behavior: intensity, duration, predictability, and controllability. The clangor found in modern cities is frequently intense, unpredictable, and largely uncontrollable. Our evidence warns that decreased tolerance for frustration, loss of efficiency, deficits in auditory discrimination, and lowered reading achievement may be the price for living in modern cities. (Glass, Cohen, & Singer, 1973, p. 99)

Intrigued by the results that Cohen and his colleagues had obtained, Bronzaft and McCarthy (1975) chose a nonlaboratory setting for their research on the impact of high-intensity, uncontrollable noise on reading skills. A New York City elementary school (PS 98) located 220 feet from an elevated subway track was selected for study. Between 9:00 A.M. and 3:00 P.M. weekdays, approximately 80 trains, or one every 4½ minutes, pass the school, raising the ambient noise level in the classrooms closest to the tracks from 59 dBA to 89 dBA. During such episodes (about 30 seconds of train noise), a teacher would be "required ... to scream in order to be heard by a student sitting 16 feet away" (p. 520). Bronzaft and McCarthy—assured by the school principal that school classes did not differ in terms of intelligence and achievement level—compared the reading-achievement scores of classes matched for grade level and teaching methods. The independent variable was classroom location in relation to the subway tracks: same (noisy) side versus opposite side of the building. Data collected in 1974 showed a significant difference between the two settings. Students on the noisy side did significantly worse on word knowledge and reading achievement tests. Furthermore, historical data obtained from school classes during the years 1971–1973 showed the same pattern of reading deficits. In 9 of 10 comparisons, noisy-side classes lagged behind their opposite side counterparts. Based on a 10-month school year, the average reading achievement deficit was 3–4 months; in one case, the noisy-side class was 5 months behind, in another 11 months behind.

In their concluding remarks, Bronzaft and McCarthy observed that PS 98 is a Title 1 school; that is, 50% of the children come from families with incomes below the poverty level. Most of the students live relatively close to the school, which is situated in one of the poorer and more noisy New York City neighborhoods. Bronzaft and McCarthy suggested that:

> This debilitating effect of noise on reading scores during the formative school years may prove irreversible even if these children attend quieter classrooms in the future. In addition, there are 54 other schools in the Metropolitan New York area that are also located within 150 yeards of elevated train tracks, and it is possible that reading scores of children in these schools may also be adversely affected by noise from passing trains. (p. 526)

Research on the effects of aircraft noise on classroom learning suggests that some communities close to busy airports are experiencing similar problems. For example, an investigation by the Jamaica Bay Environmental Study Group (1971) offered the following anecdotal data:

> The [Kennedy] airport noise has a very adverse effect on area schools. Within the impacted area . . . there are 220 schools attended by 280,000 pupils. With normal schoolroom usage, this implies about an hour's interruption of classroom teaching technique to accommodate the impossibility of communicating with pupils as an aircraft passes overhead. The noise interference with the teaching process goes beyond the periods of enforced noncommunication, for it destroy the spontaneity of the educational process and subjects it to the rhythm of the aeronautical control system. (p. 20)

Similar findings have been reported by the U.S. Environmental Protection Agency (1971) and Crook and Langdon (1974). The former study indicated that airport noise in Inglewood, California, became such a nuisance that several schools had to be relocated to quieter neighborhoods. Just as in the case of the Jamaica Bay residents, school officials in Inglewood noted that considerable time was lost not only in waiting for noisy jets to pass over, but also in refocusing the children's attention on those tasks that had been in progress before the overflight. Examining the disruption caused by jet noise near London Airport, Crook and Langdon found that speech interference provided the most useful measure of noise effects. The researchers did not observe any dramatic changes in teaching methods as noise reached peak levels; however, they did find a strong relationship between interrupted speech and peak noise levels. The sharpest increases were noted as sound levels rose from 76 dBA to 82 dBA; the percentage of times that interruptions occurred soared from less than 30 to 100.

Evidence that children with learning disabilities may be more seriously hampered by noise than children without them is documented in
two quite different studies. Hunter (1971) noted an increase in
physiological activity and a drop in performance among dyslexic children compared with their normal counterparts in controlled settings
located in the flight paths leading into the San Diego Airport. Hunter's
findings are particularly interesting when viewed in the context of research reported by Grosjean, Lodi, and Rabinowitz (1976). Their results
suggested that "backward" students were more likely to be affected by
environmental noises than advanced students in experimental tests of
"pedagogic efficiency." However, once noise levels climbed above 55
dBA, differences between the two groups tended to wash out.

Perhaps the best study to date on the impact of aircraft noise on
children is the work of Cohen, Evans, Krantz and Stokols (1980). In
contrast to earlier naturalistic investigations, which could be criticized
on the grounds that the subjects were not randomly assigned and that
the settings may have varied on other key dimensions besides noise
level, the Cohen *et al.* study used a matched-group design and attempted "to control statistically for a number of possible alternative
explanations for correlations between community noise and . . . various
criterion variables" (p. 232). The subjects were third and fourth-grade
children who attended the four most seriously noise-impacted schools
in the Los Angeles International Airport air corridor; overflights in the
area occur approximately 300 times per day, or about once every 150
seconds, with peak sound levels reaching 95 dBA. Students in "quiet"
schools—matched for age, race, and social class—served as controls.
Among the major findings:

1. Children from noisy elementary schools had higher blood-
pressure readings than did control (quiet-school) children.

2. Performance on a cognitive task showed that students from
noisy schools were more likely to fail in attempts to solve puzzles and
were less likely to persist in finding a solution:

3. Children from noisy schools performed somewhat better on a
test of susceptibility to distraction, but only for the first two years of
noise exposure; after four years of noise exposure, they performed
worse than quiet-school children, which suggests increasing difficulty in
coping with distraction over time:

4. Contrary to predictions, however, no evidence was found that
aircraft noise affected either math or reading skills.

Clearly, the key findings of the Cohen *et al.* study are the demon-
strable chronic effects of noise, particularly the impact on children's blood
pressure and their performance on cognitive tasks. Failure to replicate
the results of previous studies that showed a relationship between

transportation-related noise and reading achievement (Cohen *et al.*, 1973; Bronzaft & McCarthy, 1975) is somewhat puzzling. As Cohen *et al.* noted, however, their experimental design may not have been sensitive to subtle differences in scholastic achievement attributable to noise. Individual differences (i.e., their subjects came from different schools and different classrooms and were taught by different teachers in contrast to earlier studies, where students were taught in the same classroom by the same teachers) may in fact have washed out the main statistical effects.

Two additional points are worthy of mention. First. Cohen *et al.* performed a series of statistical tests to determine whether living in a quiet home—that is, one not subjected to intense aircraft noise—would lessen the impact of noise exposure at school. Their conclusion was that noise effects were not attenuated, suggesting that exposure at school alone might be enough to trigger the demonstrated aftereffects. Second, alluding to the ethnic mix of their sample and the observed results, they suggested the following:

> At least eight million people in this country are exposed to aircraft noise . . . , and the vast majority of noise impacted communities have racial and social class compositions more similar to the composition of the present sample than to that of the general population. . . . In combination with the laboratory noise literature, these data clearly suggest lending additional weight to the possible impact of aircraft noise on psychological adjustment and on nonauditory aspects of health. Replications of these results, however, would substantially increase their potential influence in the realms of both science and social policy. (p. 242)

CONCLUSION

More than a decade has passed since the National Environmental Policy Act was signed into law. During the early 1970s, most government agencies were simply unprepared to take on the burden of preparing technically adequate environmental impact statements; some even refused to take the NEPA process seriously. A good example is the environmental impact statement that the Pentagon prepared on the B-1 strategic bomber. As most people are aware, the B-1 was designed to be an integral part of our second-strike capability in a nuclear exchange with the Soviet Union. A summary statement in the U.S. Air Force analysis concluded, "As compared to current military aircraft, the B-1 will have less of an environmental impact." The reasons cited by the Pentagon included quieter engines, which "will not emit smoke" (Novick, 1973).

It seems clear that the development of environmental impact statements has come a long way since the B-1 bomber EIS was first prepared.

Nonetheless, questions remain about the NEPA process and the legiti-macy of social impact assessment in that process. Moreover, despite the ambiguity surrounding social impact assessment, the number of prac-titioners in the field has increased steadily over the last 10 years. The sophistication of techniques used to assess social effects has likewise increased, particularly those employed by transportation planners (see Finsterbusch & Wolf, 1977; Szalay, 1981). Indeed, it is refreshing to see social impact assessment imbedded in the planning process of transpor-tation departments such as those in California, Washington, Michigan, Colorado, and Massachusetts, to name only a few. However, in other localities with which the author is familiar, the situation is somewhat different. The problem in these areas is much more basic than methodology; in essence, it has to do with a lack of awareness and understanding of the nature and importance of social impacts. Similarly, as this chapter has attempted to demonstrate, the problem of impact equity—the distribution of social costs and benefits among various groups within our society—has not been resolved satisfactorily. In the remainder of this section, these topics are discussed briefly from the standpoint of possible remedial action and future research.

The effects of transportation noise on minority and low-income groups, particularly schoolchildren, deserve greater attention from planners and public officials alike. Despite the antipathy most agencies have to sponsoring longitudinal studies, there is a compelling need for more studies modeled after the work of Cohen *et al.* (1980). We need to know considerably more about the long-term effects of traffic noise on the childhood learning experience. The evidence to date is equivocal, or so it appears. Preliminary data collected by Lukas (1980), comparing the academic achievement of schoolchildren in relatively quiet schools to that in schools near freeways, appear to support earlier findings that traffic noise adversely affects reading achievement. The sample of chil-dren studied by Lukas was drawn from the Los Angeles Unified School District and contained disporportionately large numbers of black and Hispanic elementary students, many of whom came from low-income areas with high rates of unemployment. In this vein, it is instructive to look at the work of Herridge and Low-Beer (1973), who described the settlement of many Asian immigrants in the less expensive but very noisy areas around Heathrow Airport in London. Herridge and Low-Beer warned that we are beginning to see the creation of "noise ghettos" or "permanent noise slums." It is quite likely that similar housing pat-terns have evolved in large urban communities in this country, an in-sidious by-product of poverty with long-term effects that we still do not fully understand.

Involuntary displacement and relocation are another case in point.

The Council on Environmental Quality (1971) estimated that at the beginning of the last decade, approximately 60,000 people per year were being displaced by the construction of the interstate highway system. Many of those directly affected by highway construction were from low-income neighborhoods. Unfortunately, however, insofar as can be determined, few records exist at either the national or the state level with respect to the numbers of people displaced annually or their demographic characteristics. Former Secretary of Transportation Brock Adams (1979), citing the $80 billion spent on urban transportation projects since World War II, offered the following evaluation:

> In honor of progress, we built interstate highways designed like concrete canyons, right through our cities dividing neighborhoods and races. Once those barriers were constructed, we designed beltways that like circular magnets drew people and businesses and jobs away from the center of town. . . . Planners somehow forgot that transportation decisions are human decisions. That a decision to build a highway is a decision to tear down someone's home; that an airport may be a great municipal asset but a personal liability to those along its flight path. And yet the evidence is all around—and it screams out against the ignorance, short sightedness, and insensitivity of three decades of urban transportation decisions. (p. 3)

While one can question whether urban transportation decisions have been as callous as former Secretary Adams indicates, it is important that data on the psychological effects of forced relocation be brought to the attention of transportation planners, concerned citizens, sympathetic congressional leaders, and the courts. Archea and Margulis (1979), for example, related several instances where data on mortality rates among elderly patients subjected to involuntary relocation were instrumental in bringing about much needed changes in policy at the state level. The work of Archea and Margulis suggests that if death is a likely consequence for certain elderly people threatened with displacement, then the courts may intervene. The problem, of course, is demonstrating to decision makers that the consequences for the institutionalized elderly may also apply to elderly people displaced by transportation projects or urban revitalization—a much more difficult task than it might first appear to be.

Another important task is to see that existing guidelines on social impact assessment are clarified and strengthened. What we have now, courtesy of the NEPA, is vague, confusing, and generally unenforceable. Critical social impacts should be explicitly identified, particularly those that appear to apply in multiple settings or are frequently the result of different types of public works projects. Moreover, any federal guidelines should be common to all agencies; at present, there is little consistency across agencies with respect to the treatment of social impacts. In the meantime, if we must err in the setting of policy, it should be in favor of people, and specifically in favor of those most likely to be adversely affected by transportation projects. Do not force children to attend schools with inadequate noise shielding. Do not diplace the elderly if other reasonable alternatives exist.

Describing how proponents of Tellico Dam finally prevailed over the tiny, endangered snail darter, Peter Matthiessen (1980), also related how the last long-term residents were displaced:

> The following week, official vehicles descended upon the last holdouts in the Valley, Mrs. Nellie McCall and Thomas Moser, who were evicted from their homes by federal marshals. Mrs. McCall had been promised that her belongings would be spared, including her mother's china, but when she returned that afternoon, her house had been burned down, china and all. Mr. Moser's house, also destroyed, was the house where he was born. (p. 36)

One goal of social impact assessment should be to prevent the recurrence of this kind of American tragedy.

Acknowledgments

I am deeply indebted to Dr. Stephen T. Margulis, Center for Building Technology, National Bureau of Standards, for his comments and helpful advice on an earlier version of this manuscript. I would also like to thank Mr. Robert Lavell, formerly with the Environmental Division, Federal Highway Administration, for his assistance with the literature search provided by the Transportation Research Information Service. It should be noted, however, that the views expressed in this chapter are the author's and not necessarily those of the U.S. Fish and Wildlife Service or of any other federal agency.

REFERENCES

Abt Associates. *Socio-economic impacts related to the planning, construction and operation of urban transportation tunnel projects* (Tech. Rep. DOT-FH-11-9351). Cambridge, Mass.: Author, 1979.

Adams, B. *Urban transportation policy.* Speech presented to the Kennedy School of Government, Harvard University, Cambridge, Mass., Feb. 13, 1979.

Adkins, W. G., & Eichmann, F. F. *Consequences of displacement by right-of-way to 100 home owners* (Bulletin 16). College Station: Texas Transportation Institute, 1961.

Archea, J., & Margulis, S.T. Environmental research inputs to policy and design programs: The case of preparation for involuntary relocation of the institutionalized aged. In T. O. Byerts, S. C. Howell, & L. A. Pastalan (Eds.), *Environmental context of aging: Lifestyles, environmental quality, and living arrangements.* New York: Garland, 1979.

Bierce, A. *The devil's dictionary.* New York: Dover, 1958.

Blissett, M. (ed.). *Environmental impact assessment.* Washington, D.C.: National Science Foundation, 1975.

Bronzaft, A. L., & McCarthy, D. P. The effects of elevated train noise on reading ability. *Environment and Behavior,* 1975, *7,* 517–527.

Buffington, J. L., Meuth, J. G., Schafer, D. L. Pledger, R., & Bullion, C. *Attitudes, opinions and experience of residents displaced by highways under the 1970 relocation assistance program* (Tech. Rep. TTI-2-15-73-159-1). College Station: Texas Transportation Institute, 1974.

Burkhardt, J. E., Boyd, N., & Martin, T. *Residential dislocation: Consequences and compensation.* Washington, D.C.: National Cooperative Highway Research Program, Federal Highway Administration, 1976.

Cohen, S., Evans, G. W., Krantz, D. S., & Stokols, D. Physiological, motivational, and cognitive effects of aircraft noise on children. *American Psychologist,* 1980, *35,* 231–243.

Cohen, S., Glass, D. C., & Singer, J. E. Apartment noise, auditory discrimination, and reading ability in children. *Journal of Experimental Social Psychology,* 1973, *9,* 407–422.

Colony, D. C. Study of the impact on households of relocation from a highway right-of-way. *Highway Research Record,* 1972, *399,* 12–26.

Connor, D. M. *A community approach to social impact assessment.* Oakville, Ontario: Connor Development Services Limited, 1978.

Council on Environmental Quality. *Environmental quality: The second annual report of the Council on Environmental Quality.* Washington, D.C.: U.S. Government Printing Office, 1971.

Council on Environmental Quality. *Environmental quality: The tenth annual report of the Council on Environmental Quality.* Washington, D.C.: U.S. Government Printing Office, 1979.

Crook, M. A., & Langdon, F. J. The effect of aircraft noise on schools in the vicinity of London Airport. *Journal of Sound and Vibration,* 1974, *34,* 241–248.

Environmental Law Institute. President orders environmental review of international actions. *Environmental Law Reporter,* 1979, IX(1), 9 ELR 10001-10016.

Environmental Law Institute. *Noe v. Metropolitan Atlanta Rapid Transit Authority. Environmental Law Reporter,* 1980, X(4), 10 ELR 20247-20248. (a)

Environmental Law Institute. *Red Line Alert v. Adams. Environmental Law Reporter,* 1980, X(5), 10 ELR 20314-20316. (b)

Executive Office of the President. *Agency preparation of urban and community impact statements* (Circular No. A-116). Washington, D.C.: Author, Office of Management and Budget, 1978.

Fellman, G. Sociological field work is essential in studying community values. *Highway Research Record,* 1970, *305,* 123–132.

Fellman, G., & Brandt, B. A neighborhood a highway would destroy. *Environment and Behavior,* 1970, *2,* 281–301.

Finsterbusch, K., & Wolf, C. P. (eds.) *Methodology of social impact assessment.* Stroudsburg, Pa.: Dowden, Hutchinson and Ross, 1977.

Fried, M. Grieving for a lost home. In L. J. Duhl (ed.), *The urban condition.* New York: Basic Books, 1963.

Friedman, E. *Crest Street: A family/community impact statement* (Policy Paper No. 2). Durham, N.C.: Duke University, Institute of Policy Sciences and Public Affairs, Center for the Study of the Family and the State, 1978.

Glass, D. C., & Singer, J. E. *Urban stress: Experiments on noise and social stressors.* New York: Academic Press, 1972.

Glass, D. C., Cohen, S., & Singer, J. E. Urban din fogs the brain. *Psychology Today,* 1973, *6*(12), 94–99.

Grosjean, L., Lodi, R., & Rabinowitz, J. Noise and "pedagogic efficiency" in school activities. *Experientia,* 1976, *32,* 575–576.

Guski, R. An analysis of spontaneous noise complaints. *Environmental Research,* 1977, *13,* 229–236.

Hanly v. Mitchell, 460 F. 2d. 640, 4 E.R.C. 1152, 2 E.L.R. 20216 (2d. Cir 1972).

Herridge, C. F., & Low-Beer, L. Observations of the effects of aircraft noise near Heathrow Airport on mental health. *Proceedings of the International Congress on Noise as a Public Health Problem,* Dubrovnik, 1973, 599–607 (U.S. Environmental Protection Agency Report No. 550/9-73-008).

Horwood, E. M., Zellner, C. A., & Ludwig, R. L. *Community consequences of highway improvement* (NCHRP Report 18). Washington, D.C.: National Academy of Sciences, Highway Research Board, 1965.

Hunter, E. J. Autonomic reponses to aircraft noise in dyslexic children. *Psychology in the Schools,* 1971, *8,* 362–367.

Jamaica Bay Environmental Study Group. *Jamaica Bay and Kennedy Airport: A multidisciplinary environmental study.* Washington, D.C.: National Academy of Sciences, 1971.

Johnson, S. & Burdge, R. J. *Personal and social adjustment to reservoir development.* Lexington: Kentucky Water Resources Research Institute, 1974.

Kasl, S. V. Effects of Housing on mental and physical health. *Man-Environment Systems,* 1974, *4,* 207–226.

Kemp, B. Social impact of a highway on an urban community. *Highway Research Record,* 1965, *75,* 92–102.

Key, W. H. *When people are forced to move.* Topeka: The Menninger Foundation, 1967.

Langdon, F. J. The problem of measuring the effects of traffic noise. In A. Alexandre, J. -Ph. Barde, C. Lamure, & F. J. Langdon (Eds), *Road traffic noise.* New York: Wiley, 1975.

Leavitt, H. *Superhighway—superhoax.* New York: Ballantine Books, 1970.

Llewellyn, L. G. The social impact of urban highways. In C. P. Wolf (Ed.), *Social impact assessment.* Milwaukee: Environmental Design Research Association, 1974.

Llewellyn, L. G., & Peiser, P. G. NEPA and the environmental movement: A brief history. In *Managing the environment* (EPA-600/5-73-00l0). Washington, D.C.: U.S. Environmental Protection Agency, 1973.

Llewellyn, L. G., Bunten, E., Goodman, C., Hare, G., Mach, R., & Swisher, R. The role of social impact assessment in highway planning. *Environment and Behavior,* 1975, *7,* 285–306.

Llewellyn, L. G., Goodman, C., & Hare, G. (Eds.). *Social impact assessment: A sourcebook for highway planners* (8 vols.). Washington, D.C.: Federal Highway Administration, Environmental Division, 1981.

Lukas, J. S. *Effects of freeway noise on behavior and academic achievement of school children* (Preliminary Report). Berkeley: California Department of Health Services, 1980.

Matthiessen, P. How to kill a valley. *The New York Review,* 1980, *27*(2), 31–36.

McHarg, I. L. *Design with nature.* Garden City, N.Y.: Doubleday, 1969.

McKennell, A. C. Noise complaints and community action. In J. D. Chalupnik (Ed.), *Transportation noises: A symposium on acceptability criteria.* Seattle: University of Washington Press, 1970.

Mitchell, R.C. The public speaks again: A new environmental survey. *Resources,* 1978, *60,* 1–8.

Mogey, J., Donahue, M., & Wiersma, E. *Social effects of eminent domain: Changes in households after involuntary relocation for Southwest Expressway(I-95), Boston, 1969-1970.* Boston: Boston University, 1971.

Novick, S. Spectrum—news of the month. *Environment,* 1973, *15*(4), 21–24.

Pastalan, L. Involuntary environmental relocation: Death and survival. In E. H. Steinfeld (Chair), Action research in man-environment relations. In W. F. E. Preiser (Ed.), *Environmental design research: Vol.2. Symposia and Workshops)*. Stroudsburg, Pa.: Dowden, Hutchinson, & Ross, 1973.

Pastalan, L. *Pennsylvania nursing home relocation program interim research findings*. Ann Arbor: University of Michigan, Institute of Gerontology, 1976.

Perfater, M. A. & Allen, G. R. *Relocation due to highway takings: A diachronic analysis of social and economic effects*. Charlottesville: Virginia Highway and Transportation Research Council, 1976.

Rowland, K. F. Environmental events predicting death for the elderly. *Psychological Bulletin*, 1977, *84*, 349–372.

Schultz, T. J. Synthesis of social surveys on noise annoyance. *Journal of the Acoustical Society of America*, 1978, *64*, 377–405.

Stack, C. B., & Holt, L. R. Organizing kinfolk: Crest Street resists a highway. *Anthropology Resource Center Newsletter*, 1979, *6*, 3.

Szalay, L. Surveying public images and opinions by the Associative Group Analysis. In L. G. Llewellyn, C. Goodman, & G. Hare (Eds.), *Social impact assessment: A sourcebook for highway planners*, (Vol. 5). Washington, D.C.: Federal Highway Administration, Environmental Division, 1981.

Toffler, A. *Future shock*. New York: Random House, 1970.

U.S. Environmental Protection Agency. *The social impact of noise*. Washington, D.C.: Author, Office of Noise Abatement and Control, 1971.

U.S. Environmental Protection Agency. *The urban noise survey* (EPA 550/9-77-100). Washington, D.C.: Author, 1977.

Ward, L. M., & Suedfeld, P. Human response to highway noise. *Environmental Research*, 1973, *6*, 306–326.

Weinstein, N. D. Human evaluations of environmental noise. In K. H. Craik & E. H. Zube (Eds.), *Perceiving environmental quality*. New York: Plenum Press, 1976.

Weinstein, N. D. Individual differences in reactions to noise: A longitudinal study in a college dormitory. *Journal of Applied Psychology*, 1978, *63*, 458–466.

Weinstein, N.D. Individual differences in critical tendencies and noise annoyance. *Journal of Sound and Vibration*, 1980, *68*, 241–248.

Winder, J. S., & Allen, R. H. *The environmental impact assessment project: A critical appraisal*. Washington, D.C.: The Institute of Ecology, 1975.

Wolf, C. P. Social impact assessment: The state of the art. In C. P. Wolf (Ed.) *Social impact assessment*. Milwaukee: Environmental Design Research Association, 1974.

Wolf, C. P. Social impact assessment: The state of the art updated. *Social Impact Assessment*, 1977, *20*, 3–22.

Wolf, C. P. Getting social impact assessment into the policy arena. *Environmental Impact Assessment Review*, 1980, *1*, 27–36.

7

The Effects of a Modern Rapid-Transit System on Nearby Residents

A CASE STUDY OF BART IN THE SAN FRANCISCO AREA

MARK BALDASSARE

INTRODUCTION

During the last 50 years, the United States has increasingly relied on the automobile for local travel. Public transit has been ignored while enormous resources were poured into highway development. With a steady rise in the standard of living, more and more households have been able to afford automobiles. These events have resulted in sprawling land-use patterns outside of older cities and low-density "suburbanlike" environments in newer cities (see Baldassare, 1981). The automobile-oriented metropolitan form is now a permanent part of the landscape. However, more recent circumstances, including the energy crisis (Foley, 1976), have required urban areas to explore alternative modes of trans-

MARK BALDASSARE • Sociology Department and Center for the Social Sciences, Columbia University, New York, New York 10027. The research was supported by the U.S. Department of Transportation (DOT-OS-30176). The analysis of the survey data was conducted with Robert Knight and Sherrill Swan.

porting people. In this context, serious questions have been raised about the fiscal and social costs of building and operating mass transit systems within the new urban form. These issues are partially addressed by the Bay Area Rapid Transit (BART) impact study, which was conducted in the San Francisco metropolitan region.

Several conditions differentiate modern mass-transit systems from the subways and "els" of the Northeast and Midwest that were constructed in the early part of the century. The present-day patterns of low-density residence and decentralized industries create difficult working conditions for the fixed-rail system, which has traditionally been used to move large numbers of commuters. Construction costs are astonomical, and the possibilities of operating public transit systems without deficits seem dismal (Wachs & Ortner, 1979). It is also difficult to convince people, especially in the newly settled regions, to use public transit instead of their automobiles. Studies have reported negative attitudes towards mass transit, even among its regular users (Wachs, 1976). Of central importance to this chapter, new rail lines must be constructed through suburban single-family home environments. This raises concerns about local impacts, such as noise from passing trains and traffic problems surrounding the stations. Such conditions may result in resistance to the construction of new systems and hostility toward their operations. Widespread dissatisfaction may eventually result in social and physical decay if individuals choose to avoid living near these conditions.

The study of BART's effects on nearby residents, which is reviewed in this chapter (for more detail see DeLeuw, Cather and Company, 1977), has broad relevance for several reasons. The San Francisco metropolitan area has characteristics that make the delivery of mass transit difficult, such as large geographical size and low density. Having matured in the automobile era, the region's existing transportation system and its users are highly resistant to change. The BART system also poses possible environmental hazards for nearby residents, which have worried transportation planners in other urban areas, and the selection of study sites reflects these concerns. Thus, the information gathered has applicability to the issues of neighborhood deterioration and residents' complaints along most modern rail lines.

An example of a particular method of investigation is also provided in our discussion of the BART study. The case study describes how a social impact assessment can help determine the effects of a transportation system on nearby residents. We draw a sharp distinction between this approach, which systematically examines the responses of individuals to an environmental change, and competing models (see also

Christensen, 1976; Finsterbusch & Wolf, 1977). For example, researchers sometimes rely solely on the judgements and observations of professionals in determining impacts, even though outside experts may view events differently from those who live in the environment. Public records on the locality (e.g., crime, land use, pollution) and instrument measurements of potential stressors (e.g., noise, vibrations, traffic flow) are often considered the most dependable data on the effects of environmental changes, although there is no reason to assume that these objective factors are felt by local residents. We thus stress the importance of residents' attitudes in determining the quality of the local environment and in analyzing specific attributes that have had a negative impact (see also Stokols, 1972; Michelson, 1976).

Two factors constrain the generalizability of the BART impact study. It was, first of all, conducted only a few years after service began. We do not know if the complaints that were registered by nearby residents could be replicated today. Perhaps what were then minor annoyances may since have caused slow but steady deterioration in the neighborhood environment and the residents' attitudes. It is equally plausible that people may have adjusted to the perceived adverse impacts and are now less dissatisfied. In addition, one must keep in mind that BART was a source of great controversy in the region. Some individuals in our sample probably viewed the survey as an opportunity to vent their frustrations toward government intervention and the failures of BART's operations, rather than assessing only its effects on their localities. The opinions about social and environmental impacts may thus be overly negative.

BART AS THE MODEL OF MODERN MASS TRANSIT

The Bay Area Rapid Transit began service in 1972 and was fully operational by 1974. The system's opening symbolized the beginning of a "new generation" in American mass transit. Many believed that other metropolitan regions would follow the San Francisco Bay Area's lead and invest in expensive rail systems. There are two reasons that the overall costs and benefits of BART have been the subject of intense study over recent years. Since other muncipalities perceived BART as a model that they might emulate, there was a great demand for information about this system's operations. There was also a continuing debate about the effects of BART among metropolitan area residents, which created a need for dependable answers about its success and shortcomings. The serious commitment to evaluation eventually resulted in the finding of resources to conduct social, fiscal, and environmental impact studies. Before we examine the social controversy surrounding the system, as well as the evidence about its impact, a brief description of its characteristics will provide a background for the discussions that follow.

BART's construction and equipment costs were about $1.6 billion. It was funded primarily by local revenues. As is typical of the fiscal crisis in public transit (Ortner & Wachs, 1979), daily operating costs exceed fare collections and must be subsidized by, among other sources, a local sales tax. The BART track length is 71 miles and includes 34 stations in three counties. An approximately equal amount of the track is below ground, at ground level, and elevated. Average train speed is about 40 miles per hour, though the top speed is 80 miles per hour. The entire system is automated, with trains controlled by a central computer and tickets dispensed by vending machines. Considering the geographical size of the area and its population of 2.4 million in 1970, it is obvious that BART was envisioned as a skeletal system. Its success is dependent on commuters' journeying from their homes to a station by bus or car and, in many instances, taking a bus from their station stop to a desired destination. When our study was conducted in 1976, about 130,000 one-way trips were made each day. Train service was along four routes, basically on weekdays from 6 A.M. to midnight, and train frequency varied from 6 to 20 minutes.

An enormous amount of effort was devoted to research and development. Nonetheless, BART has always been the subject of public controversy. Many people were strongly opposed to its construction and questioned its necessity in an auto-dominated metropolitan area. Central to our interests, some communities were against its presence because they feared that it would bring environmental hazards and local deterioration. Residents of Berkeley went so far as to accept additional taxation in order to place BART below ground, so that it would be unseen and unheard.

Public opinion and media publicity did not improve when the system began operating. Technical problems and malfunctions regularly increased the commuting times of everyday riders. Numerous questions were raised about the quality of the equipment, while the strife between labor and management led to the constant threat of service disruption. It also became increasingly evident that an entire region was being given the financial responsibility for a system that served a very tiny proportion of the population. The average person did not perceive any benefits to weigh against these costs, such as reduced rush-hour traffic, better parking conditions downtown, or less air pollution. Instead, there were scattered reports of dissatisfaction with BART's impact in neighborhoods adjacent to the tracks and stations.

The most thorough evaluation of BART to date was conducted by Melvin Webber (1976). He investigated several benefits that were supposed to occur, such as a reduction in rush hour traffic and commuting time; growth in the central business district; the development of economic subcenters throughout the region; and increased land value near the system (pp. 6, 7). The data he gathered suggest that there were few gains in these realms. Total patronage was far below expectations, and BART's effects on auto traffic were negligible. There was no evidence to suggest that the system has encouraged construction in the inner city or new residential and commercial growth in the outlying areas (see also Knight & Trygg, 1977).

Webber (1976, p. 23) argued that there are three costs for commuting trips: dollar costs, time expenditures, and costs external to the transportation system. Previous research indicated that BART could not compete with buses or automobiles in terms of the dollar and time costs. To add to these criticisms, empirical information has shown that the poor in the Bay Area have disproportionately paid the operating costs for a rapid transit system that they have underutilized (Hoachlander, 1979).

The study we conducted examined the possiblity of a third type of cost, which is the annoyance that the system may represent for those who live nearby. Despite the opposition to BART's construction and the criticism of its operations that have been mentioned, one could not assume at the outset that the external costs of the BART system would be substantial. For example, the actual impact may not be very serious for most residents, or some potential benefits of having the BART facility nearby may cause others in the neighborhood to evaluate the system's overall impact more favorably. In general, an assessment of BART's impact on nearby residents cannot be offered without systematic information on the attitudes and characteristics of those living close to the system.

THE BART STUDY

RATIONALE AND APPROACH

There were several objectives that guided the BART impact study. One was to identify BART's effects on the residential environment as judged by individuals exposed to them. Another was to compare residents' evaluations with technical assessments. Examples of the latter method are instrument measurements (e.g., of noise and vibrations) and observational studies by professional planners. It was also important to specify the BART attributes that influence residents' perceptions of impacts, as well as the role of social, personal, and environmental factors. The final goal was to derive implications for future rapid-transit planning, design, construction, and operation.

The study considered residents' perceptions at 10 above-ground

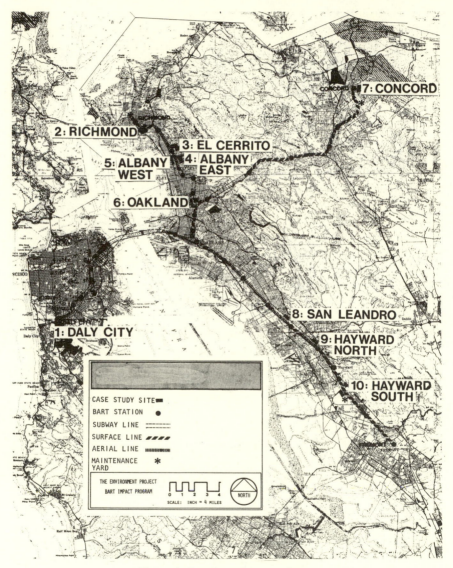

Figure 1. Location of survey sites.

sites. We did not include subway stations since visual, noise, and traffic impacts were hardly present at these inner-city sites. Three were adjacent to BART stations and seven were along the trackways (see Figure 1). The sites averaged four square blocks, and their selection was based on technical assessments of BART's impacts on the neighborhoods.

The study's central activity was a home interview survey. This survey gathered perceptions of impacts by the population living adjacent to the sites. Responses within sites and between sites were compared throughout the study. A perspective on the level and types of impacts within individual sites, as well as the influence of specific factors that varied across sites, emerged from this analysis.

THE INTERVIEW AND RESPONDENT SELECTION

Household interviews with 702 residents were completed during the summer of 1976. A sampling strategy, which maximized the number of sites that could be included, resulted in the inclusion of approximately 50 households each at six sites and 100 households each at four sites where larger samples were needed.

Earlier assessments indicated that most of BART's impacts diminish with increasing distance from the line. Interviews up to several blocks from the BART right-of-way would be required to verify this. However, a simple random sample over a wider area would include a large proportion of respondents subjected to relatively little impact, thus limiting those actually experiencing BART's impact. The first block, or "stratum," was thus oversampled, and fewer people were drawn into the sample as the distance from BART increased (i.e., 40% from the first block, 30% from the second, 20% from the third, and 10% from the fourth). Within each stratum, households were randomly selected to be included in the survey, as were household members more than 17 years old. The overall response rate was 70%.

The issues covered in the one-hour interview were numerous, and the potential impacts were so varied that we utilized both free-response items and specific questions. The residents' self-reports included four topics for questioning, which are summarized in Figure 2: general attitudes toward BART; residential mobility; specific impacts of BART; and the total neighborhood environment. The first task of this chapter is to describe the conditions within the 10 study sites. We will then be concerned with general attitudes about BART, residential mobility, and specific BART impacts. The findings are summarized, with special emphasis on differences due to the adjacent type of BART facility. These attitudinal data are then reanalyzed to determine if conditions found in some

MAJOR CAUSAL
FACTORS   MEDIATING FACTORS   RESIDENTS' PERCEPTIONS

Type of BART Facility   BART Attributes   General attitudes toward BART
                                                                          Overall satisfaction
Above-ground station   Trackway configuration   Local effects
Above-ground tracks   Train frequency   Opinion change over time
   At grade   Parking facilities   Speak out against BART
   Aerial   Linear parks
                                                                      Residential mobility
                           Environmental Differences   Prefer moving
                                                                          Prefer moving in owing to BART
                           Distance from BART   Prefer moving out owing to BART
                           Background activity
                           Housing orientation   Specific impacts of BART
                                                                          Noise
                           Demographic Differences and Personal Attitudes   Vibrations
                                                                          Traffic and parking
                           Age   Barrier to local movement
                           Sex   Privacy
                           Length of residence   Visual obtrusiveness
                           Income   Bright lights and shadows
                           Race   Crime
                           Home ownership   Land use
                           Hours away from home
                           Use of BART   The total neighborhood environment
                           Type of dwelling   Overall rating of the area
                           Orientation to BART   Best and worst things about the area
                           Powerlessness   Effects of BART's presence on the area
                           Noise sensitivity
                           Environmental concern
                           BART expectations

Figure 2. Major classes of variables in the BART study.

sites or individuals but not others (i.e., mediating factors), controlling for the type of BART facility, influence residents' reports about BART. Finally, for each site, we separately examine attitudes toward the total neighborhood environment in order to place complaints about BART in perspective and consider the overall effects of BART's impacts on the local area.

THE CASE STUDY SITES

The three station sites that were chosen are El Cerrito, Concord, and Daly City. Their users typically arrive by automobile, and thus the stations have fairly large parking facilities. The environmental impacts within the residential environments are traffic related to station attendance, automobile noise, illumination from parking lot lights, and visual exposure of parking lots and the stations (see Figure 3).

The Daly City station is at the end of BART's shortest line from downtown San Francisco and has a large number of commuter patrons who live south of San Francisco. As a result, it has the system's heaviest parking overflow problem. Concord is also a terminal station, but it is much farther from downtown and has a smaller commuter population. However, it still has a substantial problem with overflow parking in the surrounding residential neighborhood. The El Cerrito station is not a terminal station, its patronage is lower, and it has no parking problems. It is located next to a shopping center with a large parking lot and heavy traffic flow.

The residents of Concord were predominantly young white families in the lower-middle-income bracket. Much of the housing was renter-occupied, low-density, and of uneven quality. El Cerrito's respondents were among the more educated and affluent in our subject pool. Few children and a substantial elderly population were typical of this site. Most respondents were home owners and their single-family homes were in excellent condition. Daly City was a moderate-density area with an economically and racially heterogeneous population. The neighborhood contained predominantly single-family homes, with some mix in land use, and housing appeared to be slightly run-down (see Table 1).

The two at-grade line sites (Richmond, Hayward South) are fairly typical in their BART-related environmental characteristics. BART is at ground level and in already existing railroad rights-of-way. This suggests background activities potentially masking BART's adverse impacts. BART's at-grade portions have large right-of-way land requirements, which may create a substantial barrier to the community (see Figure 3).

The Richmond and Hayward South sites differ markedly in the

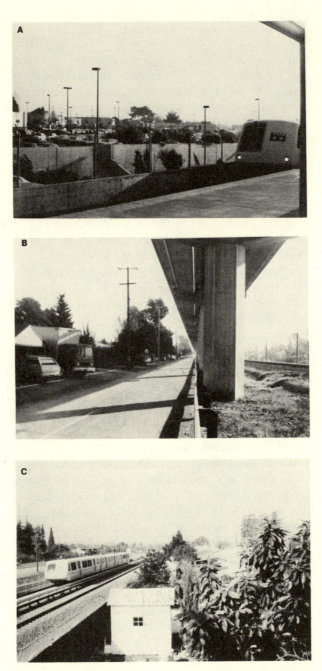

Figure 3. Examples of three site types: station, aerial, and at-grade. (A) Daly City Station. Train platform with surrounding parking lots filled to capacity. Residential area is in the background. (B) Hayward North. Houses on the left face the aerial structure. Large shadows are cast on the narrow street and front yards. (C) Hayward South. Back yards to the right face the at-grade tracks. Railroad right-of-way is fenced in.

TABLE 1

The Characteristics of Survey Respondents

	Stations			Aerial lines					At-grade lines	
	Concord	Daly City	El Cerrito	Albany East	Albany West	Oakland	Hayward North	San Leandro	Richmond	Hayward South
White (%)	93	54	80	86	91	14	96	94	10	82
Married (%)	64	52	53	60	64	35	57	82	52	76
Home owners (%)	59	68	61	73	71	49	49	92	67	96
Regular BART users (%)	20	51	31	12	8	12	7	13	17	6
Median age	33	38	49	49	57	49	51	55	38	47
Mean years of residence	8	11	9	12	14	11	10	15	10	14
Mean education index[a]	3.0	3.0	3.3	3.8	3.2	2.8	2.8	3.2	2.7	2.7
Mean income index[b]	3.8	4.0	4.3	4.4	3.7	3.1	3.3	4.7	3.2	4.4
Number of respondents	96	50	103	118	45	52	51	49	88	50

[a] The 6-point scale included: 8th grade or less = 1; high school graduate = 3; college graduate = 5.
[b] The 7-point scale included: $4,000 or less = 1; $7,000–$9,999 = 3; $15,000–$19,999 = 5; $25,000 or more = 7.

latter respect, with Richmond's residential area mainly on one side of the track, while Hayward South has residences on both sides of the tracks and a school on one side. Trains also run less frequently along the Richmond line.

The Richmond area was about 90% black with a high proportion of large families. Education and income statistics indicated that this was a disadvantaged area. Houses were predominantly single-family dwellings in run-down condition. Members of the Hayward South community were predominantly white and were employed in skilled blue-collar occupations. Many children were present, the average resident had lived there more than a decade, and the homes were uniformly well kept (see Table 1).

The five aerial sites chosen (Albany East, Albany West, Oakland, San Leandro, Hayward North) represent conditions found within residential areas. These are characterized by a relatively narrow right-of-way; easy access for automobiles across the BART tracks; heavy visual exposure of trains and the elevated structure, with consequent shadows; and problems related to the train traffic (e.g., noise, vibrations, wind, poor television reception). Our selection of aerial sites and of respondents within sites gave special weight to the viewpoint that the level of impact created by the aerial structure depends on the environmental context in which it is found.

In Albany, the BART aerial line was built with a "linear park" (a landscaped right-of-way) surrounding it. The two sites (East and West) differ in that in the former, the back yards of the homes face BART, while in the latter the front yards face BART. At the Oakland site, BART is set above the middle of a busy street with substantial traffic noise. In contrast, San Leandro and Hayward North have no linear parks and are in relatively quiet, low-density neighborhoods. For individuals living close to the BART structure, train effects and the structure's visual characteristics in the latter two areas should be particularly acute (see Figure 3).

The two Albany sites contained an older, more stable population than most other areas. Many residents were elderly and almost all were white. Income levels were among the highest in our study, and the predominant housing was small single-family dwellings of good quality. The respondents in Oakland were black, represented various age groups, and were outstandingly disadvantaged. The site had the lowest percentage of home owners, and housing quality was very poor. Almost all of the respondents in San Leandro were white, and this area was ahead of others in income, though it lagged behind many in education. This older, skilled blue-collar population was mostly composed of home owners. The condition of the housing was generally excellent, and the neighborhood appeared modest but well kept. The Hayward North neighborhood was virtually all white, with low-income residents of varying age groups. Average length of residence indicated a transient population, as did the high percentage of renters. Most dwellings were old single-family units, and housing quality appeared to be steadily declining (see Table 1).

GENERAL ATTITUDES TOWARD BART

When asked to sum up their feelings about BART, including not only its impact on the environment but also taxes, travel patterns, and anything else they considered significant, most respondents to the 1976 survey replied favorably. This finding is particularly noteworthy when we consider the general controversy surrounding BART's construction and operations. At all 10 sites, the proportion who were happy about BART was substantially higher than the proportion who were unhappy. The same held true, with minor exceptions, for the system's perceived environmental effects in and around the home. The exceptions were at two aerial line sites, where positive and negative feelings about BART's local impact were about equally balanced (see Table 2).

In order to make the issue of satisfaction more realistic, respondents were also asked whether they would have been willing to pay an extra dollar or two per month to get BART placed underground near their home. This amount is roughly what the citizens of Berkeley are paying in additional property taxes for just such a change. At 8 of the 10 sites a majority of the respondents did not support this hypothetical option.

In general, the level of acceptance of BART was highest in station-area neighborhoods. This held true with regard to both overall impressions and BART's effects in and around the home. The absolute levels of reported satisfaction at the station sites were particularly significant. While there was some unhappiness, both overall and with respect only to the environmental effects, positive responses predominated by over 2 to 1 in every case.

The highest levels of dissatisfaction were found at four of the five aerial sites, although respondents happy with BART outnumbered those who were unhappy. Between one-fourth and one-third of the respondents at any aerial site were generally displeased with BART. Several respondents at three sites were indifferent. Satisfaction with BART's more localized effects, those in and around the home, was less prevalent than feelings of overall satisfaction. However, actively negative feelings

TABLE 2

General Attitudes toward BART

	Stations			Aerial lines				At-grade lines		
	Concord	Daly City	El Cerrito	Albany East	Albany West	Oakland	Hayward North	San Leandro	Richmond	Hayward South
Overall feelings about BART (%)										
Happy	58	72	82	60	49	51	63	66	65	56
Indifferent	16	18	4	15	20	17	5	2	16	20
Unhappy	26	10	14	25	31	32	32	32	19	24
Feelings about BART's effects in and around the home (%)										
Happy	52	58	59	27	47	48	32	47	49	40
Indifferent	27	26	39	45	22	40	36	31	41	54
Unhappy	21	16	2	28	31	12	32	22	10	6
Number of cases	96	50	103	118	45	52	51	49	88	50

about these local effects were not common. Many reported noncommittal answers regarding BART's local effects, and thus outwardly positive sentiments were less common.

Negative responses to BART were less frequent at the two at-grade sites than at any of the five aerial sites. Favorable overall reactions to BART were expressed by a majority at the two sites where the BART line was at ground level. Positive feelings about BART's general impact in and around the home were expressed by fewer than a majority, displeasure was expressed by only a few, and a large proportion were indifferent.

Another issue was whether the nearest residents were substantially unhappier with BART because of their greater exposure to its impacts. The responses to the same two questions on general attitudes were investigated. Persons living next to BART reported as much satisfaction with the system as those living farther away from it. Responses to BART from the nearest stratum at the three station sites and the two at-grade sites differed very little from those for the full sites. For the aerial-line sites, first-stratum responses were more negative than the rest because of the BART train noise. As for BART's impact in and around the home, at only four sites did the percentage giving a favorable response in the first stratum depart substantially from the response for the whole site. These results suggest that BART's overall impact is not always felt most by the nearest residents.

We were interested in learning whether opinions of BART seem to have deteriorated substantially since the system opened. About half the respondents at each of the three station sites cited no change. Of the El Cerrito respondents whose attitudes did change, most reported feeling better about BART. Those at the Concord and Daly City sites are nearly evenly divided between feeling better and feeling worse. No particular changes in feelings about BART since service began were reported by about half of the respondents at all but one (Albany West) of the aerial-line sites and both at-grade line sites. At the site where opinion changes were substantial, there was little consensus about the direction of change. These results suggest that general attitudes, despite the continued controversy about BART, have been quite stable.

Finally, respondents were asked whether they had ever expressed views for or against BART, even in talking with neighbors. Very few have participated in any public actions, such as voting, signing petitions, or attending meetings, either for or against BART. The low level of active opposition, in particular, replicates the findings throughout this section of generally low levels of unhappiness with the BART system and its overall effects on the residential environment.

BART AND RESIDENTIAL MOBILITY

Another general response to BART involves residential mobility, or the reasons for moving into and out of the neighborhood and wanting to leave the present residence. BART has had an effect in this domain, though varying according to the conditions it creates within the sites. In sum, whether BART was reported as a cause of people's moving away or a reason for people's moving into the neighborhood depended on the opportunities and costs associated with being close to a specific part of the system (see also Baldassare, Knight, & Swan, 1979).

Respondents were asked whether they chose their present homes for reasons related to BART (see Table 3). Station sites had more residents citing this fact than other sites. Respondents were also asked if they knew anyone else who had moved into the neighborhood because of BART. Again, such responses occurred more frequently at station sites, while at most other sites, affirmative responses were negligible. As with individual reports of actual mobility, these respondents were more commonly in the two nearest strata. Thus, the data suggest that some have attempted to minimize their distance from BART stations in order to use the system more easily.

There were differences among sites in residents' desires to move away. However, reasons for moving were usually unrelated to the presence of BART, such as life cycle, economic status, and rates of home ownership. We also analyzed data involving those who considered moving and mentioned BART as one of the reasons (see Table 3). BART attributes seemed to influence these responses. Individuals living along aerial structures most often asserted that BART was a reason for wanting to move. BART's role at sites other than the Concord area, because noise and other costs are small in comparison, was minimal. An exception to this pattern could be seen in the Oakland aerial site, where few respondents mentioned BART, perhaps because of "background" activity (especially traffic) masking BART's train noise, or because of more pressing neighborhood problems at that site. Again, BART's impacts on moving preferences were most prevalent in the two nearest strata. Respondents were also asked whether they knew of others who had moved away from the neighborhood because of BART. Aerial sites had rates two and three times higher than at-grade sites (with the exception of Oakland, as before). However, no uniformity in responses was found for the station sites. Daly City and Concord had rates close to those of the aerial sites, while the El Cerrito Plaza station site seemed similar to at-grade sites, probably because of differences in the severity of BART-related problems (e.g., parking, traffic) favoring the El Cerrito site.

Table 3
BART and Residential Mobility

	Stations			Aerial lines				At-grade lines		
	Concord	Daly City	El Cerrito	Albany East	Albany West	Oakland	Hayward North	San Leandro	Richmond	Hayward South
Percentage that chose home because of BART	15	16	22	3	0	12	4	6	3	4
Percentage that considered moving away	40	26	26	30	24	29	37	43	43	38
Percentage that considered moving who mentioned BART	48	8	8	45	64	7	53	42	14	5
Number of cases	96	50	103	118	45	52	51	49	88	50

Again, the two nearest strata were the scenes of the greatest perceived moving activity.

We thus find differences between sites in perceived migration into and out of the neighborhood. It is also possible that BART impacts could indirectly affect housing factors such as vacancy rates, property values, and turnover rates. Given the primary importance of housing and mobility issues in individuals' experiences, this topic obviously deserves closer scrutiny and serious attention.

SPECIFIC BART IMPACTS

General responses to BART were, for the most part, indifferent or positive. We now focus on specific types of impacts that were identified in earlier technical impact studies. Whether these are in agreement with the impacts as judged by the residents themselves is an important concern (see Table 4).

Assessments of BART train noise concluded that annoying effects were present within about 500 feet of the aerial tracks. Such problems were not as likely along at-grade sites because much of the train noise is absorbed into the ground. Train traffic noise at stations, where trains move more slowly, was not particulary loud. Our survey indicated, as expected, that most respondents at aerial sites rated BART's effects on noise levels as adverse. Four of five sites showed more negative evaluations than were found in the station or at-grade sites, and there were no respondents who rated BART's effect as beneficial. Especially high proportions of those individuals within 1½ blocks rated noise as a problem. The proportions of adverse judgments declined with increasing distance from BART, even in sites that frequently mentioned bad effects. Reported behavioral changes in response to this impact were minimal and involved few respondents. The personal adjustments were found at the aerial sites with highest reported sound impact. Virtually all reactions were passive, such as stopping conversations when trains passed.

Evaluations of vibrations due to passing trains suggested that perceptible levels occur along the aerial lines. Recorded levels were not very high and not serious enough to damage nearby structures. Only those living close to the aerial line perceived adverse vibrations in and around the home. Over half the first-stratum respondents in Albany East and Albany West complained, and over a third of the first-stratum responses in San Leandro and Hayward North were also negative. Smaller proportions were found elsewhere, and the frequency of negative evaluations

Table 4

BART's Specific Impacts: Percentage Perceiving Problem as "Very" or "Somewhat Bad"

	Stations					Aerial lines			At-grade lines	
	Concord	Daly City	El Cerrito	Albany East	Albany West	Oakland	Hayward North	San Leandro	Richmond	Hayward South
Noise inside home	28	18	10	50	71	17	51	41	18	8
Vibration inside home	5	16	4	27	50	14	31	22	14	4
Traffic congestion	69	72	13	1	7	14	2	10	2	2
Parking	76	77	5	1	4	0	10	0	0	0
Barriers	51	30	1	1	2	8	4	2	16	20
Backyard privacy	12	8	4	23	18	4	20	29	10	10
Neighborhood appearance	25	16	4	15	18	12	20	23	6	2
View from backyard	6	8	7	20	14	4	16	28	10	4
Lighting at night	5	2	6	4	4	4	6	8	2	2
Shadows	5	0	4	14	16	12	16	29	1	0
Crime nearby	24	12	8	3	9	0	8	2	0	2
Change in residents	10	2	3	2	0	0	0	6	1	0
Number of cases	96	50	103	118	45	52	51	49	88	50

at all sites declined to negligible levels at greater distances. No significant levels of behavioral change in response to vibrations were found.

Earlier evaluations from the BART impact study concluded that stations with large automobile-access volumes, and especially those with inadequate parking, tended to have substantial problems. We found that most Daly City and Concord residents were unhappy with BART's effects on traffic congestion and parking. Many at these station sites also felt that the danger of traffic accidents had increased. These levels of reported adverse effects were dramatically high and did not diminish significantly up to the full four-block depth. The findings reflected overflow parking and substantial BART-related traffic at these two stations. In contrast, we observed a lack of perceived problems with parking and traffic at the El Cerrito Plaza station. Many Daly City and Concord residents changed their behavior in response to BART's traffic and parking problems, indicating a real effect on this impact. Adjustments included driving cautiously and walking carefully. These efforts involved little energy or initiative, suggesting that the problems did not disrupt neighborhood life in a major way. At worst, people felt that BART had made it more difficult to travel around their neighborhood.

The residents at at-grade sites may also experience problems with accessibility. BART's right-of-way was fenced after operation began, blocking previous automobile and pedestrian traffic. In response to earlier complaints, some pedestrian bridges were constructed. Residents' satisfaction with these structures was not known. Small but significant numbers of residents at the at-grade sites felt that the BART line was a barrier to their local movement. As perceived by at least some of the residents, BART has to some degree severed the "neighborhood." This effect was even perceived by residents who lived several blocks away. Since both Hayward South and Richmond had pedestrian bridges, we expect that this intervention mitigated more adverse effects. Thus, more problems with mobility are present in locations without this particular amenity.

Many private homes were exposed to view from the trains. This exposure was considered an annoyance for homes with back yards facing BART, since this outdoor space is especially valued and functional. However, indoor privacy was probably unaffected, since it is difficult for commuters in passing trains to peer through the windows in houses. At every site with back yards adjoining BART, a number of residents felt that this problem was "somewhat bad" or "very bad." This attitude was most evident at the aerial sites because of the high vantage point of the train riders and the extreme closeness of the tracks. To a lesser extent, a problem was also perceived by the residents nearest the at-grade lines.

Very few respondents at any sites reported any behavioral changes. Most of the changes that did occur were small, such as closing curtains, rather than building high fences or discontinuing sunbathing.

The major conclusion of earlier evaluations of BART impacts was that BART's structure and parking lots are damaging to the visual quality of the typically small-scale and personal character of low-density residential areas. However, at most sites, the majority of the respondents do not share this veiw. The visual effect of BART's architecture on the neighborhood was apparently not of particular concern to most nearby residents. It was anticipated that the persons living closest to BART, and thereby most able to see it from the home, would be strongest in their disapproval. This would be so especially for residents whose homes adjoined BART's aerial lines and station parking lots. Although the majority of respondents were indifferent to BART's visual impact, those whose back yards adjoined the BART line gave somewhat more negative evaluations. In all, most residents found the BART structures environmentally unobtrusive, if not particularly beneficial.

It was also expected that BART's very bright parking-lot lights would be viewed as having an adverse impact on the homes and yards surrounding stations. They are typically unshaded and cast light substantially beyond the lots' boundaries. Most residents were actually indifferent to the BART lighting. The aerial structures created a different problem, casting shadows on adjacent homes and yards. The shadows, in contrast to lighting, were viewed as a substantial problem where the aerial structures are sited very close to homes. Between a quarter and a half of the residents nearest BART's aerial tracks complained about this condition.

Earlier investigations of BART's effects on crime around stations, using available public records, found some increase in automobile thefts and burglaries, primarily directed at BART patrons. Among the station sites, the few adverse reactions reported by residents were outweighed by beneficial impacts, such as increased feelings of safety. This was even true at Daly City, where automobile thefts had actually risen, apparently because the victims were BART patrons rather than neighborhood residents. Concord was the exception, where some of those living across the street from the station reported bad effects of BART on crime. Despite concerns at Concord and elsewhere, few residents reported any changes in daily patterns. Those who did indicated greater caution in driving and walking. At all seven line sites, BART's adverse effects on crime were seen as insignificant.

The earlier BART impact project also included land use assessment, which indicated that since BART's construction, there have been no major changes at the study sites. Residents' perceptions of neighborhood changes were also negligible. In all, some specific impacts—such as train noise and vibrations at the aerial sites, traffic congestion and parking problems at the station sites, and barriers to movement at the at-grade sites—were perceived by residents. Other BART-related conditions were hardly noticed, and none of the specific problems was serious enough to cause widespread discontent with the nearby system.

MEDIATING FACTORS

BART ATTRIBUTES

We were able to determine the specific reasons for impact variations among sites through systematic comparisons. Attributes of BART that are present at some sites but not at others were examined as possible causes of response differences. The mediating factors considered here were trackway configuration, the presence of linear parks, train frequency, and station parking facilities. Since these are primarily design features that can be manipulated, the findings are extremely relevant to planning. General responses to BART, as well as specific perceived impacts, were used in the site comparisons.

With regard to trackway configuration, we compared aerial sites to at-grade sites. As implied earlier, those living near the aerial line were generally less satisfied with BART, and this displeasure was also found in comparisons restricted to the first sampling stratum. Residents living near aerial lines, when asked about specific BART impacts, were more often unhappy about noise, vibration, neighborhood appearance and view, and privacy than residents at the at-grade sites.

A contrast between two sites adds weights to the conclusion that at-grade lines are better received than aerial lines. The Richmond at-grade line and the San Leandro aerial line were compared since their residential conditions in relation to BART are similar. The level of overall dissatisfaction with BART and its general effects around the residence indicated greater displeasure at the aerial site. With regard to specific impacts, differences were most marked for acoustic impacts, visual impacts, and privacy. Residents at the aerial site also expressed more displeasure about the intrusiveness of the BART structure. These analyses show that trains on elevated structures cause more negative perceptions than those running at ground level. However, it is important to recall that these are relatively minor disruptions, as evidenced by the low number of residents desiring relocation or changing their activity patterns.

The only benefit of the BART facilities that could be examined was a linear park, which was present only at the two Albany sites. Responses from Albany East were compared with those from San Leandro. Both sites have back yards adjoining BART aerial tracks, similar physical structures, and comparable demographic characteristics. Albany West responses were compared with those from the Oakland site. Both have homes that face BART from across a wide street. Hayward North responses were also examined, since this site is similar to Albany West physically and demographically. In spite of positive attitudes toward the park, Albany respondents were not more positive about BART's overall effects. In fact, their responses were frequently less favorable than those for comparable aerial sites without a park. For specific impacts such as lighting and neighborhood appearance, residents of the Albany sites usually offered higher evaluations than residents without a linear park. A separate analysis of responses from the first sampling stratum shows very similar results. Most residents attributed the source of positive impacts to the linear park landscaping and lighting or to changed street conditions that were indirectly associated with the park. From these results, the perceived benefit of a linear park does not seem to offset displeasure with specific adverse impacts. The negative view of BART's impacts in Albany at least partly reflects a deep opposition to BART, as well as problems associated with specific attributes or shortcomings of planning interventions.

Technical observations led us to believe that residents are more adversely affected by BART noise where trains run more frequently, but our survey does not support this conclusion. The most comparable aerial-site pair differing in train frequency is Albany East and San Leandro. They are similar in demographic characteristics and the placement of homes in relation to the BART structure. Although trains run twice as often in San Leandro, or about once every six minutes during the day, the residents did not report that the noise was more objectionable. Even first-stratum respondents in Albany East complained more about noise than the comparable group at San Leandro.

Differences between the adequate-parking and inadequate-parking station sites, referred to in earlier discussion, were also explicitly considered. When one examines responses from the whole site and from the first stratum, persons living near the El Cerrito station site, where there is adequate parking, were happier with BART overall than were respondents from the other station sites. Variations in traffic conditions, such as safety, congestion, and parking, were even more dramatic. A majority of first-stratum respondents experiencing overflow parking felt BART's adverse impact on parking and traffic congestion, and a large proportion felt that BART had a bad effect on traffic safety. Residents of Daly City and Concord also believed that these street conditions caused the station to be a barrier in their neighborhood. Half of the Concord respondents and one-third of the Daly City respondents reported that BART had had a bad effect on their mobility, while only 1% mentioned this problem in El Cerrito. It thus appears, especially for parking facilities and trackway configuration, that BART attributes do have an influence on residents' perceptions of the system's local impact.

ENVIRONMENTAL DIFFERENCES

We made use of site comparisons here to identify the reasons for response variations where BART's attributes were similar. The mediating factors were three environmental conditions: "background" activity in the neighborhood, housing orientation, and the distance of the respondent's home from BART.

Earlier technical assessments indicated that BART's impact would be less perceptible when there was a great deal of background activity, such as auto or train traffic. This issue has important relevance regarding the exact location of transit systems. The case study sites, Richmond and Hayward South, allowed for one test of this expectation. They are in low-density suburban neighborhoods with back yards facing BART, and the BART line is parallel to an active railroad line. In Richmond, the effect of these additional trains is negligible, while the railroad in Hayward South is a double-track main line with a number of fast freight trains daily. Both at the full site and for the respondents at the first station, as expected, responses in Hayward South were consistently less negative regarding BART noise and a variety of other impacts.

The comparison of Hayward North and Oakland involved a different issue. The nearest homes at both sites face BART's aerial tracks across a street, but the street traffic in Oakland is heavy in contrast to the low activity in Hayward North. It was expected that the constant traffic activity would mask BART's sound, and the results suggest that the evaluations were consistently more positive at the site with the greater traffic noise. The findings indicate a mediating effect of generalized neighborhood activity levels—in this case, higher in Oakland and lower in Hayward North—variations that are commonly found among neighborhoods in many cities. It is also important to note that paired differences were larger for automobile background activity than for railroad noise.

Respondents whose back yards faced the BART line were considered more exposed to the system's impact. Again, we emphasize that this outdoor space was considered private and usable by the residents.

The back yards are also typically closer to the tracks than are the front yards that face the line. At closer distances, the BART structure casts shadows on yards and the noise is more prominent. A site with back yards adjoining the BART aerial line, San Leandro, was compared with Hayward North, where the nearest homes face BART. Both are in low-density areas with the same BART train frequency and adjacent railroad traffic. A second comparison involved the two contiguous sites on either side of the linear park in Albany. Results of these two comparisons suggest that BART's general effects, and its specific effects on shadows and privacy, were more adverse where back yards face BART sites. Expected effects on noise levels, on the other hand, were not supported by the data.

Technical assessments suggested that the adverse effects of BART, especially train noise, should decrease with distance from the tracks. Sound technicians predicted that noise was likely to be a problem within about one block from the aerial lines. Similarly, the visual impact of BART was expected to be blocked by other structures, so that this perceived effect would also diminish with distance. Discussions in other sections have made it clear that the perceptions of some specific impacts decrease with distance. Illustration of this tendency can also be found at three representative sites: El Cerrito Station, the Albany East aerial site, and the Richmond at-grade area. The effects of distance were generally consistent and strong. The station results appeared to be negligible after the first row of houses, and the perception of impact at the at-grade sites was also largely limited to the first row of houses. However, along the aerial lines, adverse effects were reported in substantial proportions for about 1½ blocks, with noise perceptions extending another block farther. An additional stratum was added to the Albany East sample at a distance of nearly one-half mile, and perceptible impacts were hardly evident that far from the BART line. Distance from the system, as we expected from the outset, is obviously a major factor in the perception of impact. Other environmental factors that we considered also influenced residents' attitudes and thus should influence the exact location of the trackways.

Demographic Differences and Personal Attitudes

The last type of mediating factor examined was respondent characteristics. Social status, stage of the life cycle, and time spent in the locality were of special interest. Personal attitudes and the respondent's experiences as a BART commuter were also considered.

The primary statistical procedure was stepwise regression, because the small sample sizes for the sites prevented multivariate analyses within neighborhoods. As a consequence, we conducted analyses using the total pooled sample and three subgroups based on site types (i.e., station, aerial, at-grade). We tried to replicate the results of regression analyses, whenever possible, with descriptive statistics from groups of respondents. Some comparisons were between groups, such as BART users and nonusers, within a site. When sites substantially differed in population characteristics, such as income or race, comparisons were made across sites.

Respondent characteristics were separately entered into a regression equation after dummy variables for site and stratum. Demographic factors included age, sex, years in the dwelling, annual family income, race, tenure status (owner or renter), hours spent away from home daily, orientation to BART (facing toward or away), and type of housing structure (single or multiple dwelling). Personal attitudes included measures of noise sensitivity, concern for the environment, and powerlessness. Whether or not the respondent was a BART user and whether positive expectations of BART's transportation capabilities had been fulfilled were also ascertained. We were interested in the additional variance after site and stratum that these demographic and attitudinal factors can explain. We also wanted to determine the respondent characteristics that were significantly related to perceived impacts.

General responses were first examined on items concerned with how often people noticed BART, satisfaction with BART's local effects, and the impact BART had on residential mobility. In all, most of the variance was explained by site and stratum characteristics, indicating the relative importance of physical and design features (see Table 5). Personal attitudes generally had no additional explanatory value. Only one BART-related attitude, positive expectations of the transit system, had a significant impact on perceiving satisfaction with local effects. However, use of BART was significantly associated with some of these general response items. Frequent users of BART were significantly more positive with respect to its local effects. These individuals were also more likely to choose their home for BART-related reasons. They did not, however, seem to notice BART in their local environment more than others did. Ecological comparisons replicated the findings on BART use. One station site, Daly City, included a substantially higher proportion of BART users than the other two station sites, allowing for across-site comparisons. Since there were many BART users in both Daly City and El Cerrito Plaza, it was also possible to conduct two independent within-site comparisons. In general, the results consistently indicated that BART users were more positive in their general evaluations of impacts.

TABLE 5
PERCENTAGE OF THE VARIANCE EXPLAINED BY SITE, STRATUM,
AND DEMOGRAPHIC VARIABLES

	Attitude items			
Stepwise regressions	Notice BART	BART's local effects	Noise of BART	Chose home for BART
Step 1: Site	4	9	19	4
Step 2: Site, stratum	5	10	25	5
Step 3: Site, stratum, demographics[a]	9	17	28	22
Additional variance explained by demographics	4	7	3	17

[a] Includes all of the demographic variables listed in Figure 2. Personal attitudes were not included because of low significance.

Indicators of disadvantaged status, such as income and race, had no effect on general responses to BART. Other than age and length of residence, no factors explained perceptions of BART. These two factors were particularly important at station sites. Age was relevant to local satisfaction, with residents under 30 complaining more frequently, and shorter lengths of residences tended to be associated with less hostility toward the system. The findings showing local satisfaction to be correlated with low length of residence at station sites are probably due to the fact that many recent movers chose to live near BART. These people then use the transit system fairly regularly and thus have a positive attitude toward BART. Apparently, these types of residents are middle-aged and thus account for the inverse relationship between age and local satisfaction.

Specific impacts that represented the most consistent effects of the system were next considered. Noise, the most persistent and significant adverse impact, was analyzed for all residents and separately for the three site types. For station respondents only, items concerning traffic and parking were analyzed. Perceptions of vibrations and privacy were separately examined for the aerial subgroup. Disadvantaged status was not significantly related to the perceptions of any specific impacts. There was, however, a strong tendency for respondents younger than 30 to complain more about noise, and for station residents in this age group to complain more about parking and traffic. Among station-site dwellers, perhaps for reasons related to BART use mentioned earlier, those who had a shorter length of residency tended to complain less about parking and traffic problems. Single-family home dwellers at station sites were also more likely to complain about parking and traffic problems, but they did not seem to complain more than others about noise, perhaps because traffic and parking (unlike noise) occur in residential space, and these invasions were more keenly noticed by those with high commitment to the area, namely, single-family home owners and long-time residents.

Experience as a BART commuter, unlike the role in global assessments, had no impact on specific complaints. Regarding personal attitudes, a relationship was found between noise sensitivity and perceived noise impact, but "environmental concern" had no explanatory value. We expected that people who felt powerless, because of noise and other stressors, might subsequently pay less attention to details such as BART's local impacts (see, e.g., Cohen, Glass, & Singer, 1973; Glass & Singer, 1972; Rodin, 1976). This was true of complaints about parking problems but not of perceptions of noise. In sum, physical and design features played a major role in perceptions of impact, while demographics and attitudes had inconsistent and small effects.

Importantly, this portion of the study disturbed some myths about low-income individuals, low-status ethnic groups, those who feel powerless, and the elderly. They were not less likely than others to notice the transit system or to complain about its environmental impact. If anything, there was a surprising degree of conformity across social groupings. Age differences in survey responses, which we referred to earlier, were actually due to the hypercritical attitudes of the young rather than to the underreporting of problems by the elderly. This point is reaffirmed by the findings on length of residence, which indicated that long-term residents, who often were older and typically had the strongest sense of community, were not particularly enthusiastic toward BART's local presence. It would thus be unwise to assume that certain groups will show no resistance or express no concerns over potential environmental stressors in their residential environment.

Some seemingly commonsensical and extremely useful conclusions can be drawn from the findings regarding BART use. In attempts to create favorable attitudes, efforts to convince people that the environmental benefits outweigh the costs cannot compete with the impact of regular use of the BART system. Outside of physical and design features, the best opportunities for generating satisfaction with a rapid transit system as well as minimizing criticism of its adverse local impact seem to be in attempts to ensure that it will be utilized by a broad spectrum of the population.

BART'S EFFECTS IN THE CONTEXT OF NEIGHBORHOOD PROBLEMS

In this section, we consider residents' evaluations of the total neighborhood environment. These questions allow us to place BART complaints in perspective and to compare the problems created by the system with those created by other adverse local conditions. We also recognize that how people perceived BART's specific influence on their residential area was an important facet of the investigation. This analysis was especially helpful in determining whether residents believed that BART had been the cause of local deterioration. For this analysis, we considered each site separately, examining the overall attitudes toward the neighborhood reported in Table 6 and the mean scores on items concerned with specific neighborhood attributes.

Concord was not viewed very favorably by its residents, and some of the complaints mentioned were related to the BART station's impacts. Parking and traffic in the neighborhood were the most serious problems. There was also displeasure with the way sidewalks and streets were kept, probably reflecting trash problems around the station. Despite these adverse local impacts, residents were generally positive about BART's presence, apparently because having a station nearby diminished some negative feelings toward specific environmental effects. The study sample was about evenly split among people who thought the neighborhood had got better, got worse, or remained the same since BART was built. Condition of housing was the only non-BART attribute that seemed to be a problem.

Residents of Daly City rated their neighborhood, as a whole, in slightly more favorable terms than did those of Concord. Several aspects of this area were rated unfavorably, most notably parking and traffic. Also of interest to our concern with BART's impact on stations, safety from crime was cited as a problem by one-third of the respondents. The quality of housing and landscaping was also given low marks. BART, however, was the most highly rated attribute of the area. Having BART nearby was rated as being a "very good" aspect of the neighborhood by three-fourths of the sample. In short, BART and its attributes seemed to make up the very best and the very worst aspects of this residential area. About equal percentages of people saw positive, negative, or no changes in the neighborhood environment since they had moved there. Most cited BART as a major reason for change, whether for the better or for the worse.

El Cerrito was ranked higher in neighborhood quality than any

TABLE 6
OVERALL ATTITUDES TOWARD THE NEIGHBORHOOD

	Stations					Aerial lines			At-grade lines	
	Concord	Daly City	El Cerrito	Albany East	Albany West	Oakland	Hayward North	San Leandro	Richmond	Hayward South
Pleasant location (%)										
Very pleasant	41	50	76	65	62	44	43	63	38	56
Pleasant	42	36	22	30	31	37	35	18	43	36
Indifferent	2	6	0	1	4	2	0	2	5	2
Unpleasant	9	6	2	3	2	15	16	14	11	6
Very unpleasant	6	2	0	2	0	2	6	2	1	0
Best location (%)										
Much better	31	37	47	47	36	19	24	48	21	32
Best	26	20	31	34	46	39	35	33	34	34
Same	33	35	21	16	16	42	37	19	38	34
Worse	11	6	1	3	2	0	2	0	7	0
Much worse	0	2	0	0	0	0	2	0	0	0
Neighborhood change (%)										
Better	32	38	25	22	29	31	20	35	32	20
Same	38	34	67	65	56	44	53	45	48	60
Worse	30	28	9	13	15	25	28	20	20	20
Number of cases	96	50	103	118	45	52	51	49	88	50

other site. It appeared to have had all of the benefits of being near a BART station with none of the costs. For example, few people complained about parking or saw major traffic problems in their neighborhoods. All aspects of the neighborhoods' physical and social environment were rated positively, among the highest being convenience to shopping and transportation facilities. There was almost unanimous positive sentiment about BART's local presence and about BART service. Two-thirds of the respondents reported "no change" in the character of the area since BART was built. Only 9% regarded any change as being for the worse.

The residents of Richmond viewed the neighborhood and its specific attributes in critical terms. They were unhappy with their location, complained more than other groups about issues related to accessibility, and were more concerned with crime than were the respondents at any other site. No complaints associated with ground-level tracks were reported. BART was neither a positive nor a negative feature of this particular area. About a third of the respondents thought that the neighborhood had improved in recent years, while 20% saw deterioration and about half perceived no change at all. Very few people saw BART as a factor in either favorable or unfavorable neighborhood change.

Hayward South was perceived as a moderately pleasant place to live. No particular aspects of the residential environment were described as especially good or bad. Among the most highly rated factors were the quality of neighbors and the degree of privacy in the home. Serious drawbacks were parking, traffic, and crime. These were impacts of facilities and services in the neighborhood, such as a nearby school, rather than the nearness of BART trains and ground-level tracks. BART was given high praise as a general feature of their residential environment, surprisingly, even though few residents were regular users. Two-thirds saw no recent changes in the quality of the area, while there was an even split between those seeing change for the better and those seeing change for the worse. As with aspects of environmental quality, BART was overshadowed by other causal factors in an assessment of recent changes.

Housing at both Albany sites was reportedly well maintained although the housing itself was somewhat old. Residents of Albany rated their areas very highly. Among the most favorable characteristics were convenience of shopping, the neighbors, and home privacy. Respondents at both Albany sites were unified in their complaints about BART's aerial tracks and trains, and these were the worst complaints made about any environmental feature. BART's nearby presence was rated more unfavorably here than at any other site. Despite these indications of discontent, the respondents expressed very little belief that "change" was occurring in their areas.

Ratings of the Oakland neighborhood by its residents were not as high as at most other sites. Complaints about the locale were numerous: bad landscaping, inadequate park facilities, traffic congestion, parking problems, crime, and poor schools. Despite its inner-city character, this area was also seen as being inconveniently located with respect to commercial facilities. BART was given a rather moderate rating at this aerial site. Its contribution as a neighborhood attribute placed it midway between the very good and the very bad environmental features. A number of respondents perceived change occurring in this area. Slightly more saw a change for the better rather than for the worse. Neighbors were the key causal factors cited in this change, with BART's role small and inconsistent. All in all, the residents of this area, who experienced great economic disadvantage, did not seem to find BART to be a key factor in their evaluations of neighborhood quality.

Most residents considered San Leandro a good place to live. They saw it as being extremely convenient and as having pleasant social and environmental characteristics. Crime did not appear to cause much complaint in this locale, in contrast to others, such as Oakland. The most displeasing aspects of this environment were air quality, traffic, BART, and bus service. Over half of the people noticed change in the neighborhood, and by almost 2 to 1, they saw the neighborhood improving in character. BART played a generally insignificant role in these responses. For an aerial site with seemingly detrimental BART attributes, surprisingly there was only mild anti-BART sentiment.

Hayward North was rated among the lowest of any of the study sites. Some of the worst complaints involved streets, sidewalks, parking, and traffic. The best aspects of the area involved the quality of the neighbors. BART's nearby presence elicited the most negative response of any neighborhood attribute. About half the respondents noted change, with the majority viewing the neighborhood as worse than before. BART was not mentioned often, though always cited with reference to worsening the area. All in all, the Hayward North site appeared to have many problems as a neighborhood, with BART's aerial configuration contributing to the overall sense of deterioration.

In conclusion, BART was not a major factor in evaluating neighborhood quality or recent changes in the locality. The problems of deteriorating areas, such as Richmond, Oakland, and Hayward North, were clearly separate and above the environmental impact of BART. In the same way, the presence of BART could not compete with the positive features mentioned in El Cerrito, San Leandro, and Albany. There were also cases, such as at Albany's sites, where high enthusiasm about the locality occurred in conjunction with outright hostility toward BART and its local effects. I would thus suggest that BART's influence was limited to assessments of specific local attributes. The presence of tracks and trains, however, can aggravate already existing problems and thus quicken the rate of deterioration or heighten residents' dissatisfaction. Alternatively, it may combine with existing local amenities in order to make good neighborhoods even more attractive.

CONCLUSIONS

This chapter has examined the effects of the Bay Area Rapid Transit on residential environments adjacent to the system. A social survey, which was conducted in 10 San Francisco Bay Area neighborhoods, placed the primary emphasis of our research on residents' perceptions rather than on evaluations of relevant technical data by professionals. The evidence gathered indicates that nearby residents were generally indifferent or favorable toward BART. There were even some instances where people apparently chose to live closer to the system. Despite great controversy over its operations, the presence of BART in the neighborhood thus does not appear to be a major nuisance relative to other local concerns.

Certain BART attributes, on the other hand, create specific conditions that were viewed unfavorably by residents. Noise was a major complaint along the elevated trackway, as to a lesser extent was dissatisfaction with shadows, vibrations, and lack of privacy. Traffic congestion and parking shortages were also found around several stations. BART-related problems in some cases also led to heightened preferences for moving out of the neighborhood.

However, complaining was not uniform among all residents experiencing similar BART features. Adverse impacts were mediated by local conditions and the design of the system. Background conditions, such as heavy street traffic near one aerial site, masked the noise of BART trains and thus reduced local dissatisfaction. Residents at one station site, which is provided with ample parking facilities and major thoroughfares, did not report difficulties found elsewhere. Perceptions of some specific problems also declined markedly with distance from BART. Its impact was also less notable when trains were at ground level and when tracks faced front yards. These findings indicate that certain physical and design features may mediate specific impacts of a rapid transit system.

Most social and personal factors appear to play a minor role in perceptions of BART's impacts. There is no evidence to suggest that the socioeconomically disadvantaged complain less than others or that the elderly passively accept the specific problems attributed to the system. Moreover, home owners and persons under 30 years of age are more negative in certain domains. Recent residents, especially at station sites, appeared to have more favorable attitudes toward the system's presence.

The only demographic variable that had considerable explanatory value was use of BART. This probably also accounts for the relationship between positive attitudes and recent residence at station sites, because many newcomers chose those neighborhoods so that they could more easily use BART. In general, the BART commuters tended to complain less than others about the system's local effects, so that the primary beneficiaries of BART seem to look on its presence more favorably. We can only speculate, but it appears that if a larger proportion of our respondents used BART regularly, our findings overall would have been more positive. In addition, while we have not gathered a random sample of BART users, it appears that at least this subsample of commuters living near the system saw its benefits more than its costs. The findings also present some useful information about the extent and types of problems associated with a new mass transit system. Even though the overall effects of the system may not be serious, specific complaints by nearby residents are to be expected. Noise from the moving trains and traffic-related problems around stations are among the most common annoyances. We found that several physical and design features can help to reduce the perceived impact. In general, many of the adverse effects of a system can be avoided if the placement of aerial trackways and the flow of commuters into stations are carefully planned. Regions in the market for mass transit must also consider the size of the commuting population and must vigorously attempt to recruit regular users, because widespread use may also ultimately affect the perception of the system's adverse impact. The results, however, do not necessarily apply to all other systems that are planned or are now in operation. A first consideration is where the specific neighborhoods affected by mass transit fall on the "urban" continuum. Our study areas were predominantly low-density and suburban in nature. Ambient noise and non-BART traffic congestion, in most cases, were quite low. Many residents had lived in the neighborhood for years, and the predominant housing type was the single-family home. In all probability, most of our respondents had fairly high expectations of peace and privacy. There are thus special physical, social, and perceptual features that describe these sites.

One would suggest, then, that systems that cut through "more urban" circumstances than we have described would have fewer effects, while those systems that are adjacent to even "less urban" circumstances would have a more adverse impact.

Two other considerations, in applying our findings, are specifically concerned with the system's design and its commuting population. Specifically, mass transit that predominantly runs underground does not affect nearby residents to the degree that we have reported for above-ground systems. Systems that are largely composed of elevated trackways or that involve ground-level trackways that do not offer pedestrian bridges and automobile underpasses should in general result in more problems for local residents. Finally, because BART is probably relatively underutilized as a transit system, we argue that our reports of local disruptions are more exaggerated than where people more commonly use mass transit and are more receptive to the idea of having a mass transit system.

In a more general way, the present study serves to underscore the importance of the social impact assessment. The "technical assessments" by planners did not accurately reflect the concerns raised by nearby residents. In most instances, the professionals seemed to overstate the severity of the local impact. Assumptions that we might make about residents' complaints, on the basis of adverse publicity and some anti-BART feelings expressed by Bay Area residents, also proved to be invalid. There is thus no substitute for systematic samplings of populations affected by a particular environmental change. In some cases, such as when some environmental factors are of harm to general health and well-being but are unperceived by local residents, social impact assessments should be supplemented by local officials. However, in the majority of cases where more subtle quality-of-life issues are at stake, this method provides data with direct policy implications.

Finally, many questions about the stability and the applicability of our findings require additional research. It is important to know, for example, if the general and specific attitudes toward BART mentioned several years ago have deteriorated in the interim. A follow-up study, within a time span of perhaps 10 years should concentrate on lasting environmental impact, which could surface in questions concerned with residential mobility and the total neighborhood environment. Whenever changes occur in study sites, either planned or unplanned, one also ought to be prepared to conduct a minievaluation by reinterviewing the resident population. Examples may include adding parking lots at an overcrowded station or experiencing some change in background activity at an aerial site, or even manipulating the proportion of system users in any adjacent neighborhood. This approach would offer further evidence of mediating factors. In general, the major classes of variables outlined in Figure 2 can be applied to studying other systems, though the specific design and study questions should also reflect the peculiar characteristics of the system in question. A major deficiency in the present research is its lack of longitudinal data, and thus, future efforts should at least include interviews immediately after and long after the implementation of the new transportation system.

REFERENCES

Baldassare, M. *The growth dilemma: Residents' views and local population change in the United States.* Berkeley: University of California Press, 1981.

Baldassare, M., Knight, R., & Swan, S. Urban service and environmental stressor: The impact of the Bay Area Rapid Transit on residential mobility. *Environment and Behavior,* 1979, *11,* 435–450.

Christensen, K. *Social impact of land development.* Washington, D.C.: Urban Institute, 1976.

Cohen, S., Glass, D., & Singer, J. E. Apartment noise, auditory discrimination, and reading ability in children. *Journal of Experimental Social Psychology,* 1973, *9,* 407–422.

DeLeuw, Cather, & Company. *Responses of nearby residents to BART's environmental impacts.* San Francisco, Final Report, 1977.

Finsterbusch, K., & Wolf, C. P. *Methodology of social impact assessment.* Stroudsberg, Pa.: Dowden, Hutchinson, and Ross, 1977.

Foley, D. Accessibility for residents in the metropolitan environment. In A. Hawley & V. Rock (Eds.), *Metropolitan America in contemporary perspective.* New York: Wiley, 1976.

Glass, D., & Singer, J. E. *Urban stress.* New York: Academic Press, 1972.

Hoachlander, E. G. Who pays and who rides BART: A reexamination. *Working Paper Number 309.* Berkeley, Calif.: Institute of Urban and Regional Development, 1979.

Knight, R., & Trygg, L. *Land use impacts of recent major rapid transit improvements.* Washington, D.C.: U.S. Government Printing Office, 1977.

Michelson, W. *Man and his urban environment.* Reading, Mass.: Addison-Wesley, 1976.

Ortner, J., & Wachs, M. The cost-revenue squeeze in American public transit. *Journal of the American Planning Association,* 1979, *45,* 10–21.

Rodin, J. Density, perceived choice, and response to controllable and uncontrollable outcomes. *Journal of Experimental Social Psychology,* 1976, *12,* 564–578.

Stokols, D. On the distinction between density and crowding. *Psychological Review,* 1972, *79,* 275–277.

Wachs, M. Consumer attitudes towards transit service: an interpretive review. *Journal of the American Institute of Planners,* 1976, *42,* 96–104.

Wachs, M., & Ortner, J. Capital grants and recurrent subsidies: A dilemma in American transportation policy. *Transportation,* 1979, *8,* 3–19.

Webber, M. *The BART experience: What have we learned?* Monograph Number 26. Berkeley, Calif.: Institute of Urban and Regional Development, 1976.

8

Future Transportation

ORGANIZATION OF THE DESIGN PROCESS

RICHARD M. MICHAELS

Transportation has had a fundamental influence on both the social and the economic development of society, as well as on the location and the design of the built environment. A major question for the future is whether transportation should play as central a role as it has in social organization. The answer to this question will be determined as much by changes in the social order as by transportation technology. To evaluate future transportation systems, it is necessary to place their essential purpose (i.e., accessibility) in a larger context. Therefore, the first section of this paper is concerned with the functional role of transportation in the organization of the society.

A second consideration in the future development of transportation is the characteristics of the potential users of this transportation. Transportation is a mediating system, a means of linking people and goods, and its effectiveness depends ultimately on the capabilities and limitations of the users as well as on their perceived needs and requirements, which must provide the basis for the design and operation of transportation. Such a rationale for system design is developed in the main body of the chapter.

Given an understanding of the way in which transportation has developed and the changes occurring in the society, objective functions for transportation can be defined. Similarly, given the basic user criteria

RICHARD M. MICHAELS • Urban Transportation Center, University of Illinois at Chicago Circle, Chicago, Illinois 60680.

for design, it is possible to evaluate transportation system alternatives and to speculate on systems that may meet projected mobility goals more effectively. The final section of the chapter examines these futuristic issues.

TRANSPORTATION AND SOCIAL ORGANIZATION

In any organized and technologically based society, there are three fundamental structures that underly the design of the built environment. These may be viewed as three interrelated systems: (1) production systems; (2) societal systems; and (3) infrastructure service systems. Production systems are made up of the functional units required to produce durable and nondurable goods for consumption, to transform raw materials into socially useful or desirable goods through the use of people and machines. Societal systems are the institutions that provide goods and services to consumers. Such systems are distributed so as to allow the maximum accessibility of these services to the members of society. The third element is infrastructure systems, which provide the basic resources by which both production and societal systems may function. These resources include energy, water, waste management, raw materials, and transportation, among others. Conceptually, this structural organization is shown in Figure 1. It is the interrelation among these elements that determine social organization and the structure of the built environment. The integration of these three systems determines both the wealth a society can generate and the quality of life it can provide.

Industrial societies have typically developed around production systems. The primary focus has been on providing the technology, the labor, and the infrastructure to satisfy the requirements of production. Transportation, one of the most basic of the infrastructure systems, has been designed, developed, and rationalized by production requirements. For example, one of the major determinants of urban location was the availability of transportation for linking raw materials with production systems and transferring finished goods to their markets. This requirement dictated coastal or riverine locations for industrial cities, since boat and barge were at one time the only available transportation capable of distributing the large volume of goods generated by the industrial system. This requirement was also the reason for the enormous public investment in railroads in the United States after the Civil War. Railroads had (and still have) the capacity to carry large volumes of freight at low cost. Railroad technology installed on an vast scale be-

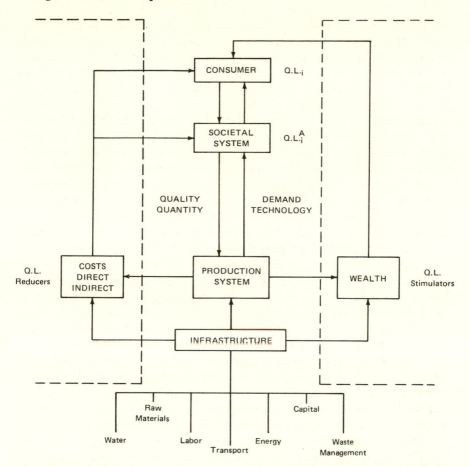

Figure 1. Social system organization. Q.L. = quality of life; $Q.L._i$ = quality of life actually obtained from societal system, i; $Q.L._i^A$ = maximum quality of life obtainable from societal system, i.

tween 1870 and 1910 allowed the development of the American industrial system. It also provided the vehicle for the creation of a new type of city.

In industrial cities, the movement of people was also largely seen as serving production goals. As industry grew, the demand for labor also grew, and it became impossible to house the work force within walking distance of the factory. One solution was to house workers in low-land-value corridors and to provide mechanical means of transportation. Mass transit technology was ideally suited to the work trip since industry was concentrated around the urban core, and a simple radial system served to link the home and the workplace. Investment in these systems was rationalized on economic grounds and led to the rapid growth of industrial cities until the middle of the twentieth century. It is important to note that it was the values of the workplace that determined transportation capacity requirements. Work hours were set by production requirements and the need for personal interaction, which led to a social agreement on the timing of work trip travel and with it the peak-hour problem. This concentration of work trips in time has dominated transportation planning and investment for nearly a half century. The work trip has also been a major determinant of the design of all transportation systems, for the focus has been on carrying the able-bodied adult population to the workplace.

It was from this interrelation of residence and workplace that the industrial city emerged. As these centers grew, the movement of people as part of the production process became a necessary component of transportation systems. Clearly, population density, residential location and structure, and the location of societal systems were determined jointly by production system requirements and transportation technology. These two factors were thus crucial determinants of the organization and construction of the built environment of industrial cities.

At some point in the twentieth century, the organization of the production system reached a level of productivity that created far more capital (time, energy, and money) than it consumed. This surplus led to a broader distribution of resources among members of society and provided a marked increase in the availability of goods and services, which, in turn, caused a change from a production-oriented to a consumption-oriented society. That is, the society developed from one based on production economics to one based on welfare economics. With this shift, different social priorities emerged so that the focus of investment—physical, economic, and social—became increasingly "qualitative." That is, the dominant concern was with the quality of life. Most of the research on quality of life over the past two decades has led to the specification of 8–12 societal systems that determine the quality of life (Baker, Dudgeon, Michaels, & Rothermund, 1978). A representative list is shown in Table 1.

A quality-of-life criterion places central concern on human needs and requirements. It also differentiates a population in terms of its accessibility to social and emotional services as well as material goods. Accessibility becomes as critical in a societal system structure as in an industrial one. For example, if people cannot reach the health care system, their quality of life is reduced. Obviously, then, transportation is a crucial factor in satisfying qualitative goals. Indeed, almost every trans-

TABLE 1
SOCIETAL SYSTEMS

Life support:
   1. Food
   2. Clothing
   3. Housing
   4. Medical care
Protection:
   5. Public safety
   6. National defense
Enrichment:
   7. Education
   8. Recreation
   9. Culture
  10. Religion

portation plan prepared by planning agencies includes some statement that the goal of transportation is to ensure access to all the systems that provide a high quality of life. In sum, the capacity to obtain any desired quality of life depends on (1) the ability of consumers to differentiate their needs; (2) the location of the societal systems that provide the means of satisfying those needs; and (3) the means of linking consumers with those societal systems.

There are two major problems that limit transportation's capacity to serve this goal. One problem is that existing transportation systems have not been designed and are not operated to serve the young, the old, the handicapped, the ill, and those without economic resources. A second problem is that quality-of-life societal systems have not set requirements for transportation services. The earlier production-oriented system specified quite precisely the access requirements for the movement of both goods and people and hence created the transportation systems that are in current use. Although it is feasible to meet the linkage requirements for each of the societal systems, this has not been done.

Of even more basic consideration are the behavioral criteria of the users of the societal systems. The quality of health care, for example, is determined by consumers' ability to recognize their health care needs, to know where they can be met, and to know how to use the health care system. Because most of the societal systems are spatially distributed and are not necessarily close to the consumer, knowledge of the means of access becomes a crucial determinant of the consumer's quality of life. It is obvious that if transportation is to serve quality-of-life goals it must be planned and designed to satisfy the requirements of both the societal systems and the users of those systems. Hence, the definition of the users needs and requirements becomes the basis for the design of transport or, more generally, access systems.

The basic approach to this kind of analysis is shown in Figure 2. The essential properties of any access system should be determined by the requirements of societal systems and of their users. Analysis of both

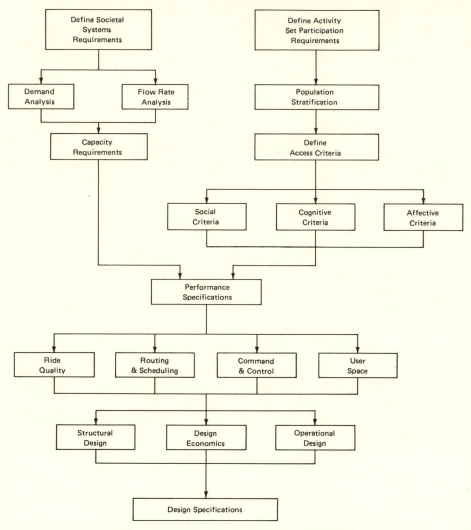

Figure 2. Design paradigm for transportation.

should lead to a specification of the performance characteristics desired from the linkage system, which are shown in the figure. It should be noted that systems developed from this frame of reference may bear little relation to existing technology. In sum, the design of future transportation should be based primarily on the goals set for such systems and on operational performance specifications.

At the present time, performance specifications have not been developed from a behavioral viewpoint. There is only agreement that the available linkage technology is inadequate. If the current transportation technology is to be adequately reorganized or replaced, it is necessary to define the design requirements starting from user behavior. There are three fundamental components of behavior that define transportation performance requirements. One component is the motivational factors that generate the demand for travel. The second component is behavioral factors that underly decisions about both where to travel and how to travel. The third component is the human factors that determine the functional effectiveness of transportation systems.

The next section is concerned with the motivational and travel demand factors. The section that follows deals with the behavioral criteria for access systems. And the section that follows that focuses on the human factors that determine transport operational characteristics.

MOTIVATIONAL FACTORS UNDERLYING TRAVEL

One way to approach transportation is to view it abstractly from the user's standpoint. Almost all studies on traveler behavior indicate that travel is a mediating activity between the needs of the individual, both internal and social, and the sources of their satisfaction, which are distributed in space. Thus, travel and transportation are mediators between needs and satisfiers. In this sense, transportation has an intrinsic cost. It delays need satisfaction and adds an increment to the energy expended to obtain satisfaction. Travel has no direct benefits; it has indirect benefits in the sense that it can increase the alternative sources of satisfaction available to the individual and the social group.

Consequently, what transportation characteristics are desired or will be acceptable must be derived from the underlying needs of people, not for travel, but for the perceived sources of need satisfaction, that is, the societal systems. This viewpoint is the general basis for defining the requirements for mobility.

In one approach, the hypothesis is essentially that individual travel behavior reflects the instrumental means of satisfying needs in time and space, as reflected by the activities in which individuals participate (Spier, 1971; Lancaster, 1970; Chapin, 1965; Jones, 1977; Dix, 1979).

Given that linkage is required for participation in these activities, the question arises: What are the behavioral criteria for an acceptable or optimal linkage system? Each activity in which the individual desires to participate has its own linkage requirements. For example, a medical emergency requires a minimum-time-delay linkage system. To satisfy the requirement or need to work, where arrival time is important, transport reliability and travel time are important, and people allocate time for travel that ideally minimizes the total psychic costs of traveling.

One approach to identifying the activities that may require transportation is shown in Table 2 (Wright, 1972). This author used a rating scale to estimate the importance of each criterion relative to each of the activities. Such a procedure is of limited utility since there is no obvioius way to translate the ratings into performance measures that can be used to design a transportation system. This is a classic problem. However, some recent work (Louviere & Norman, 1977; Levin, 1977) is moving toward this kind of translation.

One important element shown in Table 2 is open to measurement. The first column, "trip frequency," defines the number of linkages required to satisfy individual needs. In essence, the total demand for travel

TABLE 2
ACTIVITY NEEDS AND LINKAGE CRITERIA

Activity set	Trip frequency	Trip reliability	Trip length	Trip cost	Trip time	Trip urgency
Income production						
Shopping (nondurable)						
Shopping (durable)						
Shopping (impulse)						
Education (required)						
Education (discretionary)						
Social (familial)						
Social (nonfamilial)						
Social (informal groups)						
Social (formal groups)						
Recreation (spectator)						
Recreation (participatory)						
Recreation (cultural)						
Health care (nonemergency)						
Health care (emergency)						
Services (personal)						
Services (business)						

is the sum of the trips that some homogeneous subgroup of the population actually makes plus those that such a group desires to make but cannot because of inadequate transportation. Clearly, one criterion measure of transportation performance is the proportion of desired participation that is not satisfied. This may be termed *transport-constrained latent demand.*

This issue was partially approached in a study (Michaels & Weiler, 1976) of mobility of the physically handicapped. In a survey of 1,272 persons, categorized into five classes by severity of handicap, the respondents were asked to list the trips that they had made within the 48-hour period preceding the interview. This information provided a direct measure of the actual travel by the sample. These trips were combined into a six-category classification of activity. As a seperate part of the survey, the respondents were also asked to estimate their frequency of participation in 19 predefined activities over a 30-day period. This set of activities was combined with the first set of six activities, providing an indirect check on the consistency of 2- and 30-day travel. Since no significant differences were found between the two sets of recall data, the estimates of actual travel were assumed to be consistent. For the set of 19 activities, the respondents were also asked to estimate for the same 30-day period the trips they would have liked to make, providing an estimate of the desired participation in activities. Finally, the respondents were asked whether the trips desired but not made were not made because of inadequate transportation rather than lack of resources, poor health, etc. This provided an estimate of the transportation-constrained latent demand.

Given the actual travel and the latend demand, it is possible to define the total demand travel. It is composed of two parts: (1) a realized participation and (2) a latent or desired participation that is not carried out because of insufficient access capability. It is thus possible to write a general equation for total demand for travel by activity and by population subgroup. That is,

$$D_T = \underset{ijk}{\Sigma\Sigma\Sigma} \, P(\Psi_i) \, (\rho_k) \, (A_{ijk} + D_{ijk} \, C_{ijk})$$

Where

D_T = the total desired number of trips
P = population size
Ψ_i = population stratification category
ρ_k = the activity set in which people wish to participate
A_{ijk} = the actual frequency of participation in the activities: A = trips/unit time

D_{ijk} = the desired frequency of participation: D = trips/unit time
C_{ijk} = the proportion of desired trips not made because of transport inadequacy

Consistent with a need-satisfying model, one would predict that the total number of desired participatory trips would be the same within any homogeneous subgroup of the population. Further, it would be predicted that latent demand ($D_{ijk}\ C_{ijk}$) should be a measure of the inadequacies in transportation. By use of the activity set data obtained from the five classes of physically handicapped, it was possible to estimate the actual and desired participation. The results indicated no significant differences among the handicapped in terms of frequency of desired participation, but there were differences in actual participation. Further, the trips not made because of transportation inadequacies were estimated for each class of handicapped plus a control group of middle-income nonhandicapped. The results shown in Figure 3 show a direct relationship between latent demand for travel and severity of handicap. This finding indicates the relative inadequacy of existing transportation technology for this sample of the population.

This particular formulation suggests that by analyzing the latent needs as well as the manifest behavior of the individual or the household unit, a more general measure of accessibility requirements may be

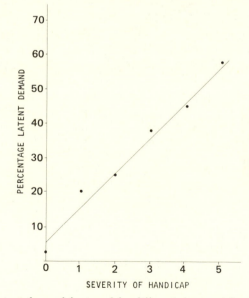

Figure 3. The latent demand for travel for different classes of the mobility-limited.

developed. Further, such an approach provides a measure of the effectiveness of the available transportation. In the case of the handicapped, it is clear that their ability to satisfy their needs is severely limited by the available linkage technology. It should not be surprising that there has been a significant political response to this group's inability to satisfy their needs.

By evaluating need structure, then, basic accessibility requirements may be derived. It is equally obvious that the needs underlying these requirements are not homogeneous over the population and depend on the social role of individuals, their physical condition, and their stage in the life cycle. In essence, the access requirements of different groups must be considered as part of the transportation design or evaluation process. It is possible, through the use of some techniques of urban demography (Shevky & Williams, 1949; Bell, 1953; Rees 1970), to define homogeneous subgroups in the population. These classification schemes provide a means of defining appropriate need sets and of identifying the linkage systems that would satisfy those needs. By starting the transportation design and planning process from this kind of behavioral frame of reference, it should be possible to specify the characteristics of systems that will satisfy human requirements for linkage. Ideally, transport should provide the opportunity for individuals and groups to satisfy their needs according to their temporal demand, should pose no barriers to users, and should offer service at a cost that does not compromise need fulfillment.

TRANSPORTATION PERFORMANCE CRITERIA

The previous discussion leads directly to the consideration of the performance criteria that transportation service must meet. In order to satisfy the quantitative and qualitative requirements for travel derived from need structure, any transportation system must satisfy basic behavioral criteria for its effective use. These criteria may be defined as cognitive, affective, and social, as shown in Figure 2.

COGNITIVE CRITERIA

For a variety of historical and functional reasons, need satisfiers are distributed in space. Indeed, it is because of the extent of this spatial distribution that mechanical means of transportation are necessary. Because satisfier sites are dispersed in space, individuals must develop some cognitive understanding of their environment. A variety of research (Stea, 1974) suggests that people's perception of location in the environment is nonlinearly related to conventional Euclidean space. Cognitive detail decreases nonlinearly from a certain few reference points (e.g., home, workplace), as well as being determined by characteristics of the trip makers, such as age, experience, length of time in the environment, and basic cognitive skills.

Some recent work (Stenson, 1978) has shown not only that is spatial recognition limited but also that distance perception is determined by cognitive structure. Thus, in large environments, points located farther from a given origin are perceived as farther away than they objectively are. As a first approximation, this distance function follows a power law.

In sum, the perception of macrospace is a major determinant of how people will use the sources of satisfaction in the environment and consequently where they will travel. In general, what may be termed *action space* is an area ideally defined by an exponentially decreasing distance function, in which perceived activity site content also decreases exponentially from the origin point.

Cognitive structure has important implications for transportation design. If the role of transport is to be the means of access for satisfying needs at places distributed in space, then how that linkage is related to the cognitive structure of trip makers determines where trips will be made and what societal systems will be used.

The distribution of trips in space is a consequence of the interaction between cognitive organization and the means of access or traverse of space. People who need clothes select a store of which they are aware; this selection is made from a small subset of possibilities that is determined by knowledge and the ability to locate the alternatives. This subset is further reduced by access capability, that is, the transportation system, vehicle, and route by which the desired site may be reached. Thus, the total set of possibilities for need satisfaction is reduced, once because of the individual's cognitive perception of the alternatives, and a second time by the relation of transportation to that cognition. It follows that a major criterion for transportation performance is how well it matches the cognitive structure of the traveler.

This discussion has focused on the behavioral factors underlying human performance in space because cognitive spatial organization has been largely neglected in transportation analysis and design, whereas other cognitive criteria have received detailed consideration in transportation. The criteria shown in Table 2 reflect the performance dimensions of importance to trip makers. Most of these have been used in transportation models as variables that determine the decision to travel as well as the choice of transportation mode. In most of these models, however, the variables have employed physical metrics (e.g, time in minutes, cost in dollars). Although these models are relatively effective in predicting mode choice, especially for work trip travel, they leave considerable room for error, in part, because they equate the physical measure of the criterion function with the psychological measure. There is no reason to believe that the human metrics of time, cost, travel time, reliability, distance, convenience, etc., bear any simple relation to conventional physical measures. Hence, any behavioral process model ultimately requires psychological metrics. The fact is that these metrics have not yet been developed in transportation. Consequently, although the cognitive criterion dimensions may have been identified, without their behavioral measure it is not possible to formulate a behavioral model of travel demand.

Affective Criteria

A second major behavioral factor is the affective criteria that underlie action in space. People select activity sites not only on the basis of such rational considerations as cost and time but also on the basis of preferences, values, and attitudes. These qualitative, emotional dimensions are as significant as cognitive factors in determining when, where, and how people will satisfy their needs. Thus the affective dimensions are also fundamental criteria for the design of transportation systems. How well such systems can satisfy the users' preferences is an important determinant of the subjective evaluation of transportation systems, which is measurable in terms of attitudes. Clearly, a transport system that allows the maximum amount of flexibility with a minimum of complexity would be most acceptable. Indeed, most attitude studies done in the 1960s indicated a significant preference for the automobile, which more nearly meets these criteria than does mass transit. More recent work on mode choice (Thomas, 1976) also suggest that trip makers employ affective analyses as a primary basis for evaluating transport alternatives.

Social Criteria

The third factor providing criteria for linkage system design is social variables. These are normative beliefs (Fishbein & Ajzen, 1976) or attitudes that determine action in time and space. Where people live and what social activities they participate in are as dependent on social as on personal values. Similarly, cognitive or affective information obtained from within the social group is a significant determinant of activity site selection and linkage system use.

People's use of particular modes of transportation is determined in part by their social context. For example, the automobile is perceived as being more secure or socially safe than public transportation (Feldman & Valenga, 1977). This attitude thus dictates when mass transit will be used and for what purposes it is acceptable. Similarly, the perceived social status of the users of a system also influences its use (Blankenship, 1976).

Social criteria are different for various homogeneous subgroups within the population. For example, there is some evidence from attitude studies that rail passengers in the United States avoid air travel in part because of their perceptions of the social status of air transport passengers.

The importance of social criteria has been overlooked in transportation system design. Satisfying these criteria may be possible only through individualized systems for certain segments of the population. In any case, careful consideration of these criteria is essential in system design.

SUMMARY

This and the previous section have described two levels of analysis of transportation. The first level provides a means of estimating the necessary quantity of linkage and the overall goals of transportation systems.

The second level analyzes the behavioral criteria—cognitive, affective, and social—that determine how and where people will seek need satisfaction. Such criteria also determine the functional characteristics that transport systems must have if trip makers are to satisfy their linkage objectives.

These criteria also suggest the close relation between transportation and land use. The spatial distribution of societal systems sets the requirement of having to travel. Having to travel establishes the need for transportation services and also the qualitative and quantitative characteristics that transportation systems must have.

USER OPERATING REQUIREMENTS

Regardless of the adaptation of transportation technology to user needs and requirements, any transport system must also be designed to satisfy the physiological and psychological properties of its users in terms of (1) a passenger space dimension, (2) a route–schedule dimension, and (3) a command and control dimension.

PASSENGER SPACE

The passenger space dimension involves consideration of the static, dynamic, and social characteristics of the transport environment. The static dimension includes seating characteristics, knee room, and the location of objects for passenger use relative to arm length and reach, etc. It also includes a definition of minimum passenger areas and volumes and aisle widths for multipassenger vehicles, as well as environmental qualities such as temperature, humidity, and air flow. Some representative values drawn from a variety of studies are shown in Table 3. These are, generally, minimum design values that provide tolerable passenger comfort for relatively short periods. It should be noted, however, that in mass transportation, these values represent a compromise between user comfort and unit vehicle capacity.

The second consideration is the dynamic characteristics of the transport environment. In general, a vehicle is a moving platform subject to linear and non-linear, repetitive, and random vectors of motion. The characteristics of these vectors depend on the design of the vehicle as well as on the characteristics of the medium in or on which it operates. Complex models have been developed to describe the dynamic behavior of transport vehicles. These models may involve equations with up to six degrees of freedom that can define pitch, roll, and yaw moments as well as the derivatives of linear motion. Further, human tolerances for all these dynamic properties have been defined over the past 40 years (Van Cott & Kincade, 1972).

TABLE 3
PASSENGER ENVIRONMENT DESIGN
CRITERIA

Variable	Criterion level
Passenger area	
Standing	3 sq. ft.
Seated	6–10 sq. ft.
Prone	18–20 sq. ft.
Passenger volume	
Standing	20 cu. ft.
Seated	25 cu. ft.
Prone	36–150 cu. ft.
Temperature	68–72°F
Humidity	45–50% RH
Air circulation	25 cu. ft./min
Ambient noise	60–65 db
Shock/vibration	0.1–0.3 g

The dynamic response of a moving vehicle to random and complex perturbations falls under the rubric of *ride quality*. Normally, the goal is relatively low levels of shock and vibration. The issue is less one of tolerance than one of subjective comfort. Again, a wide variety of research has been done over the past two decades on the ride quality on most modes of transportation. The major objective of this work has been to relate subjective judgments of ride comfort to the vehicle motion vectors. The issue is highly complex, in part, because subjective perception depends on the frequency range, amplitude, and higher derivatives, as well as on direction of motion. Ride comfort research in highway transportation, for example, indicates that passengers are most sensitive to lateral acceleration and jerk (the derivative of acceleration). Typical of research on ride quality is a study (Cooper & Young, 1978) in which a ride discomfort function was developed by relating subjective ratings to the variance of acceleration in the vertical dimension; the threshold of ride comfort was found to be .06 g vertical acceleration. It is reasonably clear that fairly precise criteria for ride quality are being developed that will provide a basis for the design of systems with acceptable dynamic characteristics.

One other aspect of the dynamic environment should be noted. There is an obvious interaction between the motion vectors of these systems and passenger stability. This interaction is determined by the vehicle control process, the passenger's location in the vehicle, and passenger orientation (i.e, seated, standing, or moving within the vehicle). When the vehicle begins to move, its acceleration and higher derivatives as well as the derived pitch, roll, and yaw moments will determine the human body response. Obviously, a standing and moving passenger is least stable. There is greater stability if the passenger is standing with some support, and the maximum stability occurs when the passenger is seated. What stresses the passenger is subjected to depends on the vehicle load factor, its design, and the control behavior of the driver. Since these factors are unpredictable, there can be significant ambiguity for passengers about the risks attendant on riding in these systems.

For physically able riders, these factors influence perceived ride comfort but generally are not directly threatening. For the physically handicapped, however, they are a real threat and are a significant determinant of their using any transport system. One study (Michaels & Weiler, 1975) defined five dimensions of the transport environment necessary to enable people to use mass transportation. By means of a categorical judgment model, it was found that the major barrier to the use of mass transit by the handicapped was the dynamics of the moving environment, rather than their access to the system. The magnitude of this barrier, as well as the attitudes of the handicapped users varied with the severity of the handicap. That is, for the severely handicapped the properties of the moving environment were the most important determinant of use, while for the least handicapped, it was the service properties that were most important.

The third dimension of transport space is a social one. In all transport systems, save the private automobile, passengers do not control who shares their space. There is ample evidence from studies on privacy (Altman, 1975) that these kinds of interactions are stressors. Further, there is evidence that mass transit riders, at least, go to considerable lengths to control encroachment on personal space (Tift, Littlejohn, Bosen, & Sherizen, 1974). Finally, one study on attitudes toward transport systems (Blankenship, 1976) indicates that different modes of transport are categorized in terms of social status. This research suggests that in the design of transport systems, social interactions are a primary consideration and are a significant determinant of whether people will use the system, for what purposes, and when. It is a reasonable hypothesis that one reason for the domination of the private automobile for all transportation purposes is its capacity to provide the user direct and complete control of social interactions in travel. There is also evidence (Margolin & Misch, 1977) that these factors are crucial in determining the ultimate effectiveness of ride-sharing programs.

ROUTING AND SCHEDULING

All transportation systems require a path for linking points, such as a track for rail vehicles, a highway for motor vehicles, or an airlane for commercial planes. For surface systems, these paths form networks that define the area of potential coverage of the system. For systems with simple point-to-point routing, such as air and marine transport, the user is not particularly concerned with the path itself; only the departure and the destination points are of concern. The traveler does have significant information-processing and management problems, but the actual travel path is a negligible consideration.

In most other transportation, routing is crucial. Highway systems, for example, are a series of links connected by nodes or junction points. The network is defined by these links and nodes. For a traveler, however, the objective is to locate a specific destination from a specific origin point. Yet, the traveler must be able to define a path or route to the destination through a network of links and nodes. In addition, the trip maker must use some criterion for the selection of one route among many. In practice, this selection process is modeled by algorithms based on the criterion of minimum travel time through the network. However, evidence suggests that at least in large networks, drivers generally do not behave to minimize travel time. Rather, they appear to try to minimize stress, and they often select routes based on direct experience or normative beliefs that may be longer in both time and distance (Michaels, 1966).

In fixed-route systems (e.g., bus systems), the routing problem for the user is even more complicated. A vehicle is assigned a fixed and predefined path from its origin to its destination. But travelers enter the system at some point on a route and have a destination that may or may not be on the path of the vehicle. How well travelers can use a fixed-route system depends very much on their understanding of the route structure and on their ability to locate activity sites, that is, on their cognitive organization of space.

Cognitive structure interacts very directly with transportation routing, especially at two levels. One is simply that route selection by a traveler hinges on a clear recognition of the destination's location relative to the structure of the network. The other is that because of general overestimation of distance, trips are perceived to be longer than they objectively are. Thus, the ability to relate travel routes to destinations is limited at best, and any transport system design in which route structure is based on Euclidean space is inconsistent with travelers' basic perceptions of space. Current transportation—and public transportation, in particular—is organized on a simple linear algebra for its route structure. Consequently, travelers must make a transformation of the linear route structure into cognitive structure. Since this cannot be done easily, use of transit systems is restricted. This is one reason that transfers among routes is as limited as it is, especially on mass transit, where only 10% of the trips involve more than a single transfer.

Scheduling refers to the temporal patterning of movement and activities. The term is used in two ways: from the standpoint of the transportation provider and from the standpoint of traveler behavior.

In the first use, the nature of the technology dictates whether the frequency of departure must be predetermined. Generally, scheduling is essential in order to ensure the maximum use of labor and equipment. The theory of the provider is a classic economic one that aims to provide maximum service at minimum cost. Consequently, the minimum number of vehicles is allocated to routes to satisfy demand. The dispatch rate may or may not be public information. It should be noted that scheduled systems have been primarily responsive to the operators' requirements, which are not always the same as those of the trip makers. One of the obvious advantages of an individually controlled system is the scheduling freedom it provides the user.

From a traveler's standpoint, trips are also time-patterned, or scheduled. In part, this scheduling is socially determined, as in work trips, and in part, it is determined by the structure of individual and household lifestyles (Dix, 1979). Essentially, individuals and households develop temporal and spatial patterns of activities that require time allocations and hence have to be time-ordered. Since these activities often require travel, transportation becomes an intregal part of the activity schedules of daily life. It follows that travelers will evaluate transport systems in part by the perceived efficiency of those modes in meeting their temporal organizations of activities. It is probably for this reason, and not because it is important in and of itself, that travel time has been found to be a dominant decision variable in mode and route choice.

COMMAND AND CONTROL

All transport systems involve the user in active or passive behavior relative to the operation of the transport vehicle. That is, the traveler must exercise continuous and discrete control over a vehicle or a large system. At one extreme, this control involves only choice, while at the other it involves direct operating control. The methodology for the human-engineering design of transportation systems is well developed (Van Cott & Kincade, 1972) and permits specification of what kinds of systems human beings control and where in the control process people should be optimally located. For all but aviation systems, however, only a limited amount of this methodology has been employed in transport design.

The other aspect of command and control is the planning of a trip. For all trips, travelers must make decisions about time, mode, and route. In addition to knowing the location of the destination, the trip maker must determine the path to the destination as well as the particular modes by which that destination can be reached. In personal transport systems as well as in mass transport, the amount of information required by users is quite large. Even if travelers have access to that information, which they normally do not, its integration for decision purposes is a complex task. Yet, it is the ability to acquire and integrate information on travel that determines whether the trip maker is in command of his or her travel.

From a subjective standpoint, these information-processing and decision rules dictate which mode of transportation the individual will use, how it will be used, and for which kinds of linkage. Although a wide variety of information-aiding techniques has been employed by all modes of transportation, including alphanumeric markings, signing, maps, color coding, human information transfers, and computer routing systems, very little systematic analysis of traveler information needs has been done in conventional transportation systems. Given the complexity of most transport systems, especially urban systems, it is not surprising that individualized modes of transportation have come to dominate travel.

ALTERNATIVE TRANSPORTATION FUTURES

The needs underlying travel require exchanges of three types: (1) information transfer; (2) materials and goods transfer; and (3) interpersonal transactions. These are not, of course, mutually exclusive sets. The transfer requirements for need satisfaction are shown in Table 4. This exchange structure involves both the production system as well as most societal systems. As may be noted, transfers involve largely interpersonal transactions. This helps explain why physical movement technologies have been a priority investment by both the public and the private sector.

Obviously, there is a large set of possibilities for access systems. However, all transport alternatives for trips fall into only three classes: (1) technologies for moving people through time rather than space; (2) technologies for physical movement; and (3) spatial or land use organi-

TABLE 4
TRANSFER REQUIREMENTS FOR NEED SATISFACTION

Activities–needs	Transfer quality		
	Information	Material	Interpersonal
Work	X	X	X
Food		X	X
Clothing		X	X
Durable goods		X	X
Education	X		X
Health care	X	X	X
Social (individual)	X		X
Social (informal group)	X		X
Recreation	X		X
Personal (services)	X		X
Personal (business)	X		X

zation. Each of these represents a different means of providing access and a basis for examining future transportation technologies.

INFORMATION TRANSFER TECHNOLOGY

As one looks closely at the requirements shown in Table 4 it is clear that many of the interpersonal trips involve significant information transfers. For example, banking is a personal business trip in which interpersonal travel is used for an information transfer. Similarly, a significant proportion of health care trips involves only information transfers yet currently demands interpersonal contact.

The more the nature of travel demand is analyzed, the clearer it becomes that much of the physical movement of people is a concomitant of moving information. Many of the needs that now motivate action in space do not inherently require physical movement. Since physical movement is a cost, any reduction in travel should provide increased resources for better satisfying manifest needs and for allowing latent needs to become manifest. Thus, reducing the quantity of physical movement would be a means of meeting the basic behavioral requirements for linkage more effectively. Thus, a major innovation in access would be to satisfying information transfer needs not by travel but by communications technology.

It is currently estimated that between 25% and 50% of all work trip travel and probably close to 50% of all household travel involves only information exchange. However, because of computer and communication technology, most of these needs can be satisfied without physical movement. It would appear absolutely inevitable that this technology will be the primary means of satisfying a significant fraction of household needs within the next two decades. When one looks at the behavioral requirements for access, it would appear that this technology can be efficiently designed to satisfy those needs and hence meet the demand for access to desired societal systems. Information-processing technology permits satisfaction of the user requirements and criteria shown in Figure 2 very directly. If interactive systems (graphic or verbal) are used, the cognitive, affective, and social criteria discussed previously can be directly satisfied. Similarly, the operating characteristics requred of linkage systems are reduced to only two major considerations: (1) scheduling and (2) command and control.

The emergence of this class of information-processing technology will not only reduce the need for physical access but is likely to change the ways in which services are provided. For example, the American Telephone & Telegraph Company has now made available an educa-

tional innovation, the "electronic blackboard." Through the telephone
system, instruction can be carried out in a conventional classroom, and
the information can be transmitted to any other location with the same
verbal interaction as in a classroom. This system is being used to provide
courses for companies in remote locations simultaneously with a regular
course. The students at the remote location cannot see or be seen by the
students or the instructor in the campus classroom, but they can hear
and be heard. This kind of distributed, but interactive, communication
process can have profound implications for the delivery of educational
services.

This is simply one example of what is happening or can happen in
the delivery of societal system services including health care, personal
business (e.g., banking), and government services. It is reasonable to
believe that the society is now at the same point relative to information-
processing technology that it was in the late 1920s relative to electric
power distribution, when about half the rural residences were without
electricity. It took about two decades to overcome this deficiency, and it
probably will take less than that to wire urban and rural residences with
extensive information-processing capability.

PHYSICAL MOVEMENT TECHNOLOGY

For the 50% of household needs that cannot be met by infomation
transfers, physical movement technology will be essential. This is likely
to involve travel for social, recreational, and other activities requiring
interpersonal transactions. These needs will have to be satisfied at locations in the larger environment. This travel may be defined in terms of
origin–destination location. Three basic trip classes are (1) intraurban; (2)
interurban; and (3) rural.

Intraurban

At present, intraurban access is provided by three different
technologies: private automobile, bus mass transit, and rail transit. Except for work trips to the central business districts of older cities with
over 1 million population, the private automobile dominates transportation in metropolitan regions. This is the case simply because in dispersed settlement patterns, the automobile is the only practicable travel
alternative. This does not mean that it is a particularly good access
technology; it is simply the best of the technological alternatives that
have been implemented on any large scale. For most population subgroups, highway transportation simply meets behavioral requirements,

access criteria, and performance characteristics better than any commercial carrier.

For intraurban transport, a variety of factors suggests that conventional highway transportation has reached the limit of its utility. Energy and other resource limitations are causing the costs of owning and operating an automobile to rise. It is projected that these costs will continue to rise, so that fewer and fewer households will be able to own cars. Finally, such a system precludes use by a significant and growing fraction of the urban population, for example, the elderly. Consequently, it is reasonable to anticipate new kinds of transport technology for individual travel.

Using the basic behavioral model, it is possible to identify the characteristics that any new system must have. It must be capable of satisfying requirements for linkage of all population subgroups, including those with physical and psychological limitations. It must be capable of responding to the users' spatial cognitive structure and of satisfying their qualitative criteria. It must allow users to direct the system to desired activity sites on a user-determined schedule. And it must meet the criteria for space and ride quality for all population subgroups.

Two kinds of systems meet these requirements. One is a personal system that would allow point-to-point linkage. Such a system, automated ground transportation (AGT), is under development. The system is comprised of a vehicle operating on a fixed guideway. The vehicle is small, lightweight, electrically powered, and generally designed to carry two to four passengers. The guideway would be an interconnected network. The command function in such a system would be adapted to the users' cognitive structure. Most such systems are conceived of as address-dispatched; that is, the user would simply code the desired destination using a keyboard built into the vehicle. Then the control system would route the vehicle to the destination, generally along a minimum time path. Such a system would not require the traveler to have a well-developed cognitive understanding of the spatial environment.

In order to serve any origin or destination within a metropolitan region, such an AGT system would require an extremely large guideway network, almost equivalent to the street network now in place. An alternative has been suggested called *dual-mode AGT*. In this design, the vehicle could be operated on the street network using electric power. The user would drive the vehicle a short distance and enter the guideway, where it would come under system control. Similarly, the vehicle would be driven from a guideway exit to the final destination. In this design, guideway spacing could be on one-mile centers, thus requiring the user to find the desired destination only within a half-mile radius of the exit point. Such a system would reduce spatial cognitive-structure demands, which could be reduced even further by the use of the automatic route guidance system to be discussed in the next section. Further, such AGT systems would satisfy the basic social and affective criteria discussed earlier. Finally, if these systems are designed to satisfy the performance dimensions, they would approach being optimal systems from a behavioral standpoint.

Considerable work has been done on this kind of system in the United States, Europe, and Japan. The Japanese have apparently solved the switching problem, which is a prerequisite to developing network systems. Further, the routing algorithms exist, as does the destination coding system. Two major problems appear to remain in single-mode AGT design. One is the distribution of vehicles in a way that satifies the time demand of users. The concept is that the traveler would move to a station point and push a vehicle call button. It is the wait time for the vehicle that is at issue. Obviously, the acceptability of the system to the user will be highly sensitive to wait time, as it is in existing systems. Dual-mode AGT would largely eliminate this problem.

The second problem is user access to the system. Most designs are conceived of as elevated structures and hence pose the same problem for physically limited travelers as do current subway systems. The problem is solvable at a price, but it must be dealt with if such systems are to satisfy the needs of all users. The dual-mode system would reduce this problem only if vehicle control were highly sophisticated.

AGT systems represent the most advanced technology for intraurban travel. They come close to providing the most user-responsive linkage system conceivable for the low-volume, short-trip travel that characterize intraurban movements. It seems inevitable that some variation of this class of technology will emerge for urban travel. The advantages in terms of externalities alone make this system extremely attractive, for example, separation of pedestrian and vehicular traffic, separation of freight and person movement, safety, personal security, pollution reduction, and energy savings. Most important, such systems can be effectively designed to satisfy behavioral requirements.

A second kind of intraurban access system would provide point-to-point service on demand for a relatively small geographic area. One such system is a dynamically routed bus system. Its dispatch and routing would be determined by calls from users and their location in time and space. Unlike in a taxi service, the calls would be consolidated on an ongoing basis, and assigned to a bus while it is en route, and the order of stops would be adjusted continuously. Ideally, each bus run would be time-optimized. Computer algorithms for real-time dispatch and routing have been developed. Demand-actuated systems would thus be multipassenger vehicles (usually with a capacity of 10–20) that would provide transport services from several origins to a single destination (e.g., a train station or an industrial plant) or to many destinations. It is obvious that the travel time by this kind of system would depend on the size of the area served by each vehicle at both the origin and the destination ends. There is some evidence to suggest that such modes could be efficient if the service area of each bus, including both origin and destination, were kept relatively small, on the order of 1–5 square miles. It should be noted that in most cases where these systems have been employed, their success has been rather modest and the cost has been quite high, probably, in part, because of too few vehicles or too great a demand, both of which lead to rapid increases in wait time, travel time and arrival time unreliability. Appropriately used, however, demand-actuated systems could efficiently serve travel needs in moderate-density subregions and do so in ways that satisfy user requirements. Obviously, such a system is most adaptable to physically limited users and also minimizes cognitive and command and control problems for all.

Although the conventional private automobile appears to be obsolescent for most intraurban travel, it is likely not to be replaced with automated systems very rapidly, certainly if the experience of the past decade is any indication. Nonetheless, external forces, mainly energy shortages, will continue to alter both the design and the use of this system. Obviously, cars are shrinking in size and weight, and new forms of motive power are under development. In addition, there are suggestions for a specialized vehicle for intraurban travel that would be very small, with a passenger capacity of no more than two persons. Such a vehicle would be very low-power, would travel at low speeds, and, whether gasoline or electric power, would use about 1,000 BTU per passenger mile, which is about a third of the current auto fleet average and about two-thirds that of a conventional bus.

When one examines the existing automobile highway system, it becomes clear that it has not been used efficiently, probably because of inadequacies in meeting the cognitive-structure and user-scheduling criteria. As was discussed earlier, the system requires users to find paths through the network in any way they can. With a limited understanding of the location of sites in macrospace, there is no reason to believe that people can find a minimum time or energy path through the network, to say nothing of using any significant proportion of activity-site alternatives. It is possible, however, to provide some form of aid in routing that could markedly increase efficiencies in automobile usage. Such a route-aiding system has been designed, and prototypes were developed 15 years ago. The system involves a transceiver on the automobile and a transceiver at each major interchange or intersection. The driver would code into the transceiver a destination address. As the vehicle approached an intersection, the address would be transmitted to a roadside computer that stored all destination codes and could compute the minimum time or energy path from that intersection. The computer would then transmit to the vehicle a simple direction, for example, "Turn right," "Turn left," or "Continue straight ahead." Thus, the system would guide the vehicle, intersection by intersection, through the network to the desired destination. Obviously, drivers would never get lost. Even if they did not follow an instruction at one intersection, they would receive another at the next intersection.

This kind of aiding system is adapted to the driver's cognitive criteria and would more effectively satisfy user needs than the current mode of operation. In addition, it has some interesting ramifications for traffic control and management in urban areas. If the destinations of vehicles entering the network were known and were transmitted to a central computer, it would be possible to route traffic on any network, since the instantaneous demand distribution would be known. This procedure would allow far more efficient use of street capacity than is now possible.

Such route-aiding systems are adaptable to mass transit as well as to the automobile, although the display of route information, as well as the input–output characteristics, would be different. Actually, such route aiding for transit would be expected to provide even greater utilization of transit capacity than of highways. Such a system, since it would meet users' needs more effectively, would markedly increase the utility of fixed-route transit.

The second area of conventional system improvement would appear to be in scheduling travel. Studies of household behavior by the New York State Department of Transportation during the 1979 energy shortage showed that households were able to reduce automobile travel on the order of 20% without significant compromise of need satisfaction. This reduction was obtained by planning travel more carefully; consolidating trips to minimize energy use; and reducing impulse trips. Thus, there appeared to be significant gains in the efficiency of automobile use by modifying household travel behavior. This finding suggests that the application of behavior modification techniques as well as informational processes can lead to substantial reductions in highway energy consumption. A recent analysis (Michaels, 1980) suggest that it may be possible to reduce urban-transport energy consumption by 20–30% with route-aiding and behavior modification techniques. There is very likely to be extensive implementation of these approaches over the next decade.

Interurban

In interurban transportation, the main focus has been on the reduction of travel time. For example, considerable development has proceeded over the past decade in this country and abroad on very high-speed trains. The designs involve the use of novel propulsion systems that theoretically can provide speeds of up to 375 kph. Such systems are conceived of for travel from center city to center city in the distance range of 150–750 kilometers. The design objective is to reduce the total travel time to city centers. In this sense, these systems are conceived of as being competitive with air travel for short to moderate-length trips (which, incidentally, account for about two-thirds of all air travel). At the upper end of the speed range, these systems probably cannot be operated on the surface and will have to be located underground.

If one examines these systems from a behavioral standpoint, the system designers seem to have focused on the functional aspects of the system rather than on traveler needs and requirements. Since the main emphasis has been on the reduction of travel time, these systems all overlook the need to integrate linkage from point of origin to the line haul terminal and from the terminal to the user's destination in order to satisfy cognitive criteria. Further, none of the proposed systems consider affective or social criteria. This disconnection in intercity transport technology explains, in part, the domination of the private automobile for interurban as well as intraurban nonwork travel.

Rural

For trips within rural areas and from urban to rural areas, the low population density and the relatively long distances to activity sites require some type of individualized system. Along with conventional automobile, development has proceeded on air-cushion vehicles and vertical- and short-takeoff aircraft. The major advantages of such systems are functional rather than behavioral. They allow rapid access to low-density areas, but they generally increase cognitive complexity for users, as well as having significant affective drawbacks. Further, the need for command and control as well as routing complexity is significantly greater than for the automobile. It is likely that such systems will emerge only for specialized purposes (e.g., emergency vehicles).

For general use, the automobile–highway system will continue to be the transport technology employed for most rural travel. There will be minor modifications in performance, safety, and the adaptability to users. Only size and weight will continue to decrease. The only other likely change will be modifications of the highway to separate passenger cars and heavey trucks. This separation will become a significant safety problem as truck sizes and weights increase and automobile sizes and weights decrease, along with their acceleration capability at highway speeds.

The problem with the private automobile is simply that people with limited physical and economic capacities are unable to use it. Alternatives for dealing with access-constrained rural residents have been suggested, and all involve use of the highway. Thus, demand-actuated systems or special-function buses as well as service-delivery programs have been considered. In all cases, these alternative would be only modest adaptations of conventional highway transport.

LAND USE REORGANIZATION

The way in which land use is organized fundamentally determines the amount of travel required to satisfy people's needs. The density of land use development and the location of the production and consumption systems determine the necessity for transportation technology. Similarly, the availability and willingness to invest in transportation have been a major determinant of land use organization. Within the constraints of transport technology, the development of the environment has proceeded on the dynamic of economic, social, and individual goals. Although largely unplanned in any comprehensive sense, the built environment has evolved from the interaction of economic and social goals with technological innovation in transportation.

Thus, over the 100-year period from 1870 to 1970, the United States went through two major phases in the organization of the built environment. The first phase was the development of the modern industrial city around the production systems, which were largely concentrated, with the commercial and financial systems, in or near the center of the city. This kind of development led to a high concentration of population around the industrial base. In major industrial cities, population densities reached 30,000–60,000 people per square mile. On the order of 65–70% of the urban work force was engaged in manufacturing-related jobs. The built environment was organized to support this industrial base in terms of housing, architecture, and public services.

Transportation was a central determinant of that structure, and the technology defined the limits of the relations between home and work-place. Mass transit, which emerged in the late 1880s was designed to serve the labor requirements of the central city. Most older cities in the northeastern United States grew along narrow transit corridors, which were extended as the urban population grew. The advent of scientific highway design—which began shortly after the turn of the century, along with the development of the internal-combustion engine—led to the creation of the bus. This innovation allowed transit to serve lower-density areas than rail transit could. Consequently, areas more distant from the city's center were opened for housing and commercial development, which occurred in successive rings around the city's center. Again, travel was oriented toward the center, and about 35% of all personal travel ended in the core.

By the end of second decade of the twentieth century, mass production of the automobile had begun, as had the change to a consumption economy. The breakdown of the industrial city also began at this time. The innovation of highway transportation, coupled with the rapid increase in disposable income, led to the second phase of urban development, that is, metropolitanization.

Metropolitan development occurred slowly, inhibited by economic depression, and World War II. Suburban development was limited and tended to be led by upper-income families. In the postwar era, the pent-up demand for housing became manifest and the major suburban development occurred. The consequences of this migration are well documented, as are its effects on cities. This revolutionary change was fueled by the growth of the highway network and auto availability. One result was almost a doubling in the percentage of personal trips by automobile and a consequent halving of travel by commercial carrier. Another result was the outmigration of business and industry from the city, so that by 1970, the total proportion of trips to the center of most major northern cities had dropped to 8–12%.

There is ample evidence (Chapin, 1965; Lansing & Barth, 1966; Lansing, et al. 1964; Lansing & Hendricks, 1967; Wilson, 1962) that the metropolitanization process was determined primarily by people's attitudes toward residential environments. The age and the stage in the life cycle of the dominant portion of the population as well as the family size desired by married couples, oriented the population toward residential evaluation. This evaluation led to desired housing size, amenities, and location preferences (Baker, Michaels, & Dudgeon, 1979). Within economic constraints (and with mortgage subsidy programs), these desired values were realizable, but at a considerable distance from the city center. In essence, new housing followed land costs and infrastructure services. By the end of the 1960s, because of new housing costs, younger and lower-income families were locating further and further from the city center leaving the economically and socially disadvantaged concentrated in the urban core. Auto ownership was a prerequisite to this migration pattern. However, given transportation and the perceived requirements for housing, the process led to continuing population growth at the periphery of metropolitan regions.

It is clear that land use development in the 30-year period between 1946 and 1976 has been dominated by the individual needs and preferences for residential quality. Land use development was also dominated by the industrial development needs of this period. The resulting highly dispersed settlement patterns in metropolitan regions depended for its success on public and private investment in highway transportation.

Although many of the consequences, positive and negative, have been noted, from the standpoint of the behavioral model discussed earlier there have been other effects of metropolitanization. One is that the satisfaction of many individual and household needs required a large expenditure of human resources in travel. A second is that the metropolitan land-use development-pattern has markedly increased the cognitive complexity of the environment, so that the information-processing burden has markedly increased. A third is that a significant minority lack access to societal systems and thus cannot fully satisfy their needs.

Land use organization is fundamentally a technological structure. Land use may be organized and integrated in any form that may be desired. Looking at the activity set shown in Table 4, it is obvious that settlement patterns (and the basic services and societal systems required by a community) can be designed at any density as well as to minimize travel (in time or distance). Transportation systems can be designed to support these settlement patterns. Further, they can be integrated into these patterns so that they more readily meet mobility requirements. The urban planning literature of the past decade or so contains many alternatives for land use organization.

Whether any major land-use reoganization will occur does not depend on transportation technology. It is clear that the technological capability now exists to meet the behavioral requirements of the people settled in any desired land use form. Although this was not true 50 years ago, the variety of linkage alternatives now available permit land use development to proceed with a reasonable certainty that satisfactory transportation can be provided.

Whether land use reorganization occurs and becomes a means of meeting linkage goals depends fundamentally on changes in the behavioral requirements for residential and employment environme. such changes are occur, then the society will enter a third phase of urban development.

Three factors have emerged in the 1980s that bear on the question. One is the marked decrease in the numbers of children desired by families. A second is the rapidly increasing proportion of the population over 55. A third is the rapid growth in single and communal units. All three of these factors suggest that the quantity of residential space required, both for house and in land area, should be less than for the past generation of large families. The demographic changes also suggest a movement toward an adult-centered rather than a child-centered social organization.

More important is whether or not peoples' attitudes toward housing have changed. Recent focus groups studies done by this author with groups 18 to 25-year-olds from mainly middle-class, white-collar backgrounds suggest that housing lifestyle expectations have changed. In general, these groups expected to live nearer to the city center, in smaller dwelling units, and in higher-density developments. Further, there was a general desire to minimize the need for transportation, expecially the need for an automobile. Finally, they expected their work lives to be less time-structured.

If these values are representative, then major changes in land use organization may be anticipated. There is some evidence already of resettlement in cities by middle-income as well as upper-income groups. New suburban housing is producing smaller dwelling units in higher-density development patterns. Further, there has been an increasing use of variable work hours.

It is extremely difficult to predict whether or how fast such changes in spatial organization may occur. Higher-density land use and integration of the societal systems within these communities will set the requirement for transportation. The conventional modes will be largely obsolete for intracommunity mobility when trips are on the order of one or two miles. The linkage system requirements will be simple to satisfy, as will intercommunity linkage. The costs associated with travel will be reduced, and direct origin–destination linkage can be provided. Many of the innovations discussed earlier would be functionally adapted to more dense and clustered land-use organizations. Certainly, higher-density development will make demand-actuated systems more efficient for both providers and users. The cost and complexity of automated ground-transportation systems would be markedly reduced and hence more economically feasible. Such reorganization would also certainly lead to the relocation of societal systems closer to the housing clusters.

Finally, since information-processing occupations account for about 50% of the work force, one would expect that multifunction computer and communication-system centers may be located within the community areas. These would afford expanded opportunity for adult interaction both at home and around the work environment, which itself would be integrated with the nonwork environment.

This scenario is a speculation at this time. From the standpoint of environmental design as well as transportation, it would be desirable to be able to make a comprehensive plan of the systems essential to meeting emerging behavioral needs and requirements, whatever they may be. It is the extent of our understanding of these needs and requirements that will determine whether we can create a human as well as a functionally effective environment that includes access systems designed specifically to satisfy basic needs.

REFERENCES

Altman, I. *The environment and social behavior: Privacy, personal space, territory, crowding.* Monterey, Calif.: Brooks/Cole, 1975.

Baker, R. F., Dudgeon, T. H., Michaels, R. M., & Rothermund, K. L. *A national transportation policy study: The societal use method.* Washington, D.C.: National Transportation Policy Study Commission, 1978.

Baker, R. F., Michaels, R. M., & Dudgeon, I. H. *The societal use method: Housing.* Washington, D.C.: National Transportation Policy Study Commission, 1979.

Bell, W. The social areas of San Francisco Bay region. *American Sociological Review,* 1953, 18.

Blankenship, D., & David, M. Discovering the rules of social interaction for carpoolers. *Public Works,* 1976.

Chapin, F. S. *Urban land use planning.* Urbana: University of Illinois Press, 1965.

Chapin, F. S., & Logan, T. H. Patterns of time and space use. In H. S. Perloff (Ed.), *The quality of the environment essays on "New resources" in an urban age.* Baltimore, Md.: Johns Hopkins Press, 1969.

Cooper, D. R., & Young, J. C. *Road surface irregularity and road vehicle ride: Part II. Riding comfort in cars driven by the public.* Crawthorne, Berkshire: Transport and Road Research Laboratory, 1978.

Dix, M. C. Structuring our understanding of travel choices. *Fourth International Conference on Behavioral Travel Modelling,* Eibsee, Federal Republic of Germany, 1979.

Feldman, L., & Valenga, L. *Security as a factor in the marketing of urban mass transportation.* Chicago: University of Illinois at Chicago Circle, 1977.

Fishhein, M., & Ajzen, I. *Belief, attitude, intention and behavior: An introduction to theory and research.* Reading, Mass.: Addison, 1976.

Jones, P. M. New approaches to understanding travel behavior: The human activity approach. *Third International Conference on Travel Behavior,* Tununda, Australia, 1977.

Lancaster, K. J. A new approach to consumer theory. In R. E. Quandt (Ed.), *The demand for travel: Theory and measurement.* Lexington, Mass.: D. C. Heath, 1970.

Lansing, J. B., & Barth, N. *Residential location and urban mobility: A multivariate analysis.* U.S. Department of Commerce, Bureau of Public Roads, 1966.

Lansing, J. B., & Hendricks, G. *Automobile ownership and residential density*. U.S. Department of Transportation, Federal Highway Administration, 1967.

Lansing, J. B., Mueller, E., & Barth, N. *Residential location and urban mobility*. U.S. Department of Commerce, Bureau of Public Roads, 1964.

Levin, I. P. Information integration in transportation decision. In M. F. Kaplan & S. Schwartz (Eds.), *Human judgment and decision processes in applied settings*. New York: Academic Press, 1977, pp. 57–82.

Louviere, J. J., & Norman, K. L. Application of information processing theory to the analysis of urban travel demand. *Environment and Behavior*, 1977, 9, 91–106.

Margolin, J. B., & Misch, M. R. *Handbook of behavioral strategies in transportation*. Washington, D. C.: George Washington University, 1977.

Michaels, R. M. Attitudes of drivers toward alternative highways and their relation to route choice. *Highway Research Record*, 1966, 122.

Michaels, R. M. Applications of behavioral science to ransportation. In R. M. Michaels (Ed.), *Transportation planning and policy making: Behavioral science contributions*. New York: Praeger, 1980.

Michaels, R. M., & Weiler, N. S. *Transportation needs of the mobility limited*. Evanston, Ill.: Transportation Center, Northwestern University, 1975.

Rees, P. H. Concepts of social space. In B. J. L. Berry & F. E. Horton (Eds.), *Geographic perspectives on urban systems*. Englewood Cliffs, N. J.: Prentice-Hall, 1970.

Shevky, E., & Williams, J. B. *The social areas of Los Angeles: Analysis and topology*. Berkeley and Los Angeles: University of California Press, 1949.

Spier, L. A suggested behavioral and approach to cost–benefit analysis. *Management Science Journal*, 1971, 17.

Stea, D. Architecture in the head: Cognitive mapping. In T. M. Lang, C. Burnet, W. Maleski, & D. Vachin (Ed.), *Designing for human behavior*. Stroudberg Pa.: Dowden, Hutchinson and Ross, 1974.

Stenson, H. *Cognitive factors in the use of transit systems*. Chicago: University of Illinois at Chicago Circle, 1978.

Thomas, K. A reinterpretation of the "attitude" approach to transport mode choice and an exploratory empirical test. *Environment and Planning*, 1976, 8, 783–810.

Tift, P., Littlejohn, S., Bosen, S., & Sherizen, S. *Coping with crime and fear on mass transit*. Chicago: University of Illinois at Chicago Circle, 1974.

Van Cott, H. P., & Kincade, R. G. (Eds.). *Human engineering guide to equipment design*. Washington, D.C.: American Institute for Research, 1972.

Wilson, R. L. Livability of the city: Attitudes and urban development. In F. S. Chapin & S. F. Weiss (Ed.), *Urban growth dynamics*. New York: Wiley, 1962.

Wright, L. N. *Behavioral model for transportation planning*. Evanston, Ill.: Transportation Center, Northwestern University, 1972.

Index